THE MAKING AND BREAKING OF THE SOVIET SYSTEM

European History in Perspective

General Editor: Jeremy Black

European History in Perspective

Series Standing Order
ISBN 0–333–71694–9 hardcover
ISBN 0–333–69336–1 paperback
(outside North America only)

You can receive future titles in this series as they are published by placing a standing order. Please contact your bookseller or, in case of difficulty, write to us at the address below with your name and address, the title of the series and the ISBN quoted above.

Customer Services Department, Macmillan Distribution Ltd
Houndmills, Basingstoke, Hampshire RG21 6XS, England

THE MAKING AND BREAKING OF THE SOVIET SYSTEM

AN INTERPRETATION

Christopher Read

palgrave

First published 2001 by
PALGRAVE
Houndmills, Basingstoke, Hampshire RG21 6XS
and
175 Fifth Avenue, New York, N.Y. 10010
Companies and representatives throughout the world

PALGRAVE is the new global academic imprint of
St. Martin's Press LLC Scholarly and Reference Division and
Palgrave Publishers Ltd (formerly Macmillan Press Ltd).

ISBN 0–333–73152–2 hardback
ISBN 0–333–73153–0 paperback

This book is printed on paper suitable for recycling and made from fully managed and sustained forest sources.

A catalogue record for this book is available from the British Library.

Library of Congress Cataloging-in-Publication Data
Read, Christopher, 1946–
    The making and breaking of the Soviet system : an interpretation / Christopher Read.
    p. cm. – (European history in perspective)
    Includes bibliographical references and index.
    ISBN 0–333–73152–2 – ISBN 0–333–73153–0 (pbk.)
    1. Soviet Union–History. I. Title. II. Series.

DK266 .R384 2000
947–dc21   00-048296

10   9   8   7   6   5   4   3   2   1
10   09 08 07 06 05 04 03 02 01

Printed in China

To my family

CONTENTS

Contents ix

ACKNOWLEDGEMENTS

My thanks are due to many friends and colleagues without whose knowledge and support a study such as this would be impossible. There are too many to name individually but I would like to mention three groups to which I owe a great deal. They are the Study Group on the Russian Revolution, the Soviet Industrialization Project Seminars of the Centre for Russian and East European Studies at the University of Birmingham and the History Department of the University of Warwick.

Specific thanks are due to the University of Warwick for the study leave and travel money devoted to this project; to the British Academy for supporting visits to Moscow and Paris; to a number of individuals for answering queries or reading parts of the draft, notably Arfon Rees, Derek Watson, Bob Service, Sheena Chapman, Mark Harrison and Roger Chetwynd. Responsibility for the final text is, of course, my own.

CHRISTOPHER READ

Part I: *Making the System*

'We, partisans of freedom, protest against all despotisms; we emphatically condemn and denounce the organisation and social tendencies of Russian despotism, as leading inevitably to the most brutalising form of communism.'

(Resolution of the French delegation at the 1866 Geneva Conference of the First Socialist International, quoted in D. McLellan, *Karl Marx: His Life and Thought* (London, 1973), p. 377)

1
BOLSHEVIK DREAMS

Even by the radical standards of the early twentieth century Bolshevism was an extreme movement. Wobblies, bomb-throwing anarchists, Fenian terrorists and Serbian Black Hand Gang members might be more violent but Bolshevism was second to none for determination, intransigence and self-confidence. In the Second International, the nominally worldwide but European-dominated organisation of socialist parties, Bolshevism had a reputation for intractable stridency, tenacious pursuit of its own ends and utter contempt for those who did not share its precise doctrines. Such characteristics were often patronisingly attributed to the rawness of Russian culture by more gentlemanly Western European socialists. Time and again they shook their heads in despair at the intense squabbles which broke out among the Russians. Its leading figures had tried to smooth things over. Bebel's offer to mediate between Bolsheviks and Mensheviks had been turned down, Kautsky, Mehring and Klara Zetkin had run into disputes in their role as trustees of party funds and Rosa Luxemburg blamed Lenin for the split.[1] One characteristic was already obvious – Bolsheviks did not believe they had much to learn from their supposed colleagues in the broader movement. Rather they saw their first duty was to denounce, with as much authority as they could muster, the 'betrayal' of socialism which they believed most other movements represented. Even before the fatal split over the First World War, Bolshevism had made its position clear. The elimination of Marxist heresy seemed to be a preoccupation at least as great as direct confrontation with the capitalist enemy. Curiously, Bolshevism's quarrelsome intransigence towards other socialists repeated arguments Marx himself had in setting up the First International. This might be something the Bolsheviks would be proud of except that they fitted the role

3

played by Marx's opponent Bakunin rather than that of Marx. Like Lenin, Bakunin was certain that he had the key to truth – notably that political struggle against church and state was the route to revolution – and he cast condescending scorn on Marx's subtleties of class struggle and economic preconditions for the successful overthrow of capitalism. Like the social democrats of 1900, Marx was pushed beyond the confines of patience and civility by the frustrations engendered by the scathing attacks of 'the Russians'.

The colossal self-confidence of Bolshevism opens up the first channel of interpretation of the success and failure of the movement and it will run through much of our story like a red thread helping us to understand the fundamental paradoxes of the Soviet experience. For example, the Soviet Communist Party brought Marxism to its highest point, but ended up killing it in the Soviet Union itself and, at least, seriously damaging it in the rest of the world. This, in itself, is related to other fundamental paradoxes to which we must return, namely that Marxist socialism was supposed to come about *after* capitalism had exhausted its formidable potential for wealth creation and had fallen victim to its own inner contradictions by which, crudely speaking, it could only accumulate capital by eventually impoverishing those who would provide the potential market for its products. If they were so impoverished that they could not buy those products then capitalism would collapse for lack of a market. One thing is clear. Even if one were to accept that Marx's predictions do seem to point to some of the basic tendencies inherent in capitalism, which has spent the last century fending off the predicted consequences through state intervention, market regulation via monopolies and global expansion, Russia was not a country at the furthest extreme of capitalist development. Rather it was a society in which capitalism had only a weak bridgehead. At the time of the revolution, Russia was, and for almost another half-century remained, a predominantly peasant country.

The Contradictions of Tsarism

If, of all the great European powers, Russia was the one which least fitted Marxist criteria for revolution, it could nonetheless be seen as the one in which revolution of some kind was the most probable. The reasons why Russia was revolutionary have been hotly debated but the most satisfactory explanations revolve around two aspects of its history. First, by the mid-nineteenth century it was economically 'backward' even though it was beginning to develop. Second, an increasingly 'modern' population was evolving within the unchanging structures of a despotic autocracy, the institutions and political culture of which had evolved to police a serf-based society and sustain a militarily-oriented dynasty. Each of these needs a brief examination before we can proceed.

By the 1860s Russia was wealthier than most countries of the world. It had a number of large industries – notably textiles, mining, metallurgy and manufacturing which employed some eight hundred thousand people[2] – the beginnings of a railway network and a military elite which, until the rude shock of the Crimean War, had basked in the reflected glory of the defeat of Napoleon's *Grande Armée*, the largest armed force the world had yet seen. How then could it be 'backward'? First and most obviously, the standard of measurement was not with the wider world but with the European powers. The Crimean War, a byword in corruption and inefficiency in British history even though Britain was the main foundation of the winning side, brought home the growing gap between Russia's miserable military efforts – resulting from poor organisation, the low quality of the serf-soldiers, poor communications and unreliable equipment – and the ability of her enemies to convey an army to the other end of the Continent and still come out on top. However, in order to be 'backward' a country (yet another paradox) needs to be partly developed, at least enough for a significant part of the population to be aware of its relative 'backwardness'. In Russia's case, the awareness of 'backwardness' permeated parts of the educated elite, including enlightened bureaucrats who saw the need to reform the system as well as radical intellectuals who, in various ways, deemed the replacement of the autocracy itself to be the prime, necessary condition for Russia's future development. Clearly Russia had some elements of progress for it to have such an educated elite. This anomalous group, usually referred to as the intelligentsia, was the pride of pre-revolutionary Russia. Its achievements in science, literature, music, the arts and, of particular relevance to the present analysis, its wide-ranging political philosophies, made their mark throughout the educated world. It was from this group that endless plans for the improvement of Russia emerged. One might very roughly divide the politically-involved intelligentsia into three broad groups: reforming state officials who wanted to make changes they saw necessary to preserve the essential strength of tsarism; constitutional reformers who wanted to introduce a rule of law and severely limit the traditional powers of the autocracy; and revolutionaries who saw the complete overthrow of tsarism and the establishment of a constituent assembly to work out an entirely new system of government for Russia as the only way forward. Within each of these groups traces of the conflicting philosophies of 'westernism' (the need for Russia to follow the path of other European powers and the United States on the road of liberalism, capitalism and rational modernisation) and 'Slavophilism' (the belief that Russia had its own path of development very distinct from those of other societies) could be found.

Second, as the previous paragraph partly implies, Russia was not a static society in the second half of the nineteenth century. Industrial, cultural, social and institutional changes were accumulating, albeit more slowly than further west. In the economic sphere, railways and modern industries began to appear alongside the traditional ones. Metalworking, mining and the oil industry all grew, drawing more and more peasants into a new urban or semi-urban way of life. An entrepreneurial class drove the process forward. Around the turn of the century large banks began to proliferate. The education system expanded to fulfil demand for engineers, lawyers, medical personnel and teachers in the new society. Villages began to feel the impact of new methods and machinery (though these last were not easily absorbed into traditional peasant or landowner agriculture) and of the migration of young people to factories and domestic service, where they underwent experiences which started a slow cultural and political revolution in the villages to which they returned. The result was that Russia became a more complex society. In agriculture, elements of capitalism – characterised by the expansion of cash crops such as sugar, flax, tea and tobacco, not to mention the vast expansion of grain exports – coexisted with time-honoured feudal remnants of strip agriculture and periodic land redistribution. The persistence of the landed estates, even though they only comprised on average some 10–15 per cent of agricultural land by 1900, was bitterly resented by the egalitarian peasantry who believed land should be shared fairly by all who worked it. The estates themselves were divided between those being farmed in a more intensive, capitalist fashion and those which were sinking into oblivion, a situation brilliantly captured in Chekhov's plays such as *The Cherry Orchard* of 1904.

While one could tease out the implications and nuances of the changes taking place at great length, the point for our present purpose is to bear in mind that the changes were being contained within a stubbornly unchanging framework of autocratic institutions and culture. As far as the former were concerned, suffice it to say that the reforms of the

1860s – which liberated the serfs from the authority of the landowners but left them indebted to the state and fixed less rigidly to their place of birth via the peasant commune, modernised military service and provided the basic framework of a completely undemocratic system of local government – were completely inadequate to deal with the problems since the real nettle – representation of at least the most powerful and wealthy members of society – was not grasped. The unsurprising failure of the reforms to achieve their objective actually made things worse in that even the tsar who granted them, Alexander II, quickly lost faith in them as new problems, particularly of terrorism, arose. His own death at the hands of revolutionary bombers opened the way for the opponents of reform to open up a full-scale counter-offensive directed at sweeping up terrorists and reversing some of the reforms. Instead of taking what one might call the German path pioneered by Bismarck, of incorporating the newly wealthy elite in the traditional framework of government, thereby holding radicals and democrats at bay, the Russian authorities declared war on all attempts to weaken the traditional autocracy and oppose every democratic initiative on the grounds that Russia had a superior, paternalistic system in which the tsar himself sought to right the wrongs suffered by all the people of Russia, no matter how humble. As one flattering courtier put it:

> In order that Russia may live in entire tranquillity and content all that is necessary is that there shall be direct relations between the Sovereign and his subjects.
>
> The Tsar can do no wrong; he stands above classes, party politics and personal rivalries. He desires the good of his people and has practically unlimited means for achieving it. He seeks nothing for himself.

The Tsar, the courtier concluded, was 'beneficence personified'.[3]

The person more responsible than any other for this reaction was Konstantin Pobedonostsev, tutor to Tsar Nicholas II and bureaucratic head of the Russian Orthodox Church from 1866 until October 1905. He, too, was responsible for cultural counter-revolution in the form of promoting the church as the source of Russianness and persecuting non-Orthodox subjects of the tsar including Protestants, Catholics and, above all, Jews, on whom the weight of pogroms began to fall from 1881 onwards. As a result, not only was Russia trying to keep the growing changes within the traditional framework of autocracy, it was trying to reshape that framework back to what it had been earlier rather than to adapt it to reality. The fundamental problem was encapsulated in the political precept Pobedonostsev had drummed into the head of Nicholas II – the fundamental duty of the tsar was to hand over his powers unimpaired to his successor. Such was the sea in which Bolshevism swam in its early, formative years.

Bolshevik Certainties – the Innocence of Inexperience

Before 1914, no one would have predicted that the Bolsheviks would come to power. They were a small, quarrelsome, fringe movement. Although Bolshevism was becoming increasingly influential among some workers, particularly in Russia's major cities, it had little influence among its more than 100 million peasants, let alone the growing middle class. Among revolutionary intellectuals it was also a minority movement.

As we have seen, it was distinguished by its fundamentalist obsession with preserving ideological orthodoxies and pursuing heresy. What was the 'truth' that the Bolsheviks believed they were realising through their revolution? The fundamental belief was that they alone held the golden key to unlocking the voracious global capitalist and imperialist system of the time and replacing it with harmonious, democratic socialism. They alone understood the true Marxist doctrine. Above all, they held unswervingly to the notion that the working class was destined, by the laws of history, to lead the transition. As a consequence they would have no truck with any part of the bourgeoisie, no sympathy for exploiters, no deference to the gentry or aristocracy and, most portentous, a deeply ingrained belief that the peasantry as a class was doomed to disappear into hostile petty-bourgeois and sympathetic rural proletarian fragments. In other words, the Bolsheviks were nothing if not class warriors, transferring many aspects of the ideology of nationalism to that of class. Where bourgeois states called on their people to sacrifice themselves for the nation – in their many millions in the First World War, which had a massive effect on this aspect of Bolshevik thinking – Bolshevism denounced the false consciousness of nationalism and urged the workers of the world to solidarity with one another in the face of the common exploiting enemy. For the Bolsheviks, class war was every bit as much a war as military warfare and a military morality, which we shall see evidenced time and time again in the formative years of the new system, underlay their strategy. As in conventional warfare, blood would be spilt, hatreds would fester, harsh discipline would have to be enforced and vast sacrifices be called for, but, also as in war, everything would be justified by the deeds of heroes and the ultimate righteousness of the cause. One could only, regretfully, harden oneself to the terrible, unavoidable costs of the struggle and not dwell on the sometimes cata-strophic mistakes because, after all, in a favourite Bolshevik saying, an omelette could not be made without breaking eggs.

Bolshevik rejection of nation had brought them into a final cata-clysmic conflict with the majority groups of the Second International as, on the eve of the First World War, most socialists, for a variety of reasons, fell in with the war policies of their respective governments and aban-doned their proclaimed ideal of international solidarity which had been at the heart of the organisation. Only fringe groups held to the original idea and spoke out against the war, arguing that the workers of Europe had no quarrel with each other. Many groups, like that around Ramsay Macdonald, also opposed the war on purely pacifist grounds. Lenin's tiny group, however, was by no means pacifist but continued to work, between 1914 and 1917, for an international, worker-based peace move-ment to turn against the imperialist warmongers and overthrow their power. The international dimension was absolutely crucial in Bolshevik thinking before October and continued to be of importance, in one way or another, throughout the life of the Soviet system. Even in its most moribund phase, the fiction that Soviet Russia led a worldwide, revolu-tionary class struggle of workers against exploiters was an integral part of communist ideology.[4]

Such was the basic faith of Bolshevism in very broad terms. Before looking at how it affected the course of events after October a few more observations about it need to be made. First, although it was interna-tional, Bolshevism also appeared to outsiders, as we have seen, to be quintessentially Russian in certain respects, not least the energy with which Bolshevik leaders held to and propagated their ideas. In this respect they mirrored the culture of the mainstream of the Russian Orthodox Church, namely that dogma must be protected at all costs. Those who did not accept the dogma were heretics and heretics must not be tolerated – rather they must be banished from the movement and their teachings uprooted among the faithful. There could be no ques-tion of dialogue with those who thought differently, no doubt about the absolute truth of the deposit of faith and no toleration of dissent.

The Bolsheviks might also be said to have 'Russified' Marxism. It may already have struck the reader as ironic that a movement which canonised

the working class and consigned the peasantry to oblivion might have little chance of influence in a Russia of over 100 million peasants and, probably, no more than five million proletarians many of whom were, in many
respects, peasant themselves. In addition, given that Marxist socialism
and communism are clearly post-capitalist social forms, why would a
party espouse them so strongly in the incontrovertibly pre- and early capitalist conditions of backward Russia? Lenin, in particular, relied on two
stratagems to resolve these apparent contradictions. First, the much-
vaunted internationalism of the Bolsheviks could be seen as a discourse
necessary to square the circle. Proposition one was that although Russia
was not ripe for Marxist revolution other parts of the capitalist world
were. Proposition two was that Russia itself was being increasingly drawn
into the global system of capitalism. This is, for example, the burden of
Lenin's well-known work of 1916, *Imperialism: The Highest Stage of Capitalism*. The conclusion to be drawn was that, although capitalism was not
dominant in Russia it could be combated there and various Marxist arguments were made to suggest that there was no reason why the initial blow
against the global system could not be struck in a place like Russia. Some,
like Bukharin and Trotsky, even argued that it was more likely to begin in
Russia. In a ringing phrase which delighted Lenin, Bukharin argued that
the chain of capitalism would break at its weakest link. Trotsky, in his theory of permanent revolution, argued that the revolution might begin in
Russia because the counter-revolutionary force of the bourgeoisie was
comparatively weaker than the revolutionary forces compared to a developed capitalist country like the United States where the bourgeoisie was
very strong, experienced and subtle in its control of society, characteristics barely present in its Russian counterpart. On the eve of October itself
Lenin justified the Bolshevik seizure of power in terms of it being the first
spark which would spread the revolution which Lenin believed to be
imminent elsewhere in Europe (particularly Germany), a belief which
guided his actions for some months to come. The corollary of this discourse, however, was clear. The revolution would not survive if it was confined to Russia. It must spread. While one might say that for Lenin this
argument remained something of a discourse which he did not ponder in
detail and was eventually ready to put at the back of his mind, one of the
most genuinely and consistently internationalist of the leaders of the
October revolution, Trotsky, spelled out its implications with devastating
clarity on the morrow of the revolution: 'Our whole hope is that our revolution will kindle a European revolution. If the rising of the people does
not crush imperialism, then we will surely be crushed.'[5]

While internationalism might be necessary to Bolshevik thinking, how did they manage to incorporate their views on peasants into their revolutionary strategy before October? Although Marx himself did not live long enough to work out his mature ideas on the peasantry, and was studying the Russian peasantry at the time of his death, his followers tended to argue that the Marxist view of the peasantry was clear. They would be wiped out by capitalism. Some would become market-oriented employers, exploiters and farmers. The majority would become workers, mostly in towns, some remaining as agricultural labourers. This was, roughly speaking, what had happened in Great Britain where, in the industrial heartland, the peasantry had been abolished and only maintained a tenuous hold in the impoverished fringes of parts of Wales, Scotland and, most of all, Ireland. As far as Russia was concerned, Lenin had claimed from early in his career, notably 1899 when he wrote *The Development of Capitalism in Russia*, that similar trends were already gripping Russia. Market-oriented cash-crop agriculture was undermining peasant subsistence agriculture. The peasantry was splitting into a proto-capitalist petty bourgeoisie, the 'wealthiest' stratum of which Lenin referred to as *kulaks*, while at the bottom, a poor peasantry was emerging as a rural exploited class and most likely potential ally of the urban workers. In between was a majority middle peasantry which oscillated between the other two, aspiring to become *kulaks* but often being threatened by economic, climatic and other circumstances with descent into the impoverished stratum. After October, as we shall see, Lenin's attitude to the middle peasantry also oscillated, but before 1917 it was clear that, in Bolshevik eyes, the existing peasantry – with their communal redistribution, strip agriculture, supposed obedience to the church and deference to tsarist authority – were clearly identified as a serious drag on progress. They would have to be eliminated for modern industry and socialism to develop. Above all, the Bolsheviks (their former allies the Mensheviks agreeing with them on this) fundamentally opposed the policy of the Socialist Revolutionaries (SRs) whose main platform was that landowner land should be given to the peasantry as the peasants themselves overwhelmingly desired and considered just. A major consequence of this argument was that the Bolsheviks identified themselves as an anti-peasant, worker party who, as a matter of course, opposed what the SRs stood for rather as government and opposition parties in parliamentary democracies routinely denounce each other's policy initiatives and rarely, if ever, agree with them. There was, however, one colossal exception to this. To the surprise of all concerned, one of Lenin's two great policy declarations in the October revolution, the Decree on Land, was a complete steal from the SRs, as vociferous critics pointed out when Lenin introduced his initiative at the Second Congress of Soviets within hours of coming to power. 'I hear voices raised here declaring both the decree and the land mandate were drafted by the Socialist Revolutionaries. Well, suppose that they were? What does it matter who drafted them?' We can doubt whether Lenin was genuinely converted, for once, to the ideas of heretics. Instead, it was a pragmatic manoeuvre designed to undermine the old ruling class; to allow the new government to establish itself by winning over the support of peasants who were, in any case, unstoppably resolved to take the land; and, specifically, to split the SR party, a fraction of which came over to ally itself with the Bolsheviks. Not coincidentally, many of the SRs who did come over were also internationalists who had denounced Russia's national war effort. While it may have worked in the short term, the decree set the scene for the first and, perhaps, worst of the Soviet government's later assaults on its own population – collectivisation. While there were, as we shall see, numerous twists and turns in Bolshevik policy towards the peasants, its fundamental belief that they were the enemies of progress and a potential source of the regeneration of capitalism in post-revolutionary Russia was shared by all sections of the party leadership, though there were immense differences about the pace and manner in which the peasantry should be transformed into modern, socialist agricultural workers. A necessary condition for such a transition was that the peasantry should give up, or pool, the land it had been given in October 1917. As we shall see, Leninist assumptions about the peasantry did not always fit the realities, particularly when it came to the issue of differentiation within the peasantry. The conflicts arising from the disparity between Bolshevik views and peasant reality were among the most severe in post-revolutionary Russia.

It follows from what we have said that, in many respects, Lenin's chief contributions to socialist theory – *The Development of Capitalism in Russia* and *Imperialism: The Highest Stage of Capitalism* – should be read not as dispassionate analyses but as particular ways of adapting Marx's ideas to the specific conditions of Russia and as necessary justifications for the very existence of a Marxist organisation in a country like Russia in the first place. The same could be said for his other two major works we have not yet had cause to refer to, namely, *What Is To Be Done?* and *State and Revolution*, as well as his main contribution to revolutionary practice, the role of the party. We will look at these shortly.

A final point. Although the Bolsheviks' faith was powerful in general terms and especially in its critique of the existing situation, not only in tsarist Russia but in the global context of rampant imperialism, the Bolsheviks spent little time in consideration of what might happen immediately after a successful revolution or how the multitude of transitional problems might be faced. However, to elaborate on this question, and to develop some of the basic ideas set out above, it is time to move on to examine Bolshevik practice once they actually came to power.

The Contradictions of the Revolution

It is not our purpose here to rehearse all the reasons why the Bolsheviks did come to power, rather it is more relevant to look at some of the aspects of their coming to power which had a lasting imprint on their evolution. In particular, we need to note that the Bolsheviks came to power through the chance conjuncture of circumstances, not through their own beloved mechanism of 'historical necessity' and they came to power despite never carrying a majority of the population with them. Let us take a look at these two phenomena.

The Path to October

Lenin's most characteristic contribution to revolutionary activity is often thought to be his idea of the party. He evolved this around the turn of the century and, in a well-known struggle in 1903, tried to impose his views on the Russian Social Democratic Party, Russia's main Marxist party, splitting it in the process into Bolshevik and Menshevik factions. Lenin strove for the rest of his life to keep the factions apart. Why was the split so important to him? In essence, Lenin called for a higher degree of commitment from party members. His opponents were prepared to allow anyone sympathetic to its aims to join the party but Lenin wanted it to be an organisation of well-informed, active militants. He did not want, in his own contemptuous words, party members who would devote only their spare evenings and weekends to the cause. He wanted people prepared to devote their whole lives, in the extreme revolutionary tradition of Chernyshevsky and others from the 1860s and 1870s. In the conditions of pre-1905 Imperial Russia, where all political parties were illegal, let alone revolutionary ones, Lenin thought such a degree of commitment was not only necessary to conduct the day-to-day struggle with the tsarist police but would also help keep the ever-present menace of infiltration by informers at bay.

In fact, it did not do so but it remained crucial to Lenin all the same. He outlined his views in a pamphlet entitled *What Is To Be Done?*, a deliberate echo of the title of Chernyshevsky's extremely influential novel (also, significantly, subtitled *Stories of New People*). The idea was still rather tentative at that stage but Lenin built elements of it into a theory of party activity which he put into rigorous practice. In a key phrase (echoing the background debate among all Marxists at the turn of the century about why the revolution they thought Marx had predicted had not taken place), Lenin stated that, left to itself, the working class could only develop 'trade-union consciousness'. It would only concern itself with improving its wages and conditions and not, as Marx had clearly expressed, move on logically to realise that only revolutionary struggle against the system itself would achieve its liberation. It was here, Lenin argued, that the party was necessary. It should be an organisation of workers who had reached revolutionary consciousness and it should be devoted to spreading that consciousness to the, as yet, unenlightened workers. In practice the party was dominated in these years by revolutionaries and working-class activists within the Russian Empire, especially after the failed 1905 revolution, who were not much moved by the Bolshevik/Menshevik split.[6] However, Lenin never admitted the intelligentsia domination of the party nor, in post-October times, its role in the leadership. Be that as it may, the role and purpose of the party defined by Lenin remained at its heart almost throughout its existence, reaching its peak under Stalin rather than Lenin. In this conception, the party was a coming together of conscious leaders of the proletarian class for the purpose of spreading that consciousness. Before 1917, this meant producing and distributing a party newspaper as its central function. After 1917 it meant using the power of the state to set up education, censorship, propaganda and agitation departments and much else, to promote the required 'proletarian consciousness'. One might speculate that the tremendous drive behind consciousness-raising was a specifically 'Russian' feature of Bolshevism picked up via the populist tradition of 'going to the people' and propaganda by word and deed. In its turn, one might trace the importance of principles and beliefs to the religious matrix of Russian thought which had not seen the separation of faith and reason which had been evolving in Western Europe through the Renaissance, the Reformation and the Enlightenment. Russian thought in many areas remained 'religious' in this sense.

Within the overarching purpose of the party Lenin and the leadership developed a wide variety of political, economic and cultural stratagems for attaining its goals. The 1905 revolution made Lenin aware of the possibility of a broad alliance of democratic forces aimed at the overthrow of tsarism and the establishment of a Constituent Assembly. Mensheviks, Bolsheviks, SRs and Liberals (Kadets) were all offically committed to a Constituent Assembly, though a few Kadets thought a constitutional monarchy might emerge. A minority of leftists who argued the time had come to admit defeat in the political struggle and urged turning to economic struggle (for better conditions and wages by means of trade unions) was roundly condemned by Mensheviks and Bolsheviks alike. Even so, Lenin sabotaged all efforts to reunite the parties. The situation changed radically in 1914 when, as we have seen, the Second International split into 'defensists' who supported their nation's war efforts and a small minority of 'internationalists' who urged workers not to participate in the war. Lenin became one of the most outspoken advocates of the latter position and, as early as September 1914 when most socialists were in depression at the disastrous turn taken by events, he proclaimed that the war opened up new revolutionary possibilities and that true socialists should proclaim the slogan 'turn the war into a European-wide civil war'. In other words, like many leftists and other rationalists since, he underestimated the deadly influence of nationalism, believing the war would awaken workers to their common plight and encourage them to band together across national boundaries in order to overthrow their evil rulers who had led them to the slaughter. Very few workers, however, blamed their own rulers for the war. Instead, they blamed the enemy and went to the slaughter, if not willingly, at least with the recognition that it was their duty to fight to defend their respective countries. Nonetheless, the split catalysed new political relationships and defensists versus internationalists became a more important division on the Russian left than that between parties.

For Lenin, the October revolution was the outcome of the logic of history. It confirmed his principles of class struggle and the near inevitability of the triumph of progressive socialism over decadent capitalism. However, close observation might suggest more mundane reasons for the Bolsheviks' success in coming to power.

The key principles behind Lenin's actions between February and October can be found in his *April Theses*, written as a guide to strategy on his journey back from exile and announced to his followers immediately upon his return. In politics, the main provisions were that no support should be given to the Provisional Government; that the party should support soviet rather than parliamentary democracy; and that the workers should make common cause in soviets with the poorest peasants and agricultural labourers. The first of these theses caused considerable controversy since it broke the united revolutionary front of the centre and the main components of the left that most activists considered necessary, at least for the time being, to hold together all anti-tsarist forces and prevent counter-revolution. With some difficulty Lenin persuaded his, as yet quite small, party to accept. His grounds for proposing it were twofold. First, in an objective sense, the new government was just as bourgeois and imperialist as its predecessor in that it remained committed to fighting the war, therefore the workers had no business supporting an unremitingly imperialist war. Interestingly, Lenin at several points did contemplate the war becoming acceptable to workers after a workers' revolution since, under such conditions, it would cease to be an imperialist war and become a revolutionary war. Clearly, Lenin still had his dream of a continent-wide civil war at the back of his mind. His second argument, which underlay many of his other policy initiatives of the time, was more theoretical. Russia, he argued, was passing from the first stage of the revolution, which put power into the hands of the bourgeoisie, to the second, socialist stage which would bring the proletariat and its allies to power. Where past policy had been geared towards preparing for the democratic overthrow of tsarism, now that goal was achieved it must refocus on the next problem, the introduction of socialism.

Before looking at further implications of this latter point, it has to be pointed out that the position of not supporting the Provisional Government was crucial in bringing the Bolsheviks to power. It led to the Bolsheviks being the only significant party not to join the broadening coalition of the Provisional Government so that the implicated parties sank as the Provisional Government sank after the Kornilov rebellion.[7] This left the Bolsheviks as the focus of the hopes of all those on the left who opposed the Provisional Government and wanted more radical action on redistribution of land, ending the war, solving the economic crisis and establishing democracy via the soviets and the long-delayed Constituent Assembly. The Bolsheviks were sufficiently shrewd (if you support them) or unscrupulous and deceptive (if you oppose them) to give the impression they were at one with these demands even when, as we have seen with the land decree, their long-term aims were completely the opposite of the popular programme.

Underlying the *April Theses* was the assumption of transition, of 'passing from' one stage 'to' the next. Since transition is what the entire Soviet experience came to be about, it is worth dwelling on Lenin's pre-October views on it for a while. First of all, no timescales were attached. Not supporting the Provisional Government did not mean it should be immediately overthrown. What cynics might think of as un-Leninist terms like 'caution', 'gradual' and 'patient' put in an appearance as does Lenin's clear belief that the Russian working class was 'backward' compared to its western counterparts. This echoed the resounding words of his 'Farewell Address to the Swiss Workers' – that it was only the chance conjuncture of circumstances, not its special qualities, which had thrust the Russian working class to the forefront of the international revolutionary movement. As Lenin had put it:

> To the Russian proletariat has fallen the great honour of *beginning* the series of revolutions which the imperialist war has made an objective inevitability. But the idea that the Russian proletariat is the chosen revolutionary proletariat is absolutely alien to us. We know perfectly well that the proletariat of Russia is less organised, less prepared and less class-conscious than the proletariat of other countries. It is not its special qualities but rather the special conjuncture of historical circumstances that *for a certain, perhaps very short, time* has made the proletariat of Russia the vanguard of the revolutionary proletariat of the whole world.[8]

There was even a thesis commenting that 'it is not our *immediate* task to "introduce" socialism', the operative words being 'immediate' and 'introduce'. Only democratic, soviet *supervision* of production and distribution were deemed to be on the cards given Russia's general unpreparedness for post-capitalist socialism. The contempt behind the word 'introduced' is particularly interesting, Lenin's implication being that socialism could only grow organically, not be artificially induced from above. Arguably, Lenin, in this phrase, was unwittingly condemning the entire Soviet experience! Incidentally, when charges of this kind were made against him he tended to argue it was the duty of a revolutionary to make revolution as best he could, not stand aside and say the time is not ripe. History was the court in which the question would be decided.

Two other aspects need to be borne in mind. Surprisingly, there is little about economic transition in Lenin's writings between the revolutions. The implication of his views – notably that, in Russian conditions, Soviet political supervision of continuing capitalism was all that was on the agenda in the short term – was expressed several times. Even when it came to supplying material resources for a potential revolutionary war, Lenin argued that political mobilisation and threats against capitalists would be sufficient. In fact, it long remained a basic aspect of Soviet 'economics' that orders from a person with a gun constituted economic policy. The only distinctly economic policy was itself institutional and revealing. It was a call to nationalise the banks. Following current socialist theory, it was argued that since, in contemporary capitalism, banks rather than individuals controlled investment, one could control this crucial component of capitalism by simply putting them under state control. Elsewhere, Lenin also appeared overly optimistic about the prospects for transition, arguing that only a soviet takeover could solve the economic mess Russia was in.[9]

A number of these themes were developed in Lenin's main theoretical work of the time, *State and Revolution*, which he composed during his renewed exile in Finland following the banning of the Bolshevik party in the wake of the July Days fiasco in which a failed attempt to seize power was blamed on the Bolsheviks and forged documents were produced by the Provisional Government intended to show that Lenin was, of all things, a German agent. The accusations have led to scholarly wild goose chases which appear to have lost little of their attraction.[10] They were also enough for the Bolshevik party to be severely inconvenienced for a couple of months, not least by its leader's withdrawal from the scene. In *State and Revolution* Lenin underlined the point about taking over the banks. He also put forward a more detailed argument about direct, post-revolutionary government through completely new institutions. His ideas were based on Marx's view, derived from observing the Paris Commune of 1871, that the problem was that, in all previous revolutions, the aim had been to take over the mechanisms of state when the point should have been to smash them. For Lenin this meant setting up soviets (though in practice he opposed the existing system between July and early September), democratising the civil service by opening all jobs up to election, rotation (that is, all citizens taking a turn) and limiting salaries to those of a skilled worker to prevent the emergence of a fat-cat administrative class. It was with these ideas in his mind that Lenin, as he laconically reported at the end of *State and Revolution*, broke off writing about revolution 'probably for a long time' and returned to the 'more pleasant and useful' business of experiencing a revolution rather than writing about it.[11] How would the real transition match up to the sketchy theories?

The simple reason for Bolshevik success in the October revolution was that they were the only party left which associated itself with popular demands, especially for a takeover of governmental power by the Congress of Soviets. Even before the Bolshevik-engineered *coup de grâce* given to the Provisional Government on 25 October 1917, the majority of congress delegates had been mandated days and weeks before to support soviet power, so low had the prestige of the Provisional Government sunk as a result of its failure to move quickly on the key issues of land, ending the war and establishing democracy, topped off by the assumed collaboration between its Prime Minister, Alexander Kerensky, and the leader of the failed counter-revolution of late August and early September, General Kornilov. In practice, the Provisional Government and Kerensky in particular had made heroic efforts to hold Russia together in the face of impending civil war, a clearly disastrous drift given Russia's struggle against Germany in the ongoing world war, but public opinion, such as it was, did not accept the slow settlement of the problems and looked for radical solutions. The collapse of the Provisional Government also pulled down the Bolsheviks' chief rivals because, although it had started out as a cabinet dominated by liberals, when it was overthrown the majority of its members were from the socialist SR (Socialist Revolutionary) and Menshevik parties. Kerensky, with considerable justification, also thought of himself as a man of the radical left rather than the liberal centre. Nonetheless, the demise of his government discredited the SRs and Mensheviks, leaving the Bolsheviks, as we have said, as the only significant party prepared to support the popular demand for soviet power. In this way, the Bolsheviks came to power through the conjuncture of events, though they themselves were inclined to argue that the laws of history, especially the unfolding logic of class struggle led by the proletariat, had impelled them into office, a misunderstanding which, in itself, had extensive consequences.[12]

Minority Status

It would be hard to judge exactly when Bolshevik popularity was at its peak in the whole period of its rule but certainly the moment when it took power must be one of the leading candidates. Few people now believe that the October revolution was no more than a coup – its mass support among Soviet Congress delegates in itself shows it was widely hoped for and welcomed. Its wide-ranging support was confirmed by its second place, with some 25 per cent of the votes, in the Constituent

Assembly elections, a figure that in practice was higher since part of the SR party, which came first in the election with around 50 per cent of the vote, had been won over to support the new Soviet government in which the splinter faction, the Left SRs, played a junior role. But whatever measure one takes, one fact remains clear. The Bolsheviks did not enjoy majority support and, as we shall see, quickly fell from their peak of support certainly by the beginning of 1918, perhaps even earlier. This leads us to an absolutely crucial consideration for our purpose of understanding the fate of the Soviet revolution. One cannot underestimate the fact that, throughout its history, Bolshevism was a minority movement. The party and state (with possibly a few exceptions such as the Second World War) never enjoyed the active support of the majority of its citizens. This fact alone helps us to understand many of the most repulsive features of the future system. It was, first and foremost, a minority dictatorship and took on dictatorial features. Between 1917 and 1989 no election of any significance was held. Only governments that think they will lose fear elections. The message is clear. In other words, arguments based on the supposedly inherently dictatorial nature of Marxism, socialism, centrally planned economies and so on often fail to take this more fundamental level of explanation into account. The Bolsheviks knew that the majority of the population in 1917 opposed them but took steps to maintain themselves in power despite that. This opened up two further aspects of the movement which cast a long shadow over its future. Bolshevism justified its acquisition and holding of power by its 'truth' and it believed its future lay in winning over the mass of the population by revealing that truth to them. If we have outlined the many paradoxes of pre-revolutionary Russia it is only right to point out the fundamental paradox of Soviet Russia – it adopted interim dictatorial methods to hold the line while it 'won over' the population but its dictatorial methods alienated much of the population and made it harder to win them over. The vicious circle that evolved meant that, instead of lightening its grip as popular support grew, the Soviet government spent decades tightening it in the face of growing opposition or indifference to its goals. We need to bear this in mind throughout most of our excursion through Soviet history.

2

The Soviet System under Lenin

The October revolution was not so much a culminating point, rather it was the first step on the sometimes heroic, sometimes catastrophic and ultimately unsuccessful long march of Soviet power. As we have seen, Lenin had not devoted much intellectual energy to post-revolutionary questions. He had only hazy expectations and optimistic assumptions about the first steps in the transition to socialism. Events turned out very differently from what Lenin had hoped. From day one of the revolution he had to backtrack and improvise. His most spectacular U-turn came on the land question. It was already a sign of the three deep problems that immediately confronted the new Soviet leader.

The first was that the revolution actually occurring – based on the self-activity of peasants, workers, soldiers and sailors – was far from that predicted or hoped for by Lenin. It was, in effect, a mass populist revolution based on small-scale communal ownership of property in land and in factories. It was much closer in spirit to the predictions of the SRs than to those of the Bolsheviks. Instead of a disciplined, worker-led movement for large-scale, socialised production there was a mass movement for direct local democracy and direct control of land and factories by the producers themselves.

Second, the assumption that, in the short and medium term, Soviet political control could supervise a continuing capitalist-led market economy pending the organic emergence of socialism proved to be a hollow dream. In practice, the capitalists and their allies, notably managers and engineers, refused to have anything to do with the new system and many even fought actively against it. These were unpromising beginnings. In order to understand the crucial first steps towards the construction of the Soviet system we need to examine the nature of these two difficulties

21

and then look at how they affected the emerging system. But before we do that we need to look at the third deep problem – the rapidly deteriorating political environment and the new government's desperate struggle to survive.

Revolutionary Wars – 1917–21

As far as the events of this complex and controversial period are concerned we can distinguish three periods: the first nine months or so before the civil war proper began; the years of civil war from June/July 1918 to the defeat of Denikin's army in January 1920 (perhaps extended to October 1920 to take in the war with Poland and the destruction of Wrangel's remaining forces in the Crimea); and, finally, the first attempts at postwar reconstruction which were abandoned in favour of the New Economic Policy (NEP) at the Tenth Party Congress in March 1921. We will take a look at the fundamental features of each of these periods.

The 'Golden Age' of Revolution

In these first few months of revolution four colossal processes took hold of Russia and transformed it. They were the peasant seizure of the land; the collapse of industry and the attempts at worker takeover of the remnants; the overthrow of the power of the traditional tsarist and emerging bourgeois capitalist elites and their expulsion to the periphery whence they formed counter-revolutionary armies to fight back; and, fourth, the establishment of a one-party Soviet state backed by its own political police and developing Red Army. Beside these, events like Russia's peace with Germany at Brest-Litovsk (March 1918) and the explosion of the Russian Empire into a multitude of as yet disorganised fragments seemed incidental, especially since the peace treaty was overtaken by events (notably the collapse of Germany in November 1918) and, by 1921, the majority of fragments had been gathered up anew in what was officially called the Soviet Union from the adoption of the constitution of 1923 onwards. Only Finland, Estonia, Latvia, Lithuania and Poland succeeded in establishing their independence.

The peasant movement had been one of the major catalysts of revolution since the spring of 1917. Peasants, other than a handful who had been serving in the mutinous guards regiments, had played no role in the February revolution but within weeks, across the whole of European Russia and some of the non-Russian areas, peasants were testing out their traditional enemies, the landowners and the state. Without much outside influence millions of peasants were beginning to work slowly towards their goals. They strengthened their village committees by throwing out hostile non-peasant elements; they forced down rents; they forced wages up; they took war prisoners off landowner estates and set them to work on the land of peasants away at the war; they encroached on gentry pasture and forest lands; they sowed their own crops on unused land and even began making inventories of landowners' estates and prevented them selling off assets which, the peasants confidently assumed, would soon be passed over to them by the new authorities or the expected Constituent Assembly. In some places there was violence but overall these momentous changes proceeded by steady, small increments which made them difficult to oppose. Troops were not much use since the peasants would simply sit out their presence and wait for them to be called away to the next local trouble spot and then carry on as before. In any case, the Provisional Government was very reluctant to use troops in the early months for fear of alienating the masses.

Observers have tended to note that the intensity of peasant action was shaped by the yearly agricultural cycle: a flurry of land encroachments (rather than full-scale seizures) in the early weeks in order to expand the area of spring sowing, a minor peak in late spring and early summer interrupted by the harvest and a final, probably more violent but smaller rise in September and October after the harvest was gathered in. The relative harshness of the last wave may be accounted for by the fact that these were probably tougher, more resistant landowners with whom accounts were being settled. However, the pattern was similar over all European Russia and to some extent beyond. The peasants were cowed by no one's reputation as they cautiously advanced their historic claim to the land and realised the police and army would not offer serious resistance. Royal estates, monastic lands, the property of the highest families were all targets. However, it must be remembered that, before October, outright land seizure had barely begun. One of many enduring myths of the revolution is that not only peasants but soldiers were caught up in an immense tidal wave of land seizures which caused troops to desert the fronts en masse. One historian puts it thus: 'The longing of the peasants in uniform to share in the seizure of land became overwhelming. The stream of soldiers to the front reversed itself. There was a backward torrent of peasants returning to the land; a dribble of deserters from the front expanded to gigantic numbers of "self-demobilised" soldiers.[1] Sadly for traditional historiography, this basic 'cause' of the October revolution was, rather, a consequence. Desertion was not the main problem facing the military before October and a high proportion of deserters returned to the line. It was mainly after October that estate seizures grew rapidly from autumn until almost all estates had been taken over by early 1918. It was also in the post-October period that the army disintegrated.[2]

In a sense, this meant the early months were a golden age for the peasants. They controlled the land. The landowners were reduced to living alongside them or had fled. The new Soviet state was as yet too weak to intervene and had in any case appeared to sanction the peasant movement. For the moment the peasants were relatively content.

However, their sense of well-being was built on a lie. Traditional Bolshevik policies were, as we have seen, deeply hostile to the traditional peasantry. The new communist authorities were determined to begin the transformation of the peasantry as soon as possible. They also had to struggle with another key problem – the production and extraction of a food surplus from the peasants. Much of the surplus had come from gentry estates and advanced capitalist cash-crop sectors of agriculture. In wartime conditions of high industrial prices the peasants had lost the incentive to market grain and even the tsarist authorities were having to contemplate forced grain requisitioning. Failure to ensure the food supply to the capital had helped bring about damaging food riots in Petrograd which had precipitated their downfall in the February revolution. The Provisional Government had faced similar problems. With the additional disruption of the October revolution and the sweeping away of the landowner sector, the danger of food shortages increased exponentially. If the peasants turned their newly acquired land to providing for their own subsistence, the cities would starve. By 1918 this was beginning to happen. It was only a matter of time before the Soviet government felt the need to intervene in the rural areas.

Ironically, the cities, supposedly the home of the revolution-leading proletariat in communist eyes, fared much worse than the countryside. The October revolution precipitated a rapid collapse of urban life in Soviet Russia. Peasant villages can, if pushed, look after themselves. Cities cannot. They are dependent on communication webs and massive interdependency as a result of their specialisation. A coal town cannot live without selling coal and having what it needs available on the market. The same goes for military, administrative, textile, metalworking and oil towns. The first step to disaster was growing disorder on the railways on which they all relied for supply and distribution. The collapse of the money economy through accelerating inflation destroyed the markets. Fleeing bourgeois managers left disruption in their wake. Cities in areas to which grain had to be imported from far away, notably Petrograd, suffered most. Cities like Moscow, which was surrounded by fairly rich agricultural provinces like Kaluga and Tambov, were at least able to scour their hinterlands for food. Those in the south, where supplies were relatively plentiful, were the least badly off. Nonetheless, cities all over the country began to break up. The first steps in industrial collapse had already begun in the early months of Soviet rule. Indeed, one could go back to 1917 to trace the beginning of the struggle for power between management and workers. The February revolution had been set against the background of a lockout of some 26 000 workers at the Putilov factory in Petrograd. By the middle of the year, employers were manipulating raw material shortages in order to shut down factories. They wanted to do this to discipline their workers and bring them back under their control because the workers were forming unions and strik-ing for better wages and conditions in the disastrous environment of wartime inflation which was cutting their already meagre living stan-dards. In response to employer shutdowns, workers stumbled into workers' control in the form of factory committees trying to keep facto-ries running and thereby protect their jobs. Here was the mundane ori-gin of the revolutionary involvement of workers. They began to support soviet power and the Bolsheviks in 1917 out of practical considerations. They thought the Bolsheviks were the most likely party to help them take over and maintain factories from which managers and capitalists alike had fled, leaving underqualified workers to cope as best they might. While Petrograd was especially affected by this process, other cities and industrial areas certainly felt the pressure of collapse and the vicious circle of class struggle. It took the form of workers, provoked by disruption of the economy which threatened wages and jobs, putting pressure on employers who responded by closures and repression. This caused further disruption, making workers more desperate and inclined to more radical action. In the wilder 'frontier' areas of Donbas mining and Urals metalworking, gunplay was not uncommon and unfortunates on either side were occasionally flung into smelting furnaces.

The October revolution served only to deepen the crisis. More of the elite fled, adding to the disruption. Chaos on the railways got worse, not least because the Bolsheviks forcibly disbanded the railway workers' union and replaced it with a tame one that would eat out of their hand. Workers themselves demanded direct takeovers of factories, something the Bolshevik leaders were unhappy about because they were afraid a spontaneous worker movement, given the relative 'backwardness' of Russian compared to, say, German workers, would leave the workers vulnerable to all kinds of harmful (meaning non-Bolshevik) influences. As we shall see, official policy was to conciliate bourgeois remnants rather than to back radical worker takeovers. Thus, for the working class, October was not much of a triumph. They had rid themselves of employers, no mean achievement, but they could only take over the rapidly sinking ships which were Russian industrial enterprises. The end of the war, economic isolation, the collapse of the national market, the unreliability of the rail network, the Soviet authorities' support for the managerial personnel and the collapse of employment and wages all made the October revolution a bitter victory for Russian workers. In the medium term, hard though it is to imagine, the situation got infinitely worse.

Ironically, the disruption of the cities and industry was a consequence of what was, from the revolutionary point of view, an undoubted achievement, the sweeping away of the old elites. The whole panoply not only of tsarist but incipient bourgeois power had also been brushed aside. The apparently all-powerful tsarist retinue of Grand Dukes, princes, princesses, noble families of ancient lineage, the gentry, the army commanders, the police force, the interior ministry with its secret police and informer network, the judiciary, the factory owners, the managers, the bankers, the respectable professional families were now nothing if they refused to go along with the new order. Even if they did, their troubles were far from over and a savage attitude to anyone who had the audacity to be born even into a fairly modest family continued to drive revolutionary vengeance at least until the time of the great purge of 1936–8. As we have already seen, the cost of this victory was to deprive Russia of many of its most educated and most skilled personnel as well as its social leeches and exploiters. It took decades to replace the lost skills and there were to be many twists and turns to make up for their absence in the short and medium term.

Civil War

Such a formerly powerful ruling class as that of Russia before the revolution was not going to accept its own obliteration without fighting back. Resistance to revolution had been its basic reflex for more than half a century. Since 1881 it had backed the tough line of Alexander III which, under Pobedonostsev's morose guidance, had instigated a stern reaction which rebounded not only in 1917 but in the 1905 revolution, a potential learning experience from which Tsar Nicholas II, Alexander's son and successor, learned nothing except that all the trouble was caused by students and Jews. Even those with tsarism's best interests at heart, like Witte and Stolypin, found their reform proposals treated almost as revolutionary blueprints. As we have already seen, the 'German model', of fusing old money with new and sidestepping parliamentary democracy, was not even contemplated by the reactionary backwoodsmen of whose club the charming, personally mild-mannered but often obstinate Nicholas was a fully paid-up member. Indeed, his overthrow in 1917 was backed by many members of the elite, including crucial figures in the army high command, who wanted to clear the decks for a more popular form of government which could reenergise the population behind the war effort. The dilemma of the right in the revolution (basically defined as those who wanted to preserve the existing distribution of power, status and, above all, property) was that it remained divided between those who saw the necessity of change in order to stave off full-blown social revolution and those who wanted to make a militant, counter-revolutionary stand. Loosely speaking, the Provisional Government represented the former, its growing enemies on the right speaking for the latter. As 1917 progressed the hard-line reactionaries became increasingly aggressive.

In political terms the civil war began long before serious fighting broke out in summer 1918. As far back as July 1917 the right had been putting pressure on the Provisional Government to assert its authority to the full. The death penalty at the front and the establishment of martial law on the railways and in Russia's major factories were its main demands. While General Kornilov, the Commander-in-Chief, was deemed to be the leader of this movement it was the cossack Ataman (Chieftain) Kaledin who put the programme forward at the Moscow State Conference in August 1917. However, it was Kornilov himself who led the ensuing attempted coup which, under the guise of moving troops to suppress the Petrograd Soviet, had a secret agenda of replacing the Provisional Government and giving 'protection', including demotion, to Prime Minister Kerensky, who only moved swiftly against his appointee when he became aware of the threat to his own power. Like most actions of the politically dumb right, the Kornilov coup rebounded spectacularly, opening the way for a rapid rise in what had appeared in many ways to be the spent force of Bolshevism and undermining the remnants of confidence in the Provisional Government which led to soviet power seeming to be the only way ahead for the mass movements of soldiers, sailors, workers and peasants which were making the revolutionary running at the time.

Kornilov was kept under light imprisonment until November when he 'escaped' to the south, formed a core anti-Bolshevik force and lead it into the early battles of what at the time was thought to be the civil war but, with hindsight, was only a foretaste. The counter-revolutionary forces got the worst of these early skirmishes, Kornilov himself being killed in one of them on 13 April at Ekaterinodar. As a result of their partly violent, partly peaceful 'triumphal march', the Soviet authorities had asserted some kind of authority over the key towns of the Russian-speaking part of the Empire. The situation in the Ukraine and other minority nationalities was too complex for us to follow in detail except in so far as it affected the general situation of what became known as the White armies.

Two related events helped restart the civil war in a big way. The western allies had, naturally, been distraught by Russia's collapse. They feared a total disaster on the eastern front would release sufficient forces for Germany and her allies to press for victory on the west. To avoid this, the allies came within a hair's breadth of sending troops to back Bolshevik resistance to Germany. It was only the Soviet government's decision to make peace at any price with Germany which aborted this policy. Out of a desire to keep the Germans occupied, to secure war materials sent to Russia which might fall into German hands and from a sense of honour to former allies, Britain and France decided to back the Whites. Unspoken hostility to social revolution and the fear of it spreading were also major motivators not only of intervention but also of the eventual peace settlement at Paris, whence the political initiatives of the Whites were directed by their emissaries and their allied quartermasters. The second event, which precipitated the actual outbreak of the civil war proper in May 1918, was the rebellion of the Czech legion which was being evacuated via Siberia in order to rejoin the war on the western front now that the eastern front had collapsed. Heavy-handed orders by Trotsky that it should disarm provoked it to rebel instead and opened the way for the Whites to take control of most of Siberia. Other peripheral forces in south Russia and the Baltic were also reactivated as a result, especially when allied equipment and even small armies began to arrive.

At the war's peak the Soviet authorities and the Red Army were pushed back into what amounted to only some 10 per cent of the territory of the tsarist empire. White armies threatened the Volga, Petrograd and even Moscow, which had become the capital on 12 March 1918 because it was deemed less vulnerable to military attack by foreign or internal enemies of the new government. The Whites believed they had built up unstoppable momentum and were dreaming of victory celebrations in Moscow. How did they fall from their apparently high-flying position?

In many ways their success was hollow and their chance of victory never good for one excellent reason. They were armies without civilian support. They believed their advance into Bolshevik-held territory would lead to them being welcomed as liberators. Instead, the population tended to treat them with sullen acquiescence at best. Even areas badly treated by the Bolsheviks were reluctant to see the Whites as anything more than another scourge. The lack of discipline of the White armies, their lack of roots in the population and their ingrained officer-class, male chauvinist, nationalist, militaristic culture meant they saw little need for subtlety in dealing with their social inferiors. Their, for many, unbridled anti-Semitism alone would have been sufficient to blacken their reputation forever were it not for Nazism which deprived them of the notoriety of being the worst twentieth-century persecutors of Jews in Europe. Contemporary estimates concluded some 115 000 Jews were killed in Ukraine alone.[3] The range of estimates today is from 50 000 to 200 000.[4] At best the Whites represented the return of empire, landlords and capitalists, an outcome devoutly to be avoided in the view of the minorities, among whom their bases were often set up, and of the peasants and workers into whose territories they advanced. With the usual political imbecility of inexperienced generals interfering in politics, they deprived themselves of any hope of popular support by suppressing the democratic remnants of the anti-Bolshevik movement. Only when they were finally on the slide did they toy with proposals for reform in the now extremely unlikely event of their victory. Only a few gullible admirers and apologists have been taken in by such death-bed conversions.

Alongside this fundamental reason, other factors in their failure are of secondary importance. They were indeed catastrophically uncoordinated, each separate force trying to outdo the others in the interests of having first pick of the spoils of victory. They were harassed in their base areas and lines of communications as they advanced by movements such as that of the peasant anarchist Nestor Makhno who dominated a large slice of the eastern Ukraine and conducted a merciless war against the old order as well as the Bolsheviks. The Reds did have certain advantages. Their 10 per cent of territory contained a much higher proportion of the population – some 50–60 per cent – as well as the bulk of the wartime military stores and the centre of the web of strategic railways along which much of the war was fought. As a result, the Reds, under Trotsky's enthusiastic leadership, were able to transfer their resources from front to front as the need became most pressing. In the crucial year of 1919 they were able to beat off Kolchak, attacking over the Urals into the Volga region, in March and April, Denikin, advancing from south Russia as far as Orel, in October and Yudenich outside Petrograd also in October. But the fundamental fact remained. Though much of the population was slow to give active support to the Bolsheviks they were, at the end of the day, more inclined to support them when the Whites threatened than they were to support the Whites when the Bolsheviks advanced. In many ways the Whites were doomed to failure from the beginning.

Post-Civil War Rebellions

In some respects the civil war might be seen to have kept the Bolsheviks in power. Left to the natural evolution of events without the blundering intervention of outdated remnants of the old order they might well have succumbed. Their popularity in the cities seems to have been in free fall in early 1918. Measures designed to increase the efficiency of factories, including high salaries for former managers, were unpopular with workers as was the increasing pressure on freely elected factory committees which were being replaced by Bolshevik-appointed replacements. In the villages, Bolshevik authority was critically thin on the ground. Among political activists, increasingly bitter divisions were opening up between the militant left and the leadership of the party which, the former said, was compromising the ideals of the revolution. The alliance with the Left SRs, which had given a fig leaf of democratic respectability, was falling apart and the naked Bolshevik one-party state was emerging. So great was Left SR disillusion that they conducted a half-hearted coup in July 1918. Lenin was shot and seriously injured by a populist terrorist. Leading Cheka officials in Petrograd were killed. In a desperate response the severely harassed authorities opened up the first red terror in which hundreds, maybe thousands, were executed.[5] The Bolshevik regime might well have found it hard to survive. However, nothing was more likely to fuse these increasingly divided elements back into a semblance of unity than the emergence of an apparently dangerous common enemy.

The absence of a serious alternative to the Bolshevik leadership meant that, for the masses and the radical left, support for the Bolsheviks was the lesser of two evils. Anarchists, SRs and Mensheviks all joined in the common struggle and, although never completely overcome, internal struggles were, for the time being, less acute. Nothing illustrates the inner tensions better, however, than the explosions of discontent which emerged after the Whites were defeated.

Throughout the civil war peasants had resisted the worst of government depredations. They had not turned up for military service when drafted (unless the Whites were around, when the response was better); they concealed the amount of crops they were growing; they even concealed land from the authorities by declaring their farms were smaller than they actually were. They switched out of requisitionable crops like wheat and rye into alternatives like millet. Above all, they tried to prevent excessive requisitioning of their produce by the new authorities. Genuine supplies for the army were usually accepted as necessary, but providing free grain for what were perceived as idle workers in the cities was bitterly resented. Their proof of idleness was the absence of any industrial goods arriving for the use of peasants in exchange for grain. Sometimes they fought off requisitioning squads though the imbalance of forces was such that, in the end, the authorities were sure to win.

In the cities, too, unrest had been endemic, driven by food shortages and job losses above everything else. There was a major incident in Astrakhan. Some 2000 people were said to have been killed and a similar number executed.[6] The Putilov factory in Petrograd was also turbulent at times, as were other factories and industrial enterprises across Russia. Given the general context of industrial collapse the unrest is hardly surprising. The number of workers in major factories fell rapidly. A loss of two-thirds of the workforce was not unusual.[7] Industrial output hit the floor by 1921 at which time it was around 16 per cent of 1912 levels.[8] Cities became depopulated as their hard-pressed, hungry citizens left for their home villages where they hoped they might be able to scrape by, the village being Russia's traditional 'social security' safety net. The population of Petrograd, which was probably the worst-hit, fell from 2.5 million in 1917 to less than 750 000 in August 1920.[9] As we shall see, it immensely complicated Bolshevik plans that they were presiding over the deindustrialisation and deproletarianisation of Russia.

In most cases, although immediate, practical concerns over jobs, hunger and food requisitioning were at the heart of the unrest, protest was also directed against the suppression of freedom of expression and of democratic institutions including soviets and genuinely representative workers' committees in factories. Their restoration was seen as an essential first step to any permanent solution. In this way, anti-Soviet political activity was the exact continuation of mass activity against the Provisional Government which had also been driven by practical concerns, the solution to which was seen to be through democratisation of Russia, through ordinary people taking power into their own hands and using it in their own interests. The protests, in other words, were not in any real sense of the term counter-revolutionary, nor did they look back nostalgically on elements of the former tsarist system. Perhaps surprisingly, given the formidable reputation of the Russian people for devotion to Orthodoxy, religion, although sometimes an element in these protests, was at best a secondary issue, perhaps because the church disgraced itself in the eyes of many through its close association with the restorationist wing of the White movement. The mass of protests aimed for the continuation and completion of the revolution of 1917, only this time it was not the Provisional Government but the Soviet government which stood in their way.

While the Whites were present these tensions tended to be diverted into a stuggle with them. Once they were on the verge of defeat, however, at the end of 1919, the tensions broke out with renewed force against the Soviet government. In West Siberia, the part of the eastern Ukraine liberated by Makhno, in Tambov and, symbolically, in Kronstadt, major rebellions broke out which the new authorities were hard put to repress. In West Siberia it took 50 000 troops.[10] Parts of Tambov were a no-go area for several months. Only the full force of the ultra-loyal Red Cavalry was able to restore order. Kronstadt was only retaken by a desperate attack across the ice by crack military units and the most loyal volunteers from the party activists present at the Tenth Party Congress. All of them were protests fuelled by the same resentments, above all, the continuation of armed requisitioning of grain and the stifling of Soviet democracy. In the absence of the Whites these anti-communist tensions came to the fore. It has also been argued that these were not simply delayed reactions against long-standing grievances but also a mass protest at the Bolsheviks' first peace-time economic experiments based on militarisation of labour and enhanced coercion of the peasantry.[11] In any case, the interaction between these protests and

Bolshevik policies was very intense. Each problem produced a policy response, each response a new problem. It is time to look at the way in which this stormy environment made a lasting mark on the evolving Soviet system.

The Foundation of the Soviet System

For the first three and a half years the eyes of the government were focused almost exclusively on survival. Nonetheless, the basic features of the Bolshevik enterprise we have already encountered began to harden while related adaptations began to evolve without really being noticed or analysed by the leadership until they, too, had become deeply rooted in the evolving system. Almost before anyone realised, features which came to dominate Soviet history were already in place. Even Lenin was unable to get on top of them.

Transition Transformed – from 'Complete Creative Freedom for the Masses' to 'Iron Proletarian Discipline'

The first few years of Bolshevik power look rather shapeless in retrospect. Between the October revolution and the Kronstadt rebellion of March 1921 and the Tenth Party Congress at the same time, many conflicting events and processes were at work and no overall pattern really emerged. At the time, party militants simply saw what they were doing as building communism but the most frequently used label was invented shortly after the period was over by an activist on the left of the party named Lev Kritsman. He called it 'war communism'. This title certainly points up the two main aspects of Bolshevik endeavour, the necessity of fighting a civil war and conducting the revolutionary transformation of the country. The title has, however, led to a debate about how much of what was undertaken was done from military necessity and how much from political doctrine. At the time few people would have made much of a distinction. The battle against the class enemy *was* the struggle for revolution. Some later scholars have mused about these years being 'a formative experience'[12] while others have completely passed them over as an interlude of internecine warfare which only gave way to serious, long-lasting action once it was over.[13] However, one of the most acute non-Bolshevik observers of the time, the writer Evgenii Zamiatin, in a remarkable 'parable' of less than two pages called *The House of God* published in 1922, made a very telling point. Ivan, he wrote, set out to build a church to be the envy of the world. But when it became difficult to raise the resources he resorted to highway robbery and murder, burying the rich, despoiled victims under the foundations. When the magnificent church was finished and dignitaries were invited from all round the world to its ceremonial inauguration, a terrible smell rose up from the foundations and drove them all away. Ivan was left alone with his monstrous creation. It is a sobering thought that even in these early days, in the time of Lenin, Zamiatin was pointing out that Bolshevik methods of violence fatally undermined their noble aims. Many have argued thus about Stalin, but about Lenin!

The years of revolutionary warfare certainly left their mark on the evolution of the Bolsheviks. But it was not so much the struggle against the Whites which was the most influential, rather it was the conflicts with the masses, who should have been their greatest supporters, which gnawed their way into the heart of the new government. The notion of a contradiction between the principles of the proletarian masses and the party was a possibility with which Lenin's political philosophy could not cope. The party was the expression of the will of the masses. If the masses disagreed with it, it must be the masses who were wrong and needed to be reeducated or, in more specifically Leninist terminology, have their consciousness raised. Trying to raise the level of proletarian consciousness, notably of its historic role as driving force behind the overthrow of capitalism and the construction of communism, had been the essence of Bolshevism from the days of its birth as a separate movement in 1902 and 1903. While any political and religious movement tries to win over converts, the degree to which this was built into Leninism put it in a class of its own. Only by keeping this in the forefront of our minds can we follow the thread running through all of Lenin's mature political theory and practice.

If Lenin, as his 1917 writings suggested, was seriously expecting the capitalists and exploiters to come along quietly because they were outnumbered then he was immensely mistaken. Instead of having to arrest a few as an example to the others and allow the people to conduct what he had called a 'gradual, peaceful and smooth' transition,[14] the whole process quickly fell apart at every level. The old order fought tooth and nail against the new authority.

First of all, cooperation with factory owners and, in many ways worse, managers, was practically nil. Key personnel simply fled to what were considered safer areas. Many who were able to do so ended up in the two-million-strong emigration which was largely composed of the upper classes. In their wake they left enterprises deprived of any moveable assets, including cash. As a result, large sectors of the economy were paralysed and workers were practically forced into taking them over and trying to keep them going as best they could. The shortage of technical and managerial skills – from electricians to accountants – left them high and dry for years.

In the countryside, the flight of landowners was less devastating for the rural economy in that peasants were self-sufficient in the skills they needed to keep their traditional economy going. However, the absorption of the remaining large estates into the peasant economy threatened overall output. All political leaders in 1917 warned against this possibility, including the Bolsheviks who included special (and largely unheeded) provisions in the Land Decree in order to prevent it. Particularly at risk was the surplus on which the non-agricultural population of the towns and the military relied for their survival. However, the impact of agricultural crisis takes months to have an effect and, for the time being, the threat was to the future harvest, not to current levels of food stocks.

The immediate hopes of smooth transition failed at two more levels which were less predictable than the opposition of capitalists and landowners. Crucial senior administrative staff in the civil service and private enterprises like banks met the Bolshevik takeover with a wall of resistance. There are many stories of newly appointed Bolshevik Commissars walking into ministries and being laughed out. Even Trotsky faced this at the Foreign Ministry. Trotsky believed his only task as Foreign Minister was, as he famously put it, simply to 'issue a few revolutionary proclamations to the peoples of the world and then shut up shop'.[15] Even though Trotsky claims he was exaggerating for effect, the naivety of this suggestion symbolises that of the whole first phase of transition. To appreciate the irony of it one only has to observe the enormous size and influence of the Foreign Ministry in the last decades of the Soviet Union when its enormous personnel overflowed one of the biggest 'Stalin wedding cake'-style buildings in Moscow and, as representatives of a joint world superpower, its personnel had to be consulted by the United States on fraught issues almost anywhere in the world. Banks also refused to join in and the new government could not lay its hands on any funds to enable it to pursue its objectives and to pay its employees.

As if this was not enough, serious working-class opposition was also threatened in the form of the railway workers, without whose cooperation the entire mobility of the country – for economic, military and private purposes alike – would come to a full stop. Their Menshevik union leadership demanded that the Bolsheviks enter into a coalition government.

Clearly things were going badly wrong and new ideas of transition had to be thought up without delay. In the short term, the Bolsheviks burst the fetters imposed by these crises in a way that became increasingly characteristic of their tactics. By a varying cocktail of deception, manipulation, mobilisation and coercion they overcame the immediate problems. For example, they appeased the railway union by engaging in negotiations to broaden the coalition. Many Bolshevik leaders hoped for success here and the emergence of a genuine coalition. When the talks broke down some major Central Committee members resigned and were bitterly denounced – in quasi-'Stalinist' terms – for their 'criminal vacillations', 'disruptive activity' and 'sabotage'.[16] Cynics might argue that the negotiations over coalition were only intended to buy time because, while they were taking place, the Bolsheviks deployed their other weapons. They denounced the existing union leadership and set up a new Bolshevik-dominated one which split the workers. Anyone who went on strike was threatened with armed retribution. The civil service strikes were dealt with similarly and some weeks after the October revolution the immediate dangers were overcome.

The same mixture was being used at this time to promote the 'triumphal march' of Soviet power. Where local soviets accepted the October revolution, all well and good, though even here Bolshevik personnel would come to dominate. Where there was resistance it was met by a number of methods. New elections, a dissolution of the recalcitrant soviet or sheer threats were usually enough. In numerous cases, however, tougher nuts had to be cracked by elite, loyal troops. Units such as the Latvian Riflemen were used for such purposes, at one moment repressing the old General Staff and replacing its former tsarist officers with reliable Bolsheviks, at another facing down democratically elected army committees which refused to accept the new Bolshevik government. As a result of this mixture, Soviet power of a sort established itself over a wide area of European Russia, Ukraine and Siberia. Usually the cities were the focus and the rural hinterland largely left to its own devices. Towns and cities elsewhere, in Poland, Finland and the Baltic States, also declared for the Bolsheviks. In the ensuing civil wars in those areas the left was eventually defeated and, in Finland, subject to merciless massacres. By the end of Russia's civil war, Ukraine was finally reunited with Russia. Siberia, Central Asia and the Caucasus had also been pacified.

However, the deeper problems of transition had to be faced and it was here, along with the associated struggle to control the masses, that many essential features of the Soviet system were born, although many had been gestating in the pre-revolutionary theories and practices of the party.

On 26 October Lenin had declared the revolution would be built on the 'complete, creative freedom of the masses' and, again, we have no reason to believe he doubted what he was saying. By spring 1918 the discourse had changed to a more threatening one of 'harmony' and, even more menacing, 'iron proletarian discipline'. In the key institutions of industrial enterprises, the military and the party as a whole, these were the new watchwords. To the leadership, their logic was irrefutable. The revolution faced multiple internal and external crises (including disillusionment with the peace of Brest-Litovsk, signed in March 1918) and it was therefore essential that, in order to stay in power, it should exert maximum control in order to get the most out of its resources. Given its minority status, with support probably eroding by the week, increasing dictatorship, as Lenin acknowledged, was inevitable. Instead of the 'gradual peaceful and smooth' transition, Lenin now stated that it was an iron law of revolutions that chaos had to be met by stern centralisation. Dictatorship, defined as 'iron rule, government that is revolutionarily bold, swift and ruthless in suppressing both exploiters and hooligans', was needed. Socialism required 'that the people unquestioningly obey the single will of the leaders of labour'.[17] In particular, bearing in mind that the civil war was in something of a lull at the time, Lenin stressed the need for subjecting the industrial economy to dictatorial control. In normal times, he argued, this dictatorship could be handled gently, like conducting an orchestra, but in revolutionary times it had to be much harsher. The centrepiece of the new dictatorship was a war on workers' control and factory committees and their replacement by 'one-person management' under which the principles of *State and Revolution* would be thrown out of the window and high salaries paid to any former manager or engineer prepared to stay on and work under the new conditions. Needless to say, most workers were opposed to shock developments of this kind and the party had to redouble its efforts to retain support in the factories.

Unholy Trinity: Productionism, Careerism, Bureaucratism

Behind the developments described above lay the logic of another set of ideas which became a bedrock of the Soviet system. In order to strengthen the proletarian revolution in Russia it was necessary to develop industry. Only *after* a highly developed, productive industry was able to meet everyone's economic needs could socialism be built and a strong, educated, advanced working class be formed to build it. Therefore, every effort must be put into increasing industrial output *at all costs* in the short and medium term in order to build the revolution in the long term. This approach, known as productionism, is the key to unlocking many aspects of Leninist, Stalinist and post-Stalinist practices in the Soviet Union. For the time being, however, it meant using every available resource, including robust coercion of economic 'saboteurs', exploiters and parasites (categories sufficiently flexible to include any critic of the new order) in order to meet economic and, once the war was back in full swing, military targets.

Incidentally, while productionism was not directly applicable to the developing Red Army as the civil war sputtered back into life, iron pro-letarian discipline and one-person management, in the form of the restoration of the authority of officers and the abolition of elections and other trappings of a democratised army, certainly were. Analogous to the managerial personnel of civilian administration and industry, former tsarist officers were encouraged to return to their duties in the new army either by a mixture of material and patriotic/revolutionary incentives on the one hand or threats to themselves and their loved ones on the other.

Underlying these developments was an implicit rather than explicit, but nonetheless truly revolutionary process. In his writings of 1917, including *State and Revolution*, Lenin had presented the worker takeover of society as a rather simple process of direct replacement of the former ruling classes by those they had ruled. Existing intermediary institu-tions, notably the state, would be 'smashed'. And yet here were the new authorities begging former army officers, industrial managers and bureaucrats, collectively know as *spetsy* from the Russian word for 'spe-cialists', to work for a new and expanding state authority. Although one should not underestimate the vastly changed conditions under which they were now working, the state was certainly not smashed, nor did it show much sign of following the more orthodox Marxist expectation that it was withering away. Although, for a time during the civil war, branches of the new system called themselves *kommunyi* (communes), they lacked the essential attributes of genuine communes, starting with democratic accountability to their members and anything resembling free elections. In practice, the state was swelling up. The main cause was the vast expansion of its responsibilities. The traditional functions of the state – diplomacy, warfare and internal policing – were being added to by a whole host of new responsibilities – financing, organising and administering all factories, mines, railways, larger farms, schools, universities, opera houses, bus and tram services, medical services including hospitals, welfare provision, sports clubs, shops. The list is endless. How was this vast array of enterprises to be supervised? Not surprisingly a vast new set of bureaucratic institutions was spawned. In the centre of things were the new economic ministries for each sector of industry, known as *glavki*, which branched out from the overarching Supreme Council for the National Economy (Vesenkha). In order to work efficiently they needed the best minds in Russia and were heavily staffed by *spetsy* willing to work for national recovery. Vesenkha employed about 3000 people in the mid-1920s, many of whom were *spetsy*. Even as late as 1929, in the fledgling State Planning Commission only 100 of 500 headquarters staff were party members.[18] The state payroll, of course, was vast since it included all industrial workers, officials and the military. The Education Ministry also had frighteningly wide responsibilities in all areas of culture. While universities retained some administrative independence until 1921–2 (despite being entirely financed by the state), schools, museums, art galleries, film studios and theatres all came under its administrative sway. It became, effectively, the monopoly patron of all the arts within a few months of October. Here, too, enormous numbers of non-Bolsheviks, including most teachers and professors, were the bedrock of the system.

At the beginning of the twenty-first century, we may be less surprised at this wide range of responsibilities since most modern states dabble in many of these areas but, in context, it was unprecedented. The First World War had dragged several combatant states into extensive economic intervention in their war economies as a logical extension of their defence role and the German example, in particular, had inspired Lenin. But no pre-war citizen expected, as we do today, that the state should deliver economic well-being. In this respect, within less than six months, the Soviet state had become an extreme example of the twentieth-century state in terms of its scope and responsibilities. Its example, particularly of state education, medical and welfare provision for all, remained as an unspoken background to the development of similar responsibilities among capitalist states hoping to preserve internal order by weaning their workers away from attraction to the revolutionary model of the Soviet Union.

In the short term, however, this sudden mushrooming of responsibilities produced acute problems for the new authorities. Their solutions further defined the embryonic system. Naturally, supervising such a vast web required the undivided attention of the most loyal revolutionaries. However, in early 1917 the party had only some 25 000 members, rising tenfold by the end of the year. True, Lenin had said that if tsarism could run the country through 130 000 landlords he could do the same with 250 000 party members but in practice it was not so easy. There were, first of all, too many priority areas. Obviously, getting the industrial economy together was one such priority but no one had much idea how it should be done, least of all in a Marxist fashion. The war was also a priority and many party members went straight to the front when they joined. Unfortunately, the war compounded the problem because it had the undesirable effect of bringing about the death of many of the party's finest volunteers.

In desperation, the supposedly lofty criteria for joining the party (which, remember, had been at the heart of Lenin's conception of it since the battle of 1903 over this very point) were progressively relaxed. Even in 1917 the flood of members into the party of roughly nine new members for every one it had at the beginning of the year had swamped it with unqualified members and its profile was little different from that of any other mass party. The need to increase membership to meet the new tasks (as well as to replace some of the best members lost in the war plus a small but increasing trickle of high-quality members leaving the party through disillusionment) was truly desperate. Party membership rose. In late 1919 it was around 350 000; 611 000 in March 1920 and 730 000 in March 1921.

The increase brought a new problem which became known as 'careerism'. It implied that many members were joining the party to secure good, supervisory jobs rather than to fulfil revolutionary ambitions. To counter this, the party always gave precedence to working-class recruits who were believed to be more likely to reflect its deeper values although, given the small size and peasant composition of the working class in Russia, even this had obvious limitations. More importantly, it also cut across the party's need for qualified personnel. So it had to recruit many 'bourgeois' and 'petty-bourgeois' members who could do the jobs it needed doing. Many of these were said to be attracted by the, albeit meagre at the time, 'fruits of office'. Victor Serge gives his impression of the atmosphere. In Moscow

> Committees were piled on top of Councils, and Managements on top
> of Commissions. Of this apparatus, which seemed to me to function

largely in a void, wasting three-quarters of its time on unrealisable projects, I at once formed the worst possible impression. Already, in the midst of general misery, it was nurturing a multitude of bureaucrats who were responsible for more fuss than honest work. In the offices of the Commissariats one came across elegant gentlemen, pretty and irreproachably powdered typists, chic uniforms weighed down with decorations; and everybody in this smart set, in such contrast with the famished populace in the streets, kept sending you back and forth from office to office for the slightest matter and without the slightest result. I witnessed members of Government circles driven to telephoning Lenin to obtain a railway ticket.[19]

Party membership in the cities could provide the best of all perks, survival through priority access to rations. In the parlous situation of civil war, it was much better to be associated with handing out the rations on which people depended than to be trying to be allocated them. Party members were not immune to the severe shortages but their chances of survival were vastly better than those of much of the urban population.

Relatively little attention has been given to these forerunners of the 'new class' of Soviet *apparatchiki* (bureaucrats)[20] but they were very important from the beginning. Every revolution had to face the dilemma of conducting a transition using the qualified personnel of the previous system. In China it crystallised into a well-known debate between 'red' and 'expert'. Ideally, the revolution needed individuals combining both qualities – revolutionary commitment and technical qualifications. For the first decades of the revolution it was almost impossible to find more than a handful of people who fulfilled both criteria (and they immediately became desperately overworked and thereby inefficient) so, while the level of expertise of working-class recruits was slowly and painfully built up, the regime had to choose.

Not surprisingly, the cry, which never died away, began to be raised that the revolution was being 'bureaucratised' and was already suffering from 'careerism'. In Soviet conditions some novel solutions were attempted.

Guarding the Guardians: The Development of Superinstitutions

First of all, some thought was given to ways of providing crash courses to provide working-class party recruits with the necessary skills. The result was two sets of institutions, workers' faculties (*rabfaky*) and party schools. The former were intended to provide basic education to get illiterate and semi-literate students to university entrance level, initially in one but later, slightly more realistically, in two years. *Rabfak* students had a considerable impact in politicising the university system in the 1920s but their educational level tended, unsurprisingly, to be below that of regular students. Party schools were crammers in which students were force-fed some 1500 hours of lectures per year on the truth as perceived by the party leadership in the form of courses on Marxist theory, current politics, history of Russia, the party programme and so on. In the early years, graduates often went straight to the civil war front. Both sets of institutions were desperately hampered by the problem they were set up to solve – shortage of qualified personnel, in this case tutors who could teach the prescribed courses. The same vicious circle bit into party efforts across the board.

Checking the quality of party members also became a priority since there were so many allegations, and many actual examples, of inappropriate candidates getting in and abusing their positions of authority. The process was known as a *chistka* – a 'cleansing' of the party. The Chinese equivalent has become known by the more poetic term 'purification' while the Russian process is usually known in English by the more sinister term 'purge'. In its first incarnation as a registration of party members, conducted in March 1919 on a broad basis, it was a routine process to throw bad apples out of the basket. Party membership fell from around 250 000 to 150 000. However, given the persistent need of the party for more and more recruits and the continuing complaints about the low level of some cadres, we can doubt that it had much effect not least because two years later, after renewed expansion, the first full-scale purge was conducted. One-fifth of the membership, around 136 000, were expelled.

Related to this was the introduction in the early 1920s of a division of the party into two categories of membership, candidate and full. Those wishing to enter the party had to go through a period of probation after which their record would be examined to see if they were satisfactory.

Purging and checking party admissions, of course, opened up the question of who was reliable enough to conduct such processes. Ensuring the political correctness of the expanding state apparatus, the peasant soldiers of the Red Army, not to mention industrial *spetsy*, former tsarist officers and the various levels of the party itself, was a major headache. In the first place, there were few material resources for spreading the new gospel. The by now party-controlled press was one channel and a mountain of pamphlets was another (though the observant reader will already have inferred that the question of who was qualified to write so much material was itself an acute one). Shortage of paper, a side effect of the general economic collapse, made it more difficult. A bold attempt to write a new catechism for Soviet times was undertaken in the form of the *ABC of Communism* which was intended to present the basic essentials of the new government's aims. It was used for party study groups but, fascinating and revealing though the document is about the party's dreams even in the crisis days of 1919 when it was written, it bears too much of the utopian intellectual characteristics of the two left-wing party activists who produced it, Nikolai Bukharin and Evgenii Preobrazhensky, for it to have been truly 'popular'. Perhaps surprisingly, it was not until 1920 that a special Agitation and Propaganda Department of the Central Committee was set up to supervise this vital activity.

While the agitprop department lay in the future, the revolution spawned a whole range of superinstitutions geared to affirming the political correctness of the growing system. In the army the unique institution of political commissars was set up. Often graduates of party schools, their task was twofold. They had to ensure that former tsarist officers toed the line and to capitalise on the presence of peasant recruits by using their time in the army for political education so that they could spread Bolshevik principles to the villages. They were key figures in their military units and could call in retribution against offenders of the highest rank. The fact that there were complaints about the low quality and inadequate supply of personnel to become commissars plus a provision in the Eighth Party Congress (March 1919) resolution 'On the Military Question' that 'the army's political sections, under the direct leadership of the Central Committee, must in the future be selective with respect to the commissars, eliminating any who were appointed by accident, who are unstable careerist elements' only underlines the same, by now familiar, vicious circle.

Within the party itself another novel control mechanism emerged, informally at first but later written down. According to this, the time a person joined the party was an objective test of their loyalty to it. It was assumed that the earlier one had joined, the more reliable one would be. Thus, the 25 000 pre-1917 members, increasingly known as 'Old Bolsheviks', were the *crème de la crème*. Those who joined before October were deemed more reliable than those who joined after and so on. The different cohorts became known as the 'party generations' and by 1921 certain key tasks were being reserved for members of particular generations. Throughout the party a member's *stazh* (length of service) was also crucial.

Obviously, the centralisation implied in the above processes meant that the central institutions of the party grew in importance and the lower-level institutions correspondingly declined. The Central Committee, itself an expanding body reflecting the growth of party responsibilities, and its even more important sub-committee, the Politburo, were the hub of the dictatorship. Even more centralised committees, like the six-member 'war cabinet' (the Defence Council, later expanded to a nine-member Defence and Labour Council) made centralisation even tighter at crucial moments. However, the focus of power was, increasingly, the Politburo rather than the Central Committee or the state institutions. The deeper the crisis the more marked the drift to centralisation. In the nine months from April 1919 the Central Committee, due to meet fortnightly according to party rules, met at five- to six-week intervals while the Politburo met every five days and the Orgburo every second day. After the Tenth Party Congress of 1921 the Politburo settled down into a pattern of twice-weekly meetings while the Central Committee, which had been meeting almost weekly in the feverish run-up to the congress, began to meet routinely about once per month. The hold of party over state institutions and the interlocking of personnel meant that, to all intents and purposes, they were one system with the party in the ascendancy. All the evidence suggests that Lenin and the leadership made less and less distinction between party and state. The party decided policy and used its power in the state to implement it.[21] The chief victim here was soviet democracy which was snuffed out by the domination of soviets by, sometimes tiny, party fractions within them. Instead of being transmission belts of popular demands from below to the top they were reversed. They spread the priorities of the elite to the masses. The whole active committee structure of 1917 was being similarly incorporated. Factory committees, army committees and the rest were all either abolished or became toothless. Trade unions were defined as a 'school of communism' at the Ninth Party Congress in April 1920 since, the argument went, in a workers' state workers did not need to be defended against their own authorities. Other semi-independent institutions were swept into the party/state maw. For example, Proletkul't, set up to develop the elements of working-class culture as a value foundation for the new society, lost its independence in late 1920. In the debate Lenin made a classic formulation of the process: '1. Proletarian culture = communism; 2. It is carried out by the Russian Communist Party; 3. The proletarian class = the Russian Communist Party = Soviet power.'[22] Where most institutions had been similarly dealt with by then it was only in 1922 that the universities finally lost all vestiges of their autonomy. Curiously, the longest holdout was the Academy of Sciences, which was not taken over until 1928–9.

It goes without saying that these deep-rooted processes were not completed without major opposition not only outside but within the party, which showed serious signs of splitting from early 1918 onwards when leftists denounced the leadership for their U-turns of giving up on international revolution and weakening the exclusively proletarian character of the new state. While the civil war kept criticism in check, it also stressed the need for even more effective vigilance and further central supervision. Here we see part of the vicious circle mentioned earlier beginning to have its baneful consequences. Centralisation and the erosion of democracy created discontent – discontent made the leadership turn to even stricter centralisation and greater discipline.

At the peak of the superinstitutions was a trio of bodies. They were the ultimate expressions of Bolshevik supervision. Two are relatively unknown and of debatable importance: these are the party's Organisation Bureau (and, from 1921 the related network of Party Control Commissions) known as the Orgburo for short, and the Worker Peasant Inspectorate, known as Rabkrin from its Russian name. The third is widely notorious, the Cheka, the secret police. These were the ultimate guards who guarded the guards. They, in turn, were under the close control of the Politburo, beyond which there was no higher earthly authority in Russia. The first two were intended to embody the correct political consciousness (membership, of course, reserved for the most reliable of the reliable) within the spheres of party and state respectively. The Orgburo, in particular, had wide powers to enforce central will on the party. It was effectively the general staff of the party and could command members to do whatever it wished, the demands the party made on its members being, of course, total. A true party member handed over body and soul to the party and was not supposed to flinch whatever task was assigned. At a more mundane level the centre could control troublemakers by sending them to undertake urgent duties in the back of beyond (something of which the Soviet Union never ran short). It could, and did, interfere extensively in the selection of delegates to crucial party conferences and congresses, thereby smoothing the way for Lenin's line to be secure against assertive oppositions. Rabkrin's purpose was to ensure that the state bureaucracy made decisions in the light of worker–peasant values, hence its name. This provided wide powers of interference in many areas though its actual influence is uncertain.[23]

It has, however, long been pointed out that the chief fish swimming through these murky waters of control was the revolutionary leadership's chief backroom boy and dogsbody, Joseph Stalin, who was appointed Party Secretary on the strength of it in 1922. He was the only individual who belonged to both the Orgburo and Rabkrin, as well as the Central Committee and the Politburo. As such, he has, to switch metaphors, been compared to a spider at the centre of the complex institutional web of the new system.

The Cheka is sufficiently well-known for us to only have to touch on a number of its salient features here. It evolved from the early hit squads of the October revolution, such as the Latvian Riflemen already mentioned, and was set up as a temporary Extraordinary Commission to Combat Counter-revolution and Sabotage on 9 December 1917. In the words of one of its founders, M. Latsis, 'It was necessary to make the foe feel that there was everywhere about him a seeing eye and a heavy hand ready to come down on him the moment he undertook anything against the Soviet Government.'[24] Its head, the 'incorruptible' of the Russian revolution, was the Polish ex-gentry revolutionary, Feliks Dzherzhinsky. From modest origins it grew and grew. While nominally supervised by the Politburo it became, as police forces often do, a law unto itself. At first it could only arrest but within a year it was also, in effect, acting as judge, jury and executioner. In any case, legality was not an issue that much bothered the Bolsheviks in the early years. They acted from 'higher' principles of revolutionary proletarian justice, and encouraged their enforcers to do the same. By August 1918, the Cheka was implicated in the first wave of mass executions, undertaken as reprisals for the shooting of Lenin, the assassination of two leading Cheka operatives in Petrograd and the tragi-comic coup attempt of the SRs.

The Cheka's effect was felt throughout the Soviet areas and the first thing the government did when it liberated a region from the Whites was to send it in to institute a political clean-up. Its brief to combat 'speculation' (otherwise known as private buying and selling) and sabotage made it an important economic agency, fitting in with Lenin's growing predilection for conducting economic policy down a gun barrel. Economic revolution, he urged, was to be promoted by exemplary confiscation of property and arrests of loosely defined 'capitalists'.[25] It began to operate harsh prison camps, one of its first major ones being the former monastery in the Solovetsky Islands in the Arctic Circle. It already showed signs of being a state within a state, its operatives living behind barbed wire with their own institutions, including relatively well-supplied canteens and even shops. It soon generated an elite *esprit de corps*. Its members saw themselves as the most selfless fighters of the revolution. Many of them were. In Ukraine, for instance, appalling White pogroms prompted many Jews to join it as the most redoubtable organisation of defence and retribution. Compared to the Whites it remained less corrupt and more politically focused from the top but, not surprisingly, it also attracted its share of sadists and adventurers whose actions further blackened its reputation. By 1922 it had become indispensable to the leadership. It was made permanent with slightly redefined powers and became known as the GPU, the first of a regular series of changes of initial down to the notorious KGB of the final decades. It became the most trusted weapon of the party up until the final collapse and, in a supreme irony, appears to have outlived the party into the post-Soviet era, even producing, in Vladimir Putin, an anti-communist president.

No institution better exemplifies the structural problems of the Bolshevik revolution and embodies its essential character. Lacking mass popular support and, even more crucial, massive Bolshevik 'consciousness' in the population, these key ingredients had to be supplied, even imposed, from above, often against the immediate interests of the classes the revolution was supposed to represent. While, in the longer term, the aim was to win over support, in the desperate conditions of civil war control had to be imposed. Violent imposition increased opposition. Opposition made it more difficult to win over the masses. The hostility or indifference of the masses strengthened the leadership's need for dictatorship. How would the authorities ever be able to lift the emphasis from coercion and iron proletarian discipline and turn it towards more peaceful 'winning over'? The end of the civil war was, perhaps, such an opportunity and it was seized upon as such. However, the situation was complicated by the fact that the overt victory in the war against the Whites overshadowed a concealed, but bitterly felt defeat at the hands of the peasantry which, for a while, took the economic initiative out of the government's hands and forced them into economic retreat (which was widely recognised as such at the time) in the form of the New Economic Policy adopted at the Tenth Party Congress in March 1921.

Defeat in the Countryside

Compared to their interventions in the urban industrial world Bolshevik policies in the countryside had been less varied. They were, however,

equally driven by a mixture of immediate need and ideological assumptions. While any regime would have imposed conscription and been
forced to requisition produce, no one but the Bolsheviks could have
thought of *kombedy*, committees of poor peasants. Though they had the
laudable aim of improving the lot of those at the bottom of the agricultural heap, preference for them undermined the support the regime
needed from middle and 'rich' peasants who were actually doing most
of the producing that was going on. The arbitrary way in which rural
'classes' were defined, plus the fact that they were used to spy on the rest
of the village and inform about who was 'hoarding' produce, meant they
were hated by most of the peasantry and did little good for the poor
themselves. Not surprisingly, they lasted less than a year, but they were
an earnest of the Bolsheviks' intentions to radicalise the rural areas and
of their continued obsession with class distinctions within the peasantry.
Many features were to reappear in the late 1920s. For the time being,
the party limited its social engineering (given that the landowners had
been dispossessed) to setting up state farms which attracted a motley
collection of members – former soldiers, a few poor peasants, some dis-
placed proletarians, rural elements who did not belong to the village
communes and who were thereby excluded from access to its land and
so on – which were granted favoured status by the regime but tended to
be unsuccessful and were resented by the commune peasants who
looked down on their poor farming methods and believed they were
wasting the land they occupied.

The majority of peasants made it clear that what they wanted was the
commune and minimal interference from outside. The ideological drives of the party could not settle for this. Throughout the 1920s the anti-
peasant attitudes of the party leadership (even though most of its
members were probably of peasant origin) came to the fore. The peasants were, they thought, the great weakness of the new system and were
a potentially dangerous, counter-revolutionary class whose demise must
be hastened at all costs. However, after abandoning the *kombedy* it was
clear that Lenin's ensuing 'turn towards the middle peasant' was
intended to lead to voluntary socialisation of the peasantry, through
observing the benefits of large-scale production, introduction of new
methods and access to machinery which larger collectivised farms would
bring. Lenin waxed enthusiastic about the new line. 'The proletariat
must separate, demarcate the working peasant from the peasant owner,
the peasant worker from the peasant huckster, the peasant who labours
from the peasant who profiteers. In this demarcation lies the *whole essence*

of socialism.'[26] His opponents, none too pleased about concessions to peasants at the best of times, were even more disappointed when, in the face of the continuing food crisis resulting from the fact that, since industry had collapsed there was nothing for peasants to buy and therefore little incentive for them to sell their produce to the state, Lenin, at the Tenth Party Congress, announced that the market would be legalised once again. The year of 1921 marked Lenin's final effort to solve the problems of the revolution.

Indeed, radical thinking was necessary. The food situation was precarious. Industry had collapsed to an unbelievable 16 per cent of its prewar output. The infrastructure was in ruins. Even the end of the civil war was a mixed blessing because it took away much of the restraint which had held back protest. In the country as a whole, as we have seen, massive rebellions broke out. Within the party a series of oppositions threatened disintegration. The thrust of the party critics was that the true democratic, proletarian values of 1917 had been catastrophically diluted. The largest of them, the Workers' Opposition, claimed the proletariat had been bound up by the evils of bureaucratisation and centralisation and should now have its freedom returned to it. The most poignant of the rebellions beyond the party, that in Kronstadt, spoke for much of the rest of the country when it claimed a new autocracy had emerged. Its solution was more radical – the restoration of multi-party Soviet democracy and the ending of the Communist Party's monopolisation of state resources to promote its own interests.

Lenin's response to party oppositions was to ban them. His response to Kronstadt was merciless repression followed by a steady stream of hundreds of executions of captured participants at the hands of the Cheka. While these gave the clearest signal that, on the political front, Lenin was determined to preserve the dictatorship at all costs, the economic concessions, he mused, might be just what was needed. Lenin fell ill in late 1921 and never fully recovered but he did, in his last writings, consider the strategy the revolution should follow. Indeed, there was much to ponder – industrial disaster, political disaffection, a growing bureaucracy, shortage of personnel, productionism, careerism, party oppositions, the persistent peasantry. The party's dictatorship – based on repression of opponents, suspension of democratic rights and values by means of force and a jealously guarded political monopoly – was already in place and Lenin saw no need to change it. It would be the mechanism of socialist transformation and he was not going to give in on that as the ban on organised opposition and the attack on Kronstadt showed.

He did, nonetheless, show an awareness of the problems of bureaucratisation and careerism in the party, but his solution, presented in his
last major article 'Better Fewer, but Better', was simply to merge the two
supervisory superinstitutions of the Rabkrin and the Central Control
Commission so that they could be run by a smaller, more carefully chosen staff. There was little new in this recipe. On one issue, however, he
seemed happier. NEP, he said, had been a fortuitous stumbling onto an
almost ideal balance of public and private enterprise from which the
party could guide society away from its private interests and demonstrate the superiority of public, socialist methods. 'All' that was needed
to complement NEP, he said, was a cultural revolution. By this he meant
a change in fundamental values, especially turning the drive for private
profit into the pursuit of the common good. Cultural revolution also
involved 'rationalising' the Russian way of life. In many respects the
1920s and beyond were an attempt to do just that. Lenin's death in
January 1924, however, meant that the task of realising it would be in
other hands.

3

THE NEP YEARS: ECONOMIC RETREAT, CULTURAL ASSAULT

It was not predestined that the hands into which power would fall would be those of Joseph Stalin. Although the ins and outs of political infighting by which he achieved his dominance are not our concern here, certain aspects of it are crucial to an understanding of our main story.

NEP and the Rise of Stalin

Many have argued that Stalin's control of the bureaucratic web gave him administrative control of the party and, by using his position to control promotions, demotions and, above all, elections within the party, he was able to 'outmanoeuvre' his rivals of whom Trotsky was in the front rank. There is a very important truth here. Stalin did convert what was seen as secondary power – administrative power – into political power. Every Soviet leader down to the end of the system did the same. Usually assuming Stalin's main position, as General Secretary, they consolidated their authority by removing opponents and appointing supporters to key institutions, notably the party Central Committee. The fact that this became the norm should point us to a crucial fact. Only in an already centralised and, at the higher levels at least, disciplined bureaucratic polity could such a process take place. It presupposes lack of power at the lower levels. Rank-and-file members played no formal role in the process, still less did the Soviet population have a say. In the 1920s, however, it was still necessary to placate or silence these groups sufficiently to make them governable. The centre did not yet have as much control as it achieved later. It therefore follows that, although it was a major characteristic of Stalin's whole political career, we must look beyond simple political intrigue to explain his rise.[1]

While Trotsky's admirer and biographer Isaac Deutscher has produced one of the most substantive accounts of Stalin's manoeuvres to explain his success, Trotsky himself, in his despair at the Stalinist turn taken by the revolution, remained true to his historical determinism. For Trotsky, more so than many other Marxists, the individual was in the grip of history, not the other way round, therefore historical forces, not backstairs deals, had put Stalin in power. Naturally, for Trotsky, they were unhealthy forces. As he contemptuously put it in 1925: 'Stalin is needed by the tired radicals, by the bureaucrats, by all the worms that are crawling out of the upturned soil of the revolution. He speaks their language and he knows how to lead them.'

Trotsky had a point, but he was not prepared to follow up its full implications. If Stalin had been brought to power by dominant historical currents, then Trotsky and the left of the party had been defeated not just by their opponent's superior skill in plotting but by the same tide of history. Many interpretations of the period overlook this, but for our purposes it is crucial. Behind Stalin and the rise of Stalinism were real historical forces. Stalinism was not just the result of one man's imposition of his policies but was shaped by the development, outcome and prospects of the revolution in the 1920s.

Lenin, as we have seen, believed that the combination of political dictatorship from the centre and the mixed economy of NEP was the form in which the transition to socialism could be established in Russia. For him, the dynamic of the relationship revolved around the continual strengthening of the public sector and the weakening of private enterprise. This would result in the growing realisation in the country, particularly among the peasants, that collective, cooperative, socialist methods of doing things were superior to the competitive, individualistic, unstable and unpredictable methods of capitalism. Here we must remind ourselves that, for any Marxist, socialism had to *outproduce* capitalism or it was nothing. Thus, economic growth was already becoming a measure of the success of transition.

Not everyone in the party shared Lenin's optimism about NEP. There was still a vociferous left in the party which continued to argue, as they had since 1918, that the leadership was taking a path of compromise and was thereby weakening the progress of the revolution. They pointed to numerous aspects of NEP which, they argued, bore out their opinion. Above all it restored market relations. Once that was the case it was, they thought, but a short step to the complete restoration of competitive, exploitative capitalist economic relations. When, in 1925, the party and government sanctioned the hiring of labour by private individuals it was seen by the left as a step too far. After all, the very essence of capitalism was exploitation and the basis of exploitation was the hiring of one person's labour to the profit of another. The prominence of bourgeois specialists and managers, the appearance of a 'middle class' of comfortably-off, educated, state and industrial administrators – often of non-proletarian background – as well as the emergence of traders known as Nepmen (though some were Nepwomen), fuelled their belief that the seeds of capitalist restoration were sprouting everywhere. They were particularly mistrustful of the village and believed that the party's policies were geared to the 'richer' peasant, the so-called *kulak*.

Interestingly, their interpretation of the way things were going was shared by some members of the former elite and ex-White Guards who thought that, in the early 1920s, Soviet Russia was being 'normalised', that is, reverting to capitalism, and many of them began to make their peace with the communists and even work in the new institutions. The communists tolerated these unlikely sympathisers, often known collectively as National Bolsheviks, because they were helpful in improving Soviet Russia's image abroad and reestablishing its newly reinstated, conventional diplomatic links with the outside world. Various National Bolshevik organisations also spread pro-Soviet propaganda and helped émigrés to return, thus partially reversing the brain and skill drain of the civil war years.

The right wing of the party, however, refuted the left's claims that it was selling out the revolution. Standing firmly on Lenin's last writings, Bukharin, himself a former leftist, argued that there was no serious alternative to NEP. While both left and right shared the same goal of achieving communism, the right was prepared to go at a much slower pace (or tempo, to introduce what was soon to become a quintessentially Stalinist term). Bukharin's encouragement to peasants to 'enrich themselves' (Guizot's words to the French entrepreneurial class in the 1840s) could hardly be expected to excite the imagination of the party's radical revolutionaries fired up with victory in the civil war and intoxicated with delusions of world revolution. Bukharin's insistence that socialism should advance in Russia at the pace of a peasant nag further inflamed the left which greatly distrusted the peasantry as a whole and the better-off peasants above all.

The overall tendency of the revolution, towards what became known as 'socialism in one country', was too much for the left to take. They did what vociferous leftists do best, that is, produced reams of sustained, critical analysis of their opponents. However, they also suffered from the usual handicaps of the extreme left, isolation from society as a whole and, at best, hazy, untried ideas about alternative policies. It was these last, above all, which doomed their attempts to take over party and government in the mid-1920s, not just Stalin's manipulation.

On top of this the leading force on the left, Trotsky, made numerous strategic errors of his own. In the forefront was his view that the party was degenerating under the pressures of careerism and bureaucratisation since it clashed with his article of faith that the party was always right. This left him in the awkward position of denouncing the very people he depended on to change the situation. Compared to Stalin, who always expressed a robust optimism about the party and working class of Soviet Russia, Trotsky's position had little appeal where it mattered.

As far as wider Russian society was concerned, in a country exhausted by war and revolution the relative relaxation of the mid-1920s and the slow return, not of prosperity but of sufficiency for almost all, were more attractive than the remote revolutionary ventures Trotsky believed to be necessary. No matter how accurate the analysis, the population as a whole, and even most of the party, did not much care about Trotsky's berating of Stalin for mishandling the Chinese revolution in 1927. Consequently, it was easy for Stalin to close down the left opposition in that year for breaking Lenin's party rules of 1921 and setting itself up as a faction. Stalin's coup also netted two of his other chief rivals, Kamenev and Zinoviev, who, though they had in many ways shared Trotsky's views, had not made common cause with him in 1923–4, when they might have tipped the balance, because they saw him as a rival for power. Even more ineptly, when it was far too late they jumped on Trotsky's rapidly sinking ship to form a united opposition in 1926. Not only did Stalin scoop the lot of them up and bring leading oppositionists to suicide and exile, he was able to strengthen the ban on factions by getting the party at its Fifteenth Congress in December 1927 to establish the rule that all members must obey the 'General Line' of the party once it was adopted. In effect, where Lenin had made organised opposition to the party line against the rules, Stalin now made individual opposition an offence.

NEP and Soviet Society

NEP may have upset many of the most dedicated members of the party but, for the mass of the population, the 1920s were a period of relief from the horrors of world and civil wars and, as we know with hindsight, from the upheavals still to come. For Russia as a whole, NEP was a period of marking time. For once, the party, sensing its weakness and distracted by internal divisions, was not trying to lead instantaneous radical change. In the absence of storms from above, the fragile flowers of Russian society, culture and economy began to bloom modestly.

At the core of NEP was steady economic recovery. From the unimaginable depths of 1921, when industry was practically non-existent, pre-war levels of production began to be reached by around 1928. Basic industries showed a remarkable ability to recover. Between 1921 and 1925 coal production increased from 9 million to 18 million tons; electricity output from 520 to 3000 million kwh; steel from 183 000 to 2.1 million tons; rail freight from 39.4 to 83.4 million tons and the grain harvest from 37.6 to 72.5 million tons.[2] The crucial transport networks – based on railways and rivers – began to meet the demand placed on them. There was even room to start some of the major industrial construction projects usually associated with the later Five-Year-Plan period, such as the giant Dnieper dam. However, the essence of NEP was not so much the large industries as the flourishing of small enterprises and petty trade. From cafés to cabinet-makers, skills and opportunities were exploited within the NEP framework. They began to soak up some of the surplus labour of the villages but by no means all of it. In the mid-1920s unemployment was a major problem and it was this which had led to the government relaxing its rules on hiring labour. All enterprises, including the larger ones in the hands of the state, had to sink or swim within the rules of market relations. At this time it was possible for state enterprises to go bankrupt and many did. Non-industrial institutions – theatres, cinemas, publishers, museums – also had to be self-supporting which meant reintroducing tickets, admission fees and prices for books, all of which had been abolished at the height of war communism. Some institutions, like the Hermitage Museum in the city of Petrograd (renamed Leningrad after Lenin's death) sold off many of the treasures accumulated in its basement to make ends meet.

NEP illustrated that socialism and the market could exist in a relatively positive relationship to each other. It was, however, a fragile relationship and was destined not to last. However, it did provide a distinctive moment in Russian history. The country was, in effect, without a stable elite in these years. The old ruling classes had been abolished as classes, although many individuals still lived on as state employees, economic and military specialists or alongside their former peasants in the villages. In Ukraine, for instance, 25 per cent of landowners were

still farming, on peasant-sized plots, in the mid-1920s. The old civil service, military, financial, industrial and professional elites had also gone.
As yet their replacements were raw and crudely trained. The party
and its attendant bureaucracy were still too small to exert a great deal of
control. As a result, Russia was a land of the *narod* and, to some extent,
the intelligentsia. Peasants, petty traders, artisans, small-scale entrepre-
neurs, private markets, cooperatives of all kinds flourished, as did
the petty criminals, conmen and swindlers of lower-class, pre-revolutionary Russia. It was a colourful, spontaneous and indubitably Russian
episode in history captured in Ilf and Petrov's vivid stories about low
life, in Vertov's documentary films, notably *The Eleventh* and *The Man
with the Movie Camera*, and recalled ambiguously as a *Golden Age* in
Shostakovich's ballet of that name. Other national cultures in Soviet
Russia shared in the same relative flourishing of popular culture
and enterprise. The relatively light touch of the party-controlled state
was permitting a hundred flowers to bloom across the land. The
weapons of control – political monopoly, the GPU, censorship, an
informer network, a near monopoly of publishing, tight control of
information, labour camps, show trials (notably of SRs in 1922) – were
all in place but their impact was considerably less heavy than it was to
become later.

The Formation of the USSR

However, significant developments were taking place at the level of party
and state. In the early 1920s the most important element was the reformation of the state structure – the founding, in July 1923, of the
Soviet Union (which is what we shall call it from this point on). The
explosion of 1917, which had blown the various national groupings of
the Russian Empire apart from one another, was replaced by a process
of reintegration. As a result of victory against the Whites and their allies,
Moscow reasserted its control over Ukraine, European Russia, Belarus,
Siberia and Central Asia. Armenia, stunned by the genocide of the war
years as a result of which between 600 000 and 2.5 million Armenians
had been massacred, had sought Russian protection from its Turkish
neighbour. It also, eventually, lost its independence in late 1920 and
early 1921. Its neighbour, Georgia, the only non-Russian area of the
former empire to establish a socialist, in this case Menshevik, government was 'mopped up' by Moscow by a combination, later to become
familiar in post-Second World War Eastern Europe, of a fake revolution

and military invasion in February 1921. The Muslim Transcaucasus –
Azerbaidzhan – was also reincorporated, not least because of its Caspian
Sea oil resources. However, significant areas were also lost to the new
Soviet Union, notably almost all of its advanced north-western border-
lands. A great swathe of territories – Finland, Estonia, Latvia, Lithuania
and Poland – became fully independent states. From having almost a
thousand kilometres of Baltic shoreline, the Soviet Union was reduced to
less than two hundred kilometres, Peter the Great's window on the west.
The Finnish border was only 30 kilometres from Leningrad, the Estonian
140 kilometres. Elsewhere there were small border rectifications.

We need to notice a number of features of the new set-up. Most obviously, it comprised a kaleidoscope of nationalities and ethnic groups
with their associated cultures – notably language, religion and way of
life. Reindeer herding, fishing and trapping were among the occupations of peripheral groups. The population lived in all kinds of homes –
wooden houses, earthen dugouts, igloos, tents. The patchwork nature of
the old Russian Empire had been recreated. There were well over a hundred languages spoken. Relations between them remained delicate but,
by and large, Soviet nationalities policy was more successful than that of
its predecessors. The new state did not attack minorities or impose one
national culture over another. It did, of course, try to impose its own new
culture over all, but within that it assisted the survival of local languages
and cultures, though in the increasingly ersatz form of official folk-song
and dance groups and so on. The yet-to-be-coined slogan 'national in
form, socialist in content' was a not inaccurate description of what
evolved, for example official ideology, such as Lenin's writings, produced ad nauseam in the local languages. By and large the nationalities
accepted the new boundaries. Only in the Muslim areas did resistance
continue sporadically into the 1930s, particularly among the mountain
peoples such as Tadzhikhs and Chechens. It was, of course, among the
Muslims and Christians of the Caucasus that the most severe national
clashes were to break out as the Soviet Union collapsed. However, even
in 1991, almost 75 per cent of voters still voted to preserve the Soviet
Union in the last *perestroika* referendum and, since then, many areas –
Belarus, Central Asia and even Ukraine – have achieved only a half-
hearted separation from Russia and each other, in itself testimony to
the degree of acceptance the borders achieved. This is also borne out by
the fact that, when the collapse came, big trouble came from the smallest nationalities – Azeris, Armenians, Georgians, Estonians, Latvians,
Lithuanians and, later, the Chechens – who amounted to less than

10 per cent of the whole population. From 1924 to 1988, the nationality issue was less prominent in the Soviet Union than either before or
since. Even the immensely complex Jewish question was less acute until
it began to be manipulated by foreign powers to weaken and undermine
the Soviet system from the 1970s onwards. Pogroms, to take the most
dramatic example, ended on Soviet territory with the civil war though
lesser forms of anti-Semitism undoubtedly survived and were given a
new lease of life in Nazi-occupied areas during the Second World War.
It was not only linguistic concessions that were made by the new constitution. Both party and state assumed federal structures which devolved
some powers to minorities, although these went against the grain of the
centralising and mobilising tendencies of the system. However, in the
NEP period there was a certain amount of regionalism within both party
and state. Ukraine, above all, began to take what would later be thought
of as its own road to socialism.

None of this, however, undermined perhaps the chief peculiarity of
the new state and party system. Like the autocracy it replaced, it was, in
essence, a bureaucracy motivated by its own agenda (or, sometimes,
agendas) rather than a reflection of the attitudes and structures of the
society over which it hovered. Contrary to the ideas expressed in the
April Theses and *State and Revolution*, the as yet relatively weak central
apparatus was upward-looking to its bosses rather than downward-
looking to its population. It continued to derive its legitimacy from its
conviction that it was more advanced than the society over which it
ruled. Although the electoral principle was firmly rooted in both party
and state practice, elections were already indices of the success of central control rather than a true measure of popular attitudes. The government did not derive any of its real power from them. Wherever it
mattered, little choice was offered to electors and, of course, only one
party was allowed to exist. Fellow-travelling 'non-party' candidates were
a fluctuating part of the system throughout but no wider choices were
offered.

One other point. It has sometimes been suggested that Soviet institutions were a front for Russian 'imperial' control of the whole country.
While it is certainly the case that Russians were disproportionately
represented in positions of power, they were not agents of Russian interest so much as party and leadership interest. As far as the ordinary
people were concerned the system lay at least as heavily, perhaps even
more so, on Russians as it did on the minorities. It was, after all, Russian
defection from the Soviet Union in 1991 that brought about its collapse.

It would be a unique metropolis that deliberately sabotaged the supposed instrument of its domination.

Of course, many of these processes, particularly the peak of centralisation, lay in the future, but it is worth laying down these background features at this point to explain the relative absence of further consideration of nationality issues in the central chapters of this study. In essence, the developing Soviet central apparatus lay heavily on them all. For the time being, and for many decades into the future, the establishment of the Soviet Union provided a stable framework for relations between the nationalities and, particularly in the 1920s, was a factor contributing to the transient stability of those years.

Party and Society in the 1920s

The Establishment of the Leading Role of the Party

The engine room of the new state and of the new system continued to be the party. While the factors we identified earlier – productionism, careerism, bureaucratisation – continued to shape the party, the peculiar conditions of NEP did create some distinctive features. Although NEP had been a 'retreat' in many areas the party, though relatively passive, was watching over a wider range of social institutions than ever. Although it had nominally withdrawn from large tracts of economic activity – which, it must be said, it had hardly controlled anyway given the massive black economy of the early years – the party was tightening its grip in other areas and establishing itself as the monopoly authority in all areas. There was hardly an institution left in the country which was not under its supervision. It had claimed what was later called 'the leading role' in society. In soviets, factories, the military, ministries, hospitals, law courts, cinemas, shops, the railways, banks, schools, it was the party that called the tune, usually through the handful of party members in each institution who belonged to it. Party fractions, acting under the direction of the party leadership, were the congealing new ruling group of the Soviet Union. As yet, inexperience, lack of skills and limited numbers meant the supervision was more light-handed than it was to become and society thrived in a more spontaneous fashion than it was to do later. Nonetheless, the basic model of party control was already in place by the early 1920s and was being strengthened by the closing down of other political parties, strict censorship and licensing of cultural institutions, the GPU, labour camps and so on. However, the scale of use of these instruments was still relatively small.

The party was, however, constantly trying to strengthen itself and consolidate its position. It was constantly recruiting new members, particularly the 'Lenin enrolment' of 1924–5 when a special effort was made to draw in more members as a national tribute to Lenin in the year after his death. But the pool from which recruits could be drawn was still small. The party's ideal – the educated, conscious 'advanced' worker – was a very scarce commodity. The fruits of office continued to attract careerists. The repopulation of the cities as industry picked up drew in new rural migrants. Recruiting from them increased the mistrusted peasant element in the party rather than the elusive truly proletarian elements. The party's turn towards enrichment and the hiring of labour made it more attractive to the even more mistrusted entrepreneurial elements of town and country who might also be recruited. Thus the party grew and its membership evolved away from its advanced proletarian ideal. Not surprisingly, the process of purging became entrenched as the party tried to square the circle of recruiting advanced proletarians in a petty-bourgeois society.

Educating a Revolutionary Elite

Already the party was deep into struggle between its revolutionary, transforming ideals and the existing culture and way of life of traditional Russia. In these years great effort was put into nurturing the required values among a new elite and then using that elite to transmit the values to the wider society. A whole range of institutions was evolved to meet the challenge. The special worker education colleges – *rabfaks* – which had been set up in 1919, had around 40 000 students by the mid-1920s. However, even here, it seems, a considerable number were from peasant and even bourgeois backgrounds. Even so, the *rabfak* graduates provided a radical leaven within higher education. Through their favoured status with the authorities, they began to undermine what was left of the authority of the traditional professoriate once the universities had lost the remnants of their autonomy in 1922, a process backed up by the expulsion of 250 university teachers deemed by the authorities to be harmful. This act alone should raise suspicions about any interpretation of the NEP period as one of real toleration. It was only toleration of those who – because of party weakness and/or because they were still of some use to the party – had not yet been silenced. For the time being the party was restricted to using the products of its proletarian education schemes to replace as many of the bourgeois specialists as it could. Indeed, the 1920s was a decade of specialists. Even in key economic institutions like the Supreme Council of the National Economy (*Vesenkha*), numerous former Mensheviks, SRs, tsarist civil servants and even the brilliant philosopher, scientist and priest Father Pavel Florensky, turned up to work energetically and conscientiously to help reestablish the Soviet Union's battered economy. The party did not yet have the skills to replace them all, though through elite institutions like the Institute of Red Professors it tried to nurture its own leading lights, a task made infinitely more difficult by the fact that it was precisely among its more educated and intellectual members that the left/right battles within the party were at their fiercest. Lower down the scale the process of 'promoting' working-class elements (*vydvyzhenie*) – what today we would call positive discrimination – did provide a fast track for rapidly educated proletarians to take over positions of authority in factories and administration to which their educational achievements and actual skills did not entitle them. Their authority could not be questioned because they had the party behind them and through them the party made its first steps towards what it finally became, the managerial elite of the new Soviet Union. It has been argued with some justification that these beneficiaries of the new system became its strongest supporters and that they reflected the robust, proletarian chauvinist values of Stalin and became, in effect, a layer of 'mini-Stalins' in important positions especially in industry and in local and regional party administration. This may be so but, as we shall see, the picture is not so simple because it appears that the blood purges of 1936–8 hit disproportionately at this layer of apparently loyal members that the party had worked so hard and doggedly to produce.

The Battle for Cultural Control: Creative Culture – the Tightening Noose

Questions of worker education bring us to one of the most discussed areas of these formative NEP years, high culture. The undoubted flourishing especially of film, literature, painting and sculpture has led many to see an alternative, more tolerant form of socialism in action in these years. Indeed, there are many great achievements associated with the names of Eisenstein, Vertov, Shub, Babel, Esenin, Mayakovsky, Malevich, Tatlin and numerous others. In some ways these years do represent an oasis of creativity between the storms of revolution and full-blown Stalinism. But two major observations have to be made to qualify such a view. First, the scope of cultural expression was narrower than during the civil war and was slowly but steadily continuing to narrow during the 1920s themselves. Second, the toleration which did exist was closely supervised and was seen by the party leadership as instrumental in establishing its goals. Let us look briefly at each of these.

Many traditional intellectual schools – liberalism, anarchism, non-Bolshevik socialism, conservatism, Christian philosophy, Nietzscheanism and so on – were able to retain corners of self-expression in parts of institutions like the universities throughout the civil war.[3] The remnants of political parties also existed for a while and it was only at the end of the civil war that Soviet Russia finally became a one-party state. A broader range of subject matter, emanating from these schools, continued to find expression in the unbelievably difficult conditions of the time. Very few outlets existed but the intellectual spectrum remained wider than in the 1920s. By the early 1920s, not only were a substantial number of those who had been responsible for this breadth expelled but great figures who had initially welcomed the revolution – Blok, Belyi, Chagall – had come to realise that the revolution they celebrated was that of the people while the one promoted by the communists was quite different. Chagall retained the light of popular revolution in his soul long after but he left Russia disillusioned in 1922. Belyi had left a year earlier and Blok had died in despair at what was happening. In fact, this became a common story for Russian culture, its most significant figures finding it impossible to live within the official confines – Zamiatin, Eisenstein, Mandelstam, Mayakovsky, even Gorky, and so on right down to the dissidents of the last decades. All testify to the continuing, and often growing, pressure from the authorities. As far as the 1920s is concerned the point is that the process of narrowing was well on the way by 1921.

It continued throughout the 1920s. Groups tolerated, often grudgingly, in the early years – like the various National Bolsheviks – were forbidden long before the Stalinist cultural revolution took hold. In 1925, to calm left/right arguments within the party, a line on literature was established in which the key word was 'supervision' exercised through 'weeding out anti-proletarian and anti-revolutionary elements' and 'fighting against new forms of bourgeois ideology', terms which became watchwords of the emerging Soviet intellectual orthodoxy. It is absolutely clear that, in any case, toleration was only extended beyond the party to those deemed to be favourable to it, to those whom the party thought it could win over, those who became known (without any pejorative over-tones) as fellow-travellers – people on the same journey though travel-ling at different speeds and in slightly different ways from the party itself. We must not lose sight of the fact that, in its own eyes, the party's success could only be achieved by winning over the population to its goals. Toleration of those closest to it seemed to be a sensible way for the party to reach a substantial number of intellectual opinion leaders.

Indeed, the cultural field in general is the main exception to what we have been saying about NEP. Where the pace of change slowed down in the political, economic and social spheres, in the cultural field the party began and sustained a major onslaught on society. Given their frustra-tion elsewhere, the cultural field offered party militants the broadest scope to assert themselves and many of them took advantage of it, throwing themselves into the expanding cultural bureaucracies. Old-style intellectuals complained that culture was becoming dominated by talentless individuals spouting half-baked theories (usually very crude versions of Marxism–Leninism). They exerted their influence over cul-ture not through their intellectual brilliance but through controlling powerful administrative positions, for instance in the various writers' organisations and journals that struggled for predominance against each other. The very issue of toleration was at the heart of these dis-putes. The strident left called ever more loudly for the closing down of journals that published the writings of fellow-travellers. Few of these left-ists are remembered today for their artistic achievements. In Nadezhda Mandelstam's ringing phrase, Russia in the 1920s was overrun with poets but there was hardly any poetry.

There were a vast number of outlets for the militants to operate in, especially education and propaganda. Although very few teachers were party members, the administration of education was dominated by a rel-atively few activists, divided amongst themselves like the rest of the party. Even priority institutions, like *rabfaks*, relied heavily on non-party teach-ers. There were even cases of non-party lecturers teaching party ideology to its future leaders! Only the elite party schools were immune from the influence of specialists. The leading figure in party educational policy, Anatolii Lunacharsky, the Minister of Education from 1917 to spring 1929, maintained a relatively tolerant line and it was his influence as much as any which held back the encroaching forces of crude party repres-sion. Even he could only restrain rather than reverse the intellectual tide.

Lunacharsky was never considered to be of sufficient importance to join the ruling Politburo, in itself a testimony to the low priority given to his area of activity. Much more important to the party leaders was the Agitation and Propaganda Department (*agitprop otdel'*) of the Central Committee set up in 1920 to coordinate the party's efforts to win over the population. It called the shots in cultural life and supervised not only the education system from kindergartens to universities and political propaganda but also censorship of all the arts, including music. Its task continued to be not only winning over the population but, in the first instance, making party members aware of what policy was and what was expected of them. To this end it published a range of journals and held short courses to train party propagandists. For the time being it remained less influential in society as a whole.

One area, however, brought headlong clashes between the party and the masses and that was religion. Where most Marxist parties were anti-religious, but fairly passive in terms of asserting their views, Bolshevism had a vehement anti-religious streak more usually associated with anarchists. It is likely that Lenin's influence was paramount here as his attitude to religion was much cruder than that of Marx himself. Certainly Lenin took Marx's phrase that religion was 'the opium of the people' as the core of his analysis, and equated religion with noxious narcotic intoxication throughout his career. Right through the Soviet period official propaganda portrayed religion as a cynical mechanism by which trickster priests, rabbis, mullahs, shamans and other 'holy' people preyed on the gullibility of believers for their own exploitative ends, that is, to take money from them and live comfortably at the expense of their followers. To see the whole religious experience of mankind in such crude terms almost beggars belief. It is perhaps partly explained by the peculiarities of the Russian situation. Leading members of the Orthodox Church had sullied its reputation by involvement in crude anti-Semitism, xenophobia, hostility to the modern world and close support of the autocracy, not to mention Patriarch Tikhon's precipitate pronunciation of anathema against the Bolsheviks in 1918. In any case, Lenin would have been well-advised to ponder the rest of the sentence from which he drew his motto. Marx had written 'Religion is the sigh of the oppressed creature, the heart of a heartless world; the spirit of spiritless conditions. It is the *opium* of the people.'[4] In other words, for Marx religion was a consolation for people downtrodden and oppressed by the alienating conditions of life.

For both Marx and Lenin the antidote to religion was knowledge, especially scientific knowledge. From its early days the new Soviet system believed it represented the triumph of science. Historical science justified its social analysis, natural science and technology would be the sinews of its superiority over capitalism. Soviet society was to be the world's first scientifically governed society. There was not the slightest idea that science and religion might be compatible. The old religions were dead. Darwin was now the gospel. It was naively assumed that by spreading scientific knowledge, all forms of religion and non-Bolshevik ideologies would wither away. The revolution was powered by the highest achievements of human reason and its fundamental truths were, in the eyes of the leaders and activists, irrefutable. Such fundamentalism, such certainty left little room in the long term for the uncharacteristic dialogue of the NEP years and foreshadowed heresy-hunting and witch-burning as the more logical outcome of its fierce self-confidence.

For the time being these dragons were only slowly awakening. From early on the party had shorn away the privileges and then the rights of the church and of believers through disestablishment, exclusion of religion from education, the redistribution of church lands and the nationalisation of church property, as well as pressure on believers to abandon their religious practices. There had been some harsh clashes between party and church, most notably in Shuia in 1922 when government attempts to take sacred objects – notably chalices, icons, icon frames and vestments – to melt down and/or sell, ostensibly to raise funds for the relief of the famine of that year, were met with determined resistance. Persecution of Catholics was also undertaken and fundamentalist Islamic practices – notably the subjection of women and the wearing of the veil – were forcibly ended. In the middle of the decade the pressure against religions was lighter, and less repressive tactics – like encouraging religious fellow-travellers such as the 'Living Church' movement – were more prominent than outright confrontation. This was, at least, more in tune with the party's own official policy on religion which acknowledged that subtlety was needed in uprooting religious prejudices and nothing would be more likely to entrench them than crude ridicule and brutal, insensitive persecution.

NEP: Temporary Retreat or Road to Socialism?

Such were the conditions of the NEP years in their ambiguity and complexity. Did they add up to an alternative path for the development of the revolution or were they simply a temporary retreat? The defeat of Trotsky, Kamenev and Zinoviev in 1927, the recovery of the economy, the relative stability, even prosperity of the mid-1920s, and the partial flourishing of society might suggest that NEP and the ideas of its archi-tect, Bukharin, were set fair to continue in the ascendant. On the other hand, by 1927–8, many party leaders were impatient with the dynamic of NEP which, they believed, was not delivering the goods. In particu-lar, there was no sign that the peasantry was being won over to socialism in significant numbers and it was also feared that industrial recovery had given way to stagnation. The ever-deepening class struggle in the field of culture had left radical militants thirsting for more action. Paradoxi-cally, despite the defeat of leading leftists in 1927, radical voices calling for a more resolute march towards socialism were stronger than ever. At the moment of its apparent triumph, the principles of NEP were about to be swept away. The fully-fledged Soviet system was about to emerge.

4

TOWARDS THE STALIN SYSTEM: THE 'GREAT TURN', 1928–32

In 1928 the Soviet Union embarked on a 'great turn', its equivalent of Mao's 'Great Leap Forward' thirty years later which was modelled on it. In a series of rapidly increasing steps the principles of NEP were abandoned. The market was marginalised – though never completely abolished – and forcible state direction became considerably more prominent. Industrialisation was speeded up through the adoption of the First Five-Year Plan in 1928. The year of 1929 saw the state embark on the enforced, rapid collectivisation of the peasantry. Accompanying these was a 'cultural revolution' which undermined the vestigial toleration of the mid-1920s and replaced it with strident leftism and visionary utopianism, themselves eventually undermined by the later turn to socialist realism. Perhaps most tragically, the new militancy was also spread via Comintern to the international arena and all communist parties were ordered to break friendly contact with all non-communists whether left social democrats, radicals, conservatives or fascists. All were to be denounced as bourgeois or petty-bourgeois and no distinctions were to be made between them. Thus, just at the crucial moment of the rise of Nazism, German communists were forced to equate socialist and democratic political parties with fascists. Had joint action against Fascism – such as the popular fronts of the mid-1930s foreshadowed by united fronts in the mid-1920s – been adopted the Nazis might not have come to power and the Second World War and the holocaust have been avoided.

For the purposes of our own argument we need to ask why the great turn was adopted, what its underlying features were and what sort of society emerged. All of these issues are, it goes without saying, highly contentious.

In 1927, around the time of the tenth anniversary of the revolution, Moscow was in the grip of a war scare. On rather insubstantial grounds based on supposed military manoeuvres and crude intelligence reports, Soviet leaders had come to the conclusion that the west was considering a renewed military intervention in Russia.[1] While the scare may have been manipulated, even constructed,[2] for propaganda purposes, the underlying issue was real enough. Were it to happen could Russia defend itself? For the legions of critics of NEP in the party, industrialisation was proceeding so slowly that it was imperilling the safety of the state. As early as 30 March 1925 Frunze, the head of the military, had raised the issue of strengthening the military with a view to countering potential British intervention in the Baltic, Poland and Romania.[3] Like any tsarist moderniser – Ivan III, Peter the Great, even Nicholas II – Stalin and his associates were pulled into state intervention in industry by the simple defence imperative. However, in 1927–8 this was only one among many reasons.

More directly influential was the evolution of NEP. It appears that once the relatively easy stage of economic recovery was achieved, and most sources agree that prewar levels of economic production had been reached by about 1928, the harder task of expanding the economy was causing the NEP mechanisms to creak. In 1928, the endemic 'scissors crises' peaked. Simply put, the problem here was that grain and other agrarian prices fell faster than industrial prices because, as we have already seen, restoration of farm output is easier than repairing the fragile web of an industrial economy which can only expand at the speed of its narrowest bottleneck. For peasants, whose entry into the market was the essence of NEP, the conjuncture discouraged them from selling since they had to market more and more to buy the same quantity of industrial goods. If they decided it was no longer worth producing for such poor returns and either retained more of the surplus in the village or did not bother to produce it at all, then the cities would go short. The name 'scissors crisis' derived from a diagram drawn to illustrate the problem which resembled a pair of scissors with agrarian prices resembling the lower, falling, blade and industrial prices the upper, rising, blade. As the scissors opened so the prices diverged. The point was to close the scissors and restore a market balance.

In the usual reflex of the party left, which politicised almost every social phenomenon, the crisis was not an economic problem but resulted from a 'grain strike', a conscious political act. The terminology betrayed a deeper issue. Within the party the peasants had not been trusted by many of the most militant activists. For them, the peasantry had been the Achilles heel of NEP. Lenin had expected NEP to draw the peasants towards socialism through the advantages of cooperation and economies of scale, enabling modernisation of the rural economy (mechanisation, greater chemical inputs, more efficient pooling of land-holdings into larger units, end of strip cultivation and so on) and the release of surplus labour for industrial projects. Instead, the village had almost turned its back on the outside world and withdrawn into inde-pendence based on its traditional institutions. The commune, rather than the local soviet (except where the latter was the commune under another name) was their key institution of self-defence. The number of cooperatives hardly changed and state farms tended to be weak institu-tions set up to provide minimal subsistence for some of the new state's dependants, notably former civil war soldiers and the unemployed, rather than local showplace farms boasting the advantages of socialist farming. Party membership in the village was very low. In 1928 there were less than 200 000 rural communists, only half of whom were farm-ers, in a population of 120 million in the countryside and out of a total of 1.3 million party members.[4] Given that the rural population was some three times larger than the urban, it is easy to see that the party leadership might become paranoid about the Soviet system's weak hold among the vast majority of Russia's population. Although probably the majority of party members were virtually peasants, they were usually ones who had left the village for the towns or the military. By the late 1920s the party was in the ironic situation of being a proletarian-oriented party, led by intellectuals, whose members were largely peasants but which had few cells in the countryside. In other words, the party and its revolution were largely urban, surrounded by a quite different revolu-tion, that of the peasants, which had got rid of landlords and tsarism, redistributed their possessions and established local self-government through the commune. The peasantry had fulfilled much of its long-held, pre-revolutionary dreams.

Unfortunately they were not the dreams of the party leaders who had quite different plans for the peasantry. The self-contained village would not do. It was believed to be engendering a new petty capitalism and thereby endangering the whole revolutionary project. Control over it had to be established. It had to be converted to socialist principles and resources released to fulfil the party's most pressing dream – industrial-isation. If Lenin's attempt at relatively gentle persuasion and belief in the demonstration effect of the superiority of socialist agriculture had failed, it was time, given the pressure of the grain crisis and the military imperative, to consider more direct methods.

In addition, with the stimulus of stagnation and the war scare, industrialisation moved further up the agenda. No one in the party opposed it, the point was how and at what pace it should be developed. The left wanted to exert ever-increasing pressure to hasten the transfer of resources from private to public. NEP was too slow. The right wanted to continue within the framework of NEP. However, the left was becoming more strident and impatient with NEP hangers-on such as the *spetsy* and Nepmen traders. It was no accident that in 1928 a show trial of *spetsy* for wrecking and sabotage in the coalmines of Shakhty presaged the change of direction.

Not everyone shared in the new logic. Bukharin, fatefully, opposed the new direction to the last. There was no clear-cut 'decision to industrialise' but the goal was being approached foothill by foothill. He spoke out against the incremental decisions which paved the way for the 'great turn'. Through 1928 he and other moderates, including Rykov and Tomsky who had been in a similar struggle over the defence of trade unions during the civil war and had ended up on the losing side on that occasion, too, fought a strong rearguard action. They were able to delay the onset of virtually forced collectivisation but gradually Stalin, Molotov, Mikoyan and Kirov wore them down. In August they published a draft First Five-Year Plan for economic development which envisaged a speeding up of industrialisation at the expense of the peasantry. Nonetheless, in September Bukharin published an article entitled 'Notes of an Economist' in which he eloquently called for continuation of the Leninist equilibrium of NEP. But by the end of the year the die was cast. Stalin manoeuvred his supporters into key positions and had some of the weaker supporters of the moderate line, like Uglanov, demoted. The moderates' last stand came in February 1929. Their increasing weakness led them into explosive and incautious language. They claimed Stalin was encouraging 'military–feudal' exploitation of the peasantry. Stalin's response was swift. Bukharin, Rykov and Tomsky were dismissed from their key positions, Bukharin as editor of *Pravda* and head of Comintern, Tomsky as trade union chief and Rykov as head of the Russian Council of People's Commissars. Bukharin was dismissed from the Politburo, as was Tomsky, though none of them was expelled from the party. Even so, the way was clear for a much more ambitious Five-Year Plan, with fantastic targets for industrial output and labour productivity. In the frenetic atmosphere of the time the plan targets were raised and raised again. In town and country the pressure increased relentlessly. In late 1929 the twin slogans 'Eliminate the *kulaks* as a class' and 'Fulfil the Five-Year Plan in four years' became the mantras of the mobilising bureaucracy.

In addition to the political shift the changes represented, notably the end of the last substantial opposition to Stalin, they left a legacy of further bitterness. Heated language had been used by all sides. Fatally, as it turned out, the right opposition had opened conversations with the remaining disgraced leftists, Kamenev and Zinoviev. Trotsky, himself, was finally exiled at this point. The contents of dissident talks, including Bukharin's description of him as 'Genghis Khan with the telegraph', had made their way to Stalin to be filed in that cavernous section of his mind marked 'awaiting retribution'. The sense of danger, panic, internal disorder and the emergence of potentially disloyal 'enemies of the people' in high places laid the first foundations of the purges. The apparently absurd linking of left and right oppositions in the later show trials had its roots in the supercharged realities of the last struggle against Stalin.

Once made, the decisions were implemented with the full force the new party/state could muster. Industrialisation was pushed ahead, the peasantry was directly attacked, a cultural revolution was conducted. Soviet society buckled under the triple onslaught.

Each assault had two phases. In the first, massive mobilisation around radical, even utopian, goals, linked to slogans of renewed class struggle against kulaks, Nepmen, *spetsy* and the rest, created so much disorder that there had to be a reduction of tempo to avert disaster. Thereafter there was a restoration of part of what had been abolished in the first phase. The transition between the two phases came at different times in each area. In agriculture the slowdown came in March 1930 but in the other two sectors it was only in 1931 and 1932 that partial reversal replaced the initial attack. However, it should be emphasised from the outset that key political targets, notably the breaking of the peasantry, the Nepmen and *spetsy* of all kinds, were achieved in that, as we shall see, even when individuals were sometimes restored to their positions and the tempo of transition was reduced, the conditions to which they returned were vastly different from those they had originally been expelled from. The power of the apparatus had increased exponentially.

In phase one tactics in all three areas were rather similar. Massive exhortation and encouragement of radicals, particularly among young men and women, encouraged them to change the face of the Soviet

Union and break the ties of backwardness. In factories, construction
sites, colleges, universities, the Academy of Sciences, intellectual unions,
farms and villages a similar scenario developed. A sometimes very small
minority of enthusiasts was unleashed to revolutionise their institutions.
Where local support was lacking, notably in many villages, volunteer
squads were raised in cities and launched at the target. Elsewhere,
knowledge that they could call on the police or even the army to back
them up was often sufficient to diffuse opposition.

The best-known of these processes is that which hit the peasantry in
the autumn and winter of 1929–30. The main features have long been
known from Merle Fainsod's pioneering work based on the Smolensk
archives, captured by the Nazis in 1941 before the local communist
authorities could destroy them. In 1945 they fell into American hands
and have been available to scholars since the 1950s. Fainsod's picture is
one of brigades of young urban workers and Komsomol volunteers
descending on the village – full of ideological enthusiasm and an extraordinary high level of youthful self-righteousness – in order to bend the
villagers to the will of the party. Village meetings were railroaded into
joining collective farms. Once taken the decision was forcefully implemented, sometimes with police and army involvement. There were
many reports of volunteer brigades getting out of control, beating peasants up (all opponents could conveniently be labelled 'kulaks'), stealing
clothes people were actually wearing, taking food from ovens and many
more offences. Naturally the peasants resisted. They slaughtered livestock rather than allow it to be collectivised. They defended many fellow villagers accused of being kulaks and sheltered members of their
families. There is no evidence to support the official view that the village
was divided against itself on class lines. By and large the villages united
against the violent intruders. The chaos grew so rapidly that by early
1930 not only the spring sowing but also the stability of the countryside,
perhaps even of the regime, was endangered. The army was being called
in more and more frequently to deal with uprisings of which 1678 were
recorded in the peak months of January to 15 March 1930.[5] Army chiefs
warned that the soldiers would not indefinitely support violent repression of their own kind. The policy had to be changed.

The story was the same elsewhere. Militants were given their head but
the disasters they wrought had to be reined in. In factories, young militants supported new work practices designed to bulldoze through the
limitations of the low productivity of Soviet labour and to bring new
industries and factories into existence almost through willpower alone.

In industry, the extremes of madness were ended when the plan was declared 'by and large fulfilled' after four and a quarter years, that is, in early 1932, but periodic reversion to the similar methods such as 'storming' to meet targets and the encouragement of norm-busting Stakhanovites from 1935 on became endemic to the system.

In the cultural sphere, organisations like the League of Militant Godless launched a major attack on religion but the damage done by their direct assault added to the chaos and opposition to the government. In universities, respected professors were sent into exile. Established writers were declared to have been superseded, their places taken by party faithful who were often intellectually ill-equipped for their jobs. Leopold Averbakh was a typical example. He had been a firebrand member of various 'proletarian' literary movements of the 1920s and had fought against compromise with fellow-travellers and specialists. The renewed class war slogans, under which Stalin's second revolution was conducted, made characters like Averbakh into apparent natural leaders of the new cultural revolution. Moderates were thrown out of organisations, silenced, even sent to camps in extreme cases. 'Bourgeois' intellectuals were uprooted in science, history, architecture and every other field of intellectual endeavour.

Blind party loyalty and extreme enthusiasm for the new line were the order of the day. The slogan 'There is no fortress the Bolsheviks cannot storm' was interpreted almost literally in all fields. Like its Maoist successors, the Great Leap Forward and the Great Proletarian Cultural Revolution, the movement was based on breaking 'objective' social and economic laws by organised effort of the will, by simply ordering people to do things so that, as the policy of the time made clear, it would be possible to increase savings and investment massively at the same time. In Bukharin's memorable phrase, the basis of the plan was to 'build today's factories with tomorrow's bricks'.

Nonetheless, in the turmoil of these years the main pillars of the Soviet system were consolidated. First of all the events should be seen as the continuation of the process of centralisation of power which had been going on from day one of the Bolshevik revolution. The central leadership came out of the struggle immensely more powerful than it had been before the struggle began. By 1932, through the unique mechanism of economic ministries, the planned economy and its chief coordinating instrument, the State Planning Commission (Gosplan), the central authorities tried to control every economic enterprise in the Soviet Union from bomb production to the sale of shoe laces. While

managers still retained much influence there is no doubt that, ultimately, all economic authority lay with the centre which could and did
override opposition in priority areas. In the countryside, the traditional
peasant communities had been smashed. The *mir* was no more. Religion
had been undermined. More positively, small-scale strip cultivation had
also gone. Henceforth the peasants were incapable of further 'grain
strikes' and, even though collectivisation is rightly maligned for its overall economic inefficiency, it did provide a reliable mechanism for state
procurement of agricultural produce. It broke the peasantry and it broke
the rural stranglehold over economic progress as the party perceived it.
While Russian towns certainly did not start flowing with milk and honey
they were supplied steadily with minimum necessary rations, allowing a
vast stream of people to enter the urban workforce. During the years of
the first plan the industrial workforce grew to 22 million people, double
what was expected. The system also guaranteed the supply of a large
army and, in wartime, was one of the sinews of victory. At the terrific cost
of short-term famine and long-term underproduction, collectivisation
established a mechanism for the state to exact, in Stalin's word, 'tribute'
(*dan'*) from the peasantry. So successful was it in providing relatively reliable supplies that the Germans kept it in place under their occupation
when disbanding the collectives might well have been a major means of
winning over support from the Soviet population. However, like the
Soviet leadership, the Nazi occupiers were not interested in compromise. Both regimes were concerned to impose their power over the population on their own terms, even if it meant courting unpopularity and
failing to achieve maximum economic efficiency. In this sense, purely
economic analyses of industrialisation and collectivisation miss the
point. They were not intended simply to maximise economic output,
but to do so while maximising central control over the country. Where
the two were in conflict, the political imperative was paramount.

Of course, the political and the economic had already been brought
together in the phenomenon of productionism. The new Soviet state
bore its imprint, and that of its equally deep-rooted cousin, bureaucratisation, and brought both to new levels. The new party apparatus
was to concern itself less and less with politics, more and more with management. In this sense, not only was the second revolution the end of
the peasantry, it was also the final act in the history of the political intelligentsia and brought about its replacement by a technical one. This
was a by-product, almost, of the fundamental processes shaping the new
system, the system which has dominated and bedevilled Russia from

then right down to the twenty-first century as post-Soviet Russia contin-
ues to struggle with its legacy. What was the essence of the new system?

One way to understand it is to see the emerging model as that of a
new hierarchical society bringing all its component parts into a direct
relationship with one another.[6] At the top of the hierarchy stood the
party. As in the 1920s this meant primarily the leadership – the
Politburo and the Central Committee. Even Stalin still had to have these
on his side in the early 1930s and, arguably, even later, though unques-
tionably, his personal power rose rapidly in these years. Below the party
was the state. The state had been thoroughly transformed into the
errand-boy of the party, a process reaching back to the first days of the
October revolution. Ministers were less important than their party counterparts. Ministries, spreading their tentacles through the entire economy and therefore the entire society, followed party leadership
instructions. It was here that the great innovation began to take hold.
The main mediating force between party, state and people was the plan.
The leadership established the plan's priorities; the ministries worked
out the details; the State Planning Commission (Gosplan) mediated and
then drafted the plan; the ordinary party membership acclaimed it and
exhorted the population to fulfil it; the people settled down to work
within its context. While the actual system was as yet (indeed, always)
imperfect, the model was very much in place.

Its ideological driving force was, of course, productionism. The drive
for an advanced industry was equated with continuing the revolution.
Only on the basis of a Soviet economy which outpaced capitalism could
the utopian, self-managed society of socialism emerge. Indeed, the propaganda of the First Five-Year Plan period took productionism as its key
theme. Although less intense at other times, it remained at the top of
the ideological agenda, some observers even arguing that Gorbachev's
perestroika was focused on giving one more neo-Stalinist heave to the
groaning mechanism of the Soviet system. Be that as it may, it is unques-
tionable that we must look at the evolution of the Soviet system from
1928 on through the prism of this party–state–plan–population model
with the emergence of productionism as its rationale.

One does not have to look very far to see that an obvious consequence
of this state of affairs is further bureaucratisation. The hierarchical chain
of command and the nature of the operations conducted by party, state
and plan bodies spawned a vast 'new class' of administrators, beholden,
like most administrators, to their superiors more than to those whom
they were administering. None of Lenin's principles for controlling the

emergence of careerists which he expounded in the *April Theses* and *State and Revolution* was applied, with the inevitable consequence that the new bureaucratic class rapidly transformed itself into not exactly a ruling class, since power resided with the party leader and his associates, but into a privileged elite managerial class which we will look at in more detail later. For the moment, however, let us note that the new circumstances produced it and that its existence – as an appointed rather than, in any meaningful sense, an elected group of people – strengthened the deeply anti-democratic instincts of the party leadership. It is also worth commenting that the phenomenon of bureaucratisation is often seen as the primary cause of the degeneration of the revolution, particularly by Trotsky and his followers, one of whom, James Burnham, turned the initial ideas into a broad critique of the anti-democratic tendencies of what he saw as *The Managerial Revolution* which blighted corporate capitalism as much as Soviet communism. Bruno Rizzi also warned of *The Bureaucratisation of the World*. However, we should remember that it is a mistake to see bureaucratisation as primary in Soviet conditions. Rather it is a consequence of the elitism, minority status and productionism of communism. In other words, it is a logical outcome of the kind of revolution conducted by the Bolsheviks, not an unfortunate side effect without which the revolution would work better. To avoid it the revolution would have had to be very different and be led by a group with a very different outlook. The bureaucratisation of the revolution, in other words, is a clear consequence of Leninism, heightened by, but not solely attributable to, Stalinism. Clearly those within the Bolshevik tradition, like Trotsky, could not go this far in their critique of bureaucratisation and for that reason their analysis remains ultimately unconvincing, though helpful in pointing to the phenomenon itself.

Another as yet unappreciated aspect of the First Five-Year Plan period is the way in which the cultural revolution which accompanied it resulted in the suppression of the last vestiges of *organised* intellectual independence and squashed the final remnants of civil society, understood as organised, at least semi-independent, high cultural life outside the state. In 1929 the last relatively independent intellectual institution, the Academy of Sciences, was fully taken over by the party. Elsewhere, semi-independent unions of writers, artists and so on were broken up. For a while, utopian leftists from the party enjoyed a brief ascendancy. In the intellectual sphere as in the economic sphere the extremes of madness had to be reined in. Discredited figures, like the historian E. V. Tarlé, returned from camps. Militants like Averbakh were sent to them. For

someone so young – he was barely into his thirties when arrested –
Averbakh had done incredible damage. Leftist historians like Pokrovsky
were also undermined as their opponents became more favoured.
Similar reversals were occurring right across the spectrum. Some historians have seen these as restoration of the previous status quo or even as
'immediate improvement – not only in comparison with the period of
cultural revolution, but also in comparison with NEP' in that, for example, harassment by leftist groups was now reined in.[7] However, such a
judgement is somewhat overoptimistic. The conditions under which
individuals returned were quite different. Before 1928 the institutions
and organisations through which intellectuals operated had been much
freer, especially from direct party control. The various organisations of
writers, cinematographers, architects, lawyers and so on had been set up
to represent the largely non-party membership and negotiate with the
party. The post-cultural revolution model was based on direct party control with less freedom of action for non-party members.[8] To operate as
an intellectual it was increasingly expected that a person should be a
party member, so here, too, the political dimension of the Stalin revolution was apparent. In fact, not all intellectual organisations were transformed at the same time. The Union of Film Workers was formed in
1934 but lawyers were not finally incorporated into a union until 1939.
However, by the mid-1930s all the major intellectual and professional
groups were in party-dominated unions, Musicians', Artists', Architects'
and Writers' Unions being organised in 1932. Aspects of the new
dispensation will be discussed below.

The Emerging Model

In the agricultural, industrial and cultural fields the Stalin revolution
had had an enormous impact, not least in vastly extending the tentacles
of party/state power into every area of social life and many areas of private life. For the time being however, the would-be totalitarian monster
was held in check by its own inefficiencies. Workplace control was
diluted by the immense demand for labour. If a worker was in trouble in
one place she or he could move elsewhere, the 'totalitarian' workbook
imposed on every worker turning up later or not at all. Many restrictions
could be avoided by moving around the country in the milling chaos
that accompanied these great events. Equally, one might fall foul of the

authorities in an arbitrary way for happening to be in the wrong place at the wrong time but that, too, showed that the system was still too ramshackle to be called truly totalitarian, even though it would have liked to be. There was a host of problems – unfamiliarity with the new system on the part of its implementors (that is, local police and party officials); the impossibility of keeping up with the avalanche of often contradictory decrees and directives sent out by a multitude of conflicting authorities; traditional cultural survivals of religious values and bonds, especially among sectarians; kinship, family and accustomed ways of doing things such as arguing one's way through hostile authorities, bribery (though this might be increasingly risky), influence (*blat* in Russian), mutual favours and so on. All these factors moderated the ferocity of the new system. However, as time went on it became increasingly organised though one should not overestimate the hold of the central authorities, especially in the provinces. Even as late as 1937 the British Embassy official and later long-serving Conservative MP Sir Fitzroy Maclean tells how, having been refused permission by the authorities in Moscow to travel to sensitive areas like Central Asia and the Caucasus, he simply went and bluffed his way through. On one occasion he was intercepted and arrested by an NKVD patrol while riding in the Caspian region. He satisfied them of his bona fides by 'translating' a pass to the May Day parade in Moscow as though it were a permit from the Foreign Minister Litvinov allowing Maclean to visit the frontier zone patrolled by the non-Russian-reading border troops who had arrested him. After hearing the contents of the 'translation' the platoon became sheepish and tried to persuade Maclean not to report the incident in Moscow and to convey their good wishes to Comrade Litvinov.[9] Elsewhere, whenever questioned, he simply waved his passport and asserted his right to be there. One would have needed much more convincing forgeries to get away with that ten years later.

Despite these weaknesses in practice, there can be no doubt that a new, powerful system had been formed in the years from 1928 to 1932. The chain of agrarian backwardness had been ruthlessly broken and the Soviet Union opened up an extraordinary spurt of industrial growth and an unprecedented cascade of workers into the cities. Although the majority of the population remained rural for another twenty years or so the tide was now turning inevitably towards industry and the city and a new way of life, and new social classes, especially the burgeoning millions of administrators and their families, began to develop new cultures, which we will examine in the next chapter.

While the totalitarianism of this system was restricted in practice by its inefficiencies, there can be no doubt that, as a model, party/state control was intended to penetrate into all areas of life, even to return to more 'utopian' collective models of the family where eating, washing and child-rearing would be more collective activities. Women would not be expected to stay at home to look after the family. Instead, although large families were still encouraged, mothers were supposed to leave household tasks to crèches, canteens and laundries and go out to work. The drive for this was not motivated so much by a concern for the liberation of women, rather it arose out of productionist motives of mobilising every available source of labour for economic production. Shortage of resources for consumer services, like canteens, crèches and laundries, tended to undermine the success of such drives, more often than not leaving working-class families with the worst of both worlds, the need for both parents to work, the lack of services and, in some cases, apartments without kitchens in areas without canteens.

The system that had emerged was very far from the utopian ideals which had inspired the revolutionaries who had led the Soviet Union to its current state. Rather than see a new breakthrough into the future – a continuing theme of official propaganda – it was instinctive on the part of many observers to evoke comparisons with the worst of Russia's past. Stalin was 'the last of the Tsars', a latter-day Ivan the Terrible or Peter the Great, imposing terrific sacrifices on self and country in the name of greatness. Others have seen a new serfdom. At one extreme were peasants who adapted the Russian initials VKP, which stood for 'All Union Communist Party', to read 'The Second Serfdom' (*Vtoroe krepost'noe pravo*). At the other, the Austrian economist Friedrich Hayek concluded from an apparently superficial study of Russian conditions that socialism in general was *The Road to Serfdom*, a system by which the state enserfs the whole population. His book became a founding text of the 1980s New Right in Britain and the United States.

The connection between Soviet socialism and serfdom does, perhaps, have something to it but as historians we should see the connection being the opposite to that proposed by Hayek. It was not socialism which opened up the road to a new serfdom, rather it was the late survival of serfdom which opened up the road to a Stalinist-style socialism. Although serfdom was officially abolished in 1861 many aspects of its culture and institutions survived into the twentieth century. The autocracy, for instance, was a governmental system devised to control a serf society and a state service society through official patronage and interference in all areas and harsh police discipline and labour camps to back up its authority. Popular attitudes to the state – mainly well-justified mistrust – pervaded Russia before its revolution and continue down to the present. In a society where the state has largely brought repression, misery, taxation, conscription and disillusionment it would have taken a miracle for a new attitude to emerge in the revolution. The narrowness of Russian 'civil society' before 1917 and the weakness of basic liberal values – with absence of respect for a just and democratically arrived-at system of law in the forefront – meant that there was no national democratic tradition on which the socialist revolution could build. In its place there was a political culture of despotism, chauvinism, racism, anti-westernism and messianic complacency. Even work attitudes showed the serf imprint – do as much as you can on your own behalf (for example, in the black economy), as little as possible for the employer or the state. Russian productivity down to the present shows traces of this.

Such was the atmosphere in which the Bolshevik revolutionaries were brought up. Although they opposed many of these phenomena in theory, certain aspects crept into their own intellectual make-up, for example contempt for liberalism as hypocrisy without seeing that, for instance, Marx incorporated many aspects of liberalism (liberty, fraternity, equality) in the foundations of socialism. Bourgeois hypocrisy lay less in the values than in the failure to apply them fully, notably in the sphere of property relations. One might even hypothesise that it was the Bolsheviks' very lack of westernism – which was much more a feature of Menshevik, Kadet and even Socialist Revolutionary intelligentsia leaders – that helped mark them out for power. Stalin himself was one of the least westernised of the Bolshevik leaders.

Once in power the undemocratic way of doing things reasserted itself. Although there was an immensely lively grass-roots democracy, particularly in 1917, democratic institutions at the national level had never been allowed to take root, in the name of defence of divine right by the tsars, in the name of the true ideology by the Soviet leaders. In this respect both tsarist and Soviet regimes resembled each other as 'theocracies' motivated by their possession of 'religious' truths and using their great ideological organisations – the church for one, party propagandists for the other – as their main legitimising cultural props. The basic institutions of Soviet rule – informers, political police, labour camps, a dominant military – were all extensions of tsarist precedent. The fact that they were vastly more widespread is not the point. The culture of using such institutions was *inherited* by the Soviet regime, not *invented* by them – it was, in a sense, the way things were done in Russia. Popular acquiescence in the enormities of state rule was also bred in the vestiges of a serf culture. It was not the lesson of 1917 but the lesson of a millennium that one kept one's head down when the bosses were on top of things. One worked around the system, evaded it, migrated from it, but head-on challenge was likely to be useless and only to be embarked upon *in extremis* or when the bosses appeared to have lost their grip.

It follows from this that it is a mistake to see the Stalin system, still less socialism in general, as a return to serfdom. Rather, the Stalin system was a type of socialism adapted to (or perhaps, more appropriately, deformed by) Russian conditions. It was not a universal but a Russified form of Marxism. It was the socialism of a society that had not overcome the legacy of serfdom, the socialism of a pre-capitalist country, the socialism of an economically backward, autocratic, serf culture.

Such were the fundamental features of the emerging Soviet model. Models, however, tend to be static. History, especially Soviet history in the 1930s, was dynamic. In the fast-flowing currents of history the model would be thoroughly tested and, where necessary, modified. But its main aspects and its goals would remain the same for some time yet.

5

STALINISM TRIUMPHANT

By late 1932 Stalin stood triumphant. He had taken enormous risks in promoting full-scale industrialisation and collectivisation but, in his terms, they had paid off. Where the peasants had forced Lenin to retreat after the civil war, they had now been ruthlessly broken as an independent force in Russian life – a truly historical achievement in that the peasantry had, hitherto, been the bedrock of Russian society. With great effort the oversized supertanker that was Russia had been forced to make a decisive change of course. The rural 'veto' on industrial development had been smashed. The Soviet Union was, henceforth, to become ever more industrial. In the process, Stalin's power in the party had become unchallengeable. Had he failed, his critics would have struck back ruthlessly but he had, it seemed, confounded them. He had wrecked the '*smychka*', the alliance with the peasantry that Lenin had come to believe was essential. But Stalin had survived. It was the peasantry which had been forced to give way. He had outdone the industrialisers in boldness and left them floundering. Trotsky was in foreign exile. Bukharin, Kamenev and Zinoviev lived on in Moscow but were politically broken. Stalin had surrounded himself with like-minded Politburo and Central Committee colleagues who became increasingly sycophantic. New, hard, men emerged – Molotov, Kirov, Ordzhonikidze – cut from the same tough, 'practical' cloth as Stalin himself. They were devoted Leninists largely up from the back streets, lacking, in most cases, the intellectual finesse of higher education. They had been formed in the university of civil war and class struggle, like their leader. No matter that the country was actually in turmoil, that many areas were soon to tip into devastating famine that took millions of lives. No matter that more sensitive souls in the party were horrified by the costs of 'success' and voiced criticisms of the leadership. Stalin was beyond the reach of all this. The party leadership, by and large, was not going to shed tears over the distress of the, in their view, historically doomed peasantry if the development of the all-important working class was thereby assured. Short-term misery should not be allowed to short-circuit long-term joy. From the standpoint of 'history' the literally dying groans of a dying class were, for the party faithful, a regrettable but inevitable cost of progress.

Who was Stalin?

Victorious though he was, Stalin had only just emerged from the shadows and, although the cult of his personality was to grow to monstrous proportions, he was, as yet, relatively little-known to the country. His complex, paradoxical character and the lack of hard information about many aspects of his life, especially his early years, have made him equally difficult for historians to know. In a curious inversion, the anti-cult of his personality – that is, that everything he did was wholly evil – has come to dominate his critics as surely as the positive cult took over his supporters. In the light of new evidence and the subsiding passions of the post-Cold War era, can we form a more nuanced and realistic view of Stalin?

There seems little doubt that, at this stage, and probably throughout his adult life, Stalin saw himself first and foremost as a revolutionary and we should do the same. His commitment to revolution was the foundation of every other aspect of his personality. Though we know very little about the origin of his revolutionary commitment, what we do know suggests it was strong from his early youth. It may be that Stalin is the prime example of tsarism sowing the dragon's teeth that brought about its own destruction in that it appears that Stalin's first steps into revolution arose from nationalist disturbances in his native Georgia provoked by the attempted Russification of the province in the 1890s and the harsh regime of the Georgian monks in whose charge he was in 1894–9. Be that as it may, he spent the years up to 1912 (by which time he was 32) as a provincial activist and labour organiser in the Caucasus and south Russia, notably the oilfields. Many legends persist, notably that he was involved in bank robberies and may have been a tsarist police agent. Whatever the truth, there is nothing to shake the view that even if he was involved in such activities they were an extension of his revolutionary commitment. After all, many revolutionary organisations fund themselves by robbery and fraud and have convoluted relations with the police forces set up to keep them under surveillance. Compared to the evidence for his revolutionary commitment the case against its being genuine looks very flimsy.

Three aspects of his early life need to be noted for our purposes. First, his experiences in places like the oilfields of Baku exposed him to some of the rawest forms of capitalist exploitation exercised by Russian and foreign companies. Wages were poor, jobs insecure and the work was very dangerous. Injury led to dismissal without compensation or health-care. We might surmise that Stalin's life-long adherence to proletarian chauvinism – the belief that small though it was, the working class of Russia was tough enough to face anything without condescending help from do-gooders and intellectuals – and his hatred of the upper classes and especially imperialism for their hypocrisy and veneer of civilisation built on ruthless exploitation, owed much to these early experiences. If, later on, the bourgeoisie was going to squeal because the boot was on the other foot, Stalin was not going to be sympathetic. Second, Stalin absorbed essential elements of Georgian culture which remained with him throughout his life and to which we will have to return. Third, it is important to note that Stalin's rise from provincial obscurity, like most of the decisive moments of his early career, was indissolubly linked with his acquaintanceship with Lenin. His first, and thereby most important in many ways, step from provincial obscurity came in 1906 when, at the Fourth Party Congress in Stockholm, he attracted Lenin's attention, not least because Stalin was the only Bolshevik representative from Baku and the Caucasus at the congress and he wanted to use him as a strate-gic wedge to drive into the Menshevik domination of the region. Several of Stalin's crucial promotions – cooption to the Central Committee and appointment as *Pravda* editor in 1912 and as General Secretary in 1922 – were brought about by Lenin's influence. Throughout these years Stalin was one of Lenin's closest personal aides. After Lenin had fallen ill and withdrew from active politics it was Stalin who liaised between him and the rest of the party leaders. It was in these difficult circum-stances that, in the winter of 1922/3, the only shadow fell across their relationship. In an outburst of rage at Lenin's wife Krupskaia because she had been encouraging Lenin to overwork and because Lenin heard that Stalin had been riding roughshod over fellow Georgians in the party, Lenin began to seek ways of removing Stalin from his post as General Secretary, though not, it seems, from the Politburo or Central Committee. A great 'what if' controversy has resulted from these late efforts by Lenin. Many writers and activists at the time, not least Trotsky,

who had most to gain, have argued that had Lenin succeeded then the
rise of Stalin and Stalinism would never have taken place.[1] In the event,
Lenin's health took a serious turn for the worse and Stalin – who had
apologised profusely to Lenin and to Krupskaia – continued in post. We
have no way of knowing what might have happened. Lenin had had personal and political spats with almost all his associates and had continued
to work with them. Compared to the decade of separation, political
antagonism and verbal recrimination between Lenin and Trotsky prior
to 1917 the affair seems trivial. Within the context of Lenin's long-
standing close relationship with Stalin the moment of dispute seems
evanescent. Had Lenin, in his last days of relative lucidity, finally spot-
ted flaws in Stalin to which he had been blind for fifteen years when he
was well? Was it the whim of a sick and dying man? We can never know,
but we do know that Lenin trusted Stalin perhaps more closely, up to
that point, than any other of the leaders. What was it that Lenin saw in
Stalin, beyond that first recognition of him as a useful political pawn in
south Russia?

Lenin was surrounded by followers and associates but Stalin seems to
have stood out for two related reasons. First, he was a practical person
rather than an intellectual and, second, he was the most personally loyal
of Lenin's immediate circle. In fact, Stalin practically idolised Lenin,
possibly even changing his revolutionary codename from Koba (the
name of the Georgian 'Robin Hood') to the more familiar Stalin because
it echoed Lenin's own pseudonym.[2] The combination was irresistible to
Lenin. Here was an unquestioningly loyal person who actually got
things done and did not dispute principles or split hairs in a way that
frequently frustrated Lenin. Stalin was Lenin's political fixer. For example, before the vital Tenth Party Congress Lenin was worried that he
might face close votes on the crucial issues of adoption of NEP, party
discipline and the Workers' Opposition. We even have his back-of-an-
envelope style calculations of what majorities he might expect. He need
not have been concerned. Stalin was at work. As one of Lenin's opponents, the Democratic Centralist Rafailov, complained, the Central
Committee and the Organisation Bureau of the party had intervened to
invalidate the election of oppositionists and substituted candidates of
their own. For Rafailov, it was Stalin who was at work here, packing the
congress with supporters of Lenin.[3]

Politically speaking, the link, while useful to Lenin, was irreplaceable
for Stalin. Curiously, Lenin's death did not so much weaken it from
Stalin's point of view as strengthen it. After all, there was no real Lenin

to threaten it any more as he had done in 1922/3. Instead, Stalin was able to go about inventing a new Lenin and establishing himself as the high priest of the evolving cult. Lenin might be dead but Leninism would live forever. Stalin lost no time. He took a prominent role at Lenin's funeral, delivering a solemn series of vows reminiscent of the style (though obviously not the content) of the Orthodox liturgy. While this, in itself, was not crucial it did allow him to upstage his arch-rival Trotsky who accepted Stalin's advice not to rush back from convalescence to attend the funeral. His absence was noted and provided material for rumours and slanderous whispering campaigns against him. Stalin was also one of the prime movers of the idea, repulsive as it was to Lenin's widow Krupskaia and many other friends and colleagues, of embalming Lenin's body and displaying it in a specially constructed mausoleum in Red Square. It was from the podium of the mausoleum that Stalin came to project many aspects of his political personality and his body even came to rest beside that of his leader for seven years after his own death.

While the funeral and the mausoleum were symbolic, Stalin was also involved in more substantial efforts to create a Leninism after Stalin's own heart. He had already begun with a series of lectures in April 1924 to just his kind of audience, working-class militants following a party training course at the Sverdlov University. He called the lectures *The Foundations of Leninism*. In them and other works of the period Stalin defined his own political characteristics in the form of Leninism. What were the features emphasised by Stalin? Above all, three areas were given prominence and they came to dominate Stalin's political thinking throughout his career. These were class struggle, socialism in one country and Bolshevik morality. To understand Stalin, Stalinism and the Soviet system as he built it, we need to take a closer look at each of these.

First, class struggle. For Marx, who made this idea the bedrock of his interpretation of all human history, the concept of class struggle was subtle and complex. But Marx was a thinker more than an activist. Lenin reversed the proportions in being an activist first and thinker second. This led to him simplifying many of Marx's complex ideas and reducing them to cruder versions. When it comes to Stalin, however, who was an activist with no serious claims as a philosopher, the crudity factor is even more in evidence. A simple division of the world into bourgeois and proletarian forces was enough for Stalin. The countryside, as Stalin imagined it, seems to have been populated with peasants and *kulaks*. Stalin reduced the concept to Manichaean contrasts of black and white, good and evil. Stalin's judgements on internal and external policies revolved around simple opposites. Class was the guiding principle of his world-view. Stalin's views on class, like those of many other party members, can best be described as 'proletarian chauvinism'. The workers and their interests and outlook were the touchstone of any principle or policy. A consistent belief in the tough qualities of the formerly humiliated and exploited working class (probably picked up from his time in south Russia, as we have seen) remained one of Stalin's most enduring and personal characteristics. His first serious clash with Trotsky and, partly, with Lenin came over this issue when, during the civil war, a military specialist named Sytin, a former tsarist officer, was sent to assist Stalin. Stalin had him sent back, preferring to rely on his less expert but more politically reliable party associates. Only Lenin's authority was able to smooth over the associated recriminations between Stalin and Trotsky. Throughout the 1920s too, Stalin made threatening speeches about toleration of bourgeois specialists as managers, engineers and teachers, preferring instead the rough and ready, less educated but fully committed working-class militants of the party. One of the first signs of his growing authority and of the looming change of direction was a trial of 'bourgeois' engineers accused of sabotaging the mines of Shakhty in 1928. Proletarian chauvinism runs like a red thread through Stalin's career.

Like any other Marxist, for Stalin class took precedence over nationality. Class divisions in society were real, national divisions were artificial and doomed. This may sound an odd thing to say about someone who is usually thought of as the fount of 'Soviet patriotism' and national struggle during the Second World War. However, the paradox can be explained, indeed, has to be explained, because the predominance of the class principle in Stalin's outlook has often been underestimated and his supposed preference for nationalism and patriotism overemphasised. For instance, Trotsky abused Stalin for abandoning international revolution but even when Stalin dominated the international communist movement and its agency Comintern the class principle still ruled. The Comintern line might be 'class against class' as in the 'third wave' of 1928–32 or it might be class collaboration as in the 'united front' policies of the 1920s and the 'popular fronts' of the 1930s, but class remained at the heart of the analysis. Class, too, was at the heart of Stalin's 'Soviet patriotism'. This is best explained by focusing on the quintessential Stalinist concept of the 1920s – 'socialism in one country'.

As we have seen, it was assumed that Russia's revolution would be a spark to set off similar upheavals elsewhere and that, for it to survive,

world capitalism would have to be overthrown. By 1921 it was clear that
hopes of revolution elsewhere were unrealistic and, rather than arriving
at the concept intellectually, Bolsheviks had to adjust to reality and face
indefinite isolation in what was deemed, not incorrectly, to be a hostile
world. In many ways, 'Stalinism' is the system's adjustment to this reality – a paranoid vision of the outside world and a bluff confidence in the
qualities of the Russian worker to get through regardless. The emergence of socialism in one country was an elaboration of these features.

Certain aspects of Lenin's theory and practice fed into it, above all
Lenin's adaptation of Marxism to, at best, an early capitalist society
rather than a mature one, encapsulated in his reply to Sukhanov who
had accused him of deviating from Marxism. Lenin replied that there
was nothing in Marx to say one could not start with the political revolution and then use that platform to build the economic, social and cultural dimensions. Of course, Stalinism was exactly that, revolution
driven politically by the party and state or, in familiar terminology, revolution 'from above'. But, as we have seen, Lenin had already made, in
practice as much as theory, another major adaptation which Stalin
incorporated and took to new levels – productionism. For Lenin, anything which built up the economy – including such apparently regres-
sive policies as reintroducing wide wage differentials, bringing back
specialists, reintroducing 'iron proletarian discipline' in the factories,
dallying with Taylorist work practices to maximise worker productivity –
had to be taken up. Many leftists in the party objected to these various
'betrayals'. Perhaps oddly, even though he was to adopt many aspects
of Leninist productionism, Stalin was more 'Marxist' than Lenin in
the sense that he was, as we have also seen, prepared to rely more on
the rough and ready untutored working class than on better-educated
'specialists' and 'class enemies'. The way was thus open for Stalin to
combine, as he did in 1928–32, a line of turning to the proletariat and
proclaiming class struggle against specialists in industry and kulaks in
the village with all-out breakneck industrialisation. It was also here that
class and national themes intertwined. It was the collective achievements
of the cosmopolitan working class and its developing intelligentsia of
Soviet Russia (guided, of course, by the wisdom of the party) which was
eulogised in Soviet 'patriotism', not the traditional values of the feudal
and capitalist elites of tsarist Russia. Indeed, in a key speech of 1931 he
claimed that the Russian people would have the strength to succeed in
building a powerful Russia where its elite predecessors had been endlessly kicked around by their neighbours. In Stalin's words, 'One feature

of the old Russia was the continual beatings she suffered for falling behind …. In the past we had no fatherland, nor could we have had one. But now that we have overthrown capitalism, and power is in the hands of the working class, we have a fatherland and we will defend its independence.'[4] In other words, it was a very new, class-based form of patriotism. It was also from here that Soviet 'messianism' also developed in that, in Stalin's eyes, the achievements of Soviet workers were a beacon to their class sisters and brothers elsewhere as much as they were a warning to the bloated capitalists of Stalin's imagined world.

The third major concept which Stalin developed in his new form of 'Leninism' was Bolshevik morality. In many ways, it was their political morality which had distinguished the Bolsheviks from most of the rest of the revolutionary intelligentsia. One can find many similarities of ideas and theories which ran across political divisions. However, most party leaders of the left adhered to what we might call common standards of decency of the time so that, for instance, honesty, trustworthiness, respect, bonds of family and friendship, honour, were part and parcel of their lives as they were for early Marxists such as Plekhanov. Nonetheless, it was Plekhanov himself who proclaimed that the good of the revolution was the highest law. In the hands of Lenin this principle was taken to extremes more reminiscent of the morality of ultra-revolutionaries like Nechaev and Bakunin than of Marx.

Stalin certainly picked up this pragmatic morality or lack of it but gave it an additional spin in two directions. Perhaps even more than Lenin he equated revolution with war and saw the morality of class struggle being more akin to the morality of wartime than of peace. In particular, as in war, the struggle might lead to innocent people getting hurt – 'collateral damage' in today's euphemism – but losses, casualties and even atrocities did not outweigh the good of the cause. They were regrettable, but unavoidable. Like a military leader, Stalin and the party chiefs had to keep their minds on the goal of ultimate victory and not be deflected by the costs to their own side and to the war's victims in general. Where imperialist guns, gunboats and, later, bombers indiscriminately pounded soldiers and civilians – men, women and children – into submission, so the revolution would, while taking every care to avoid unnecessary damage, prioritise victory over everything else. The rub came in the term 'unnecessary'. Who was to judge what was and was not 'necessary'? 'Necessity' became a key term in Stalinist discourse.[5] Party leaders, too, were expected to give everything to the cause. Family life was secondary to politics even to the extreme of Politburo members' close relatives, even wives, being held in the Gulag. Stalin, in a notable example from wartime, did not exert privilege for his own family, in that he refused to exchange his own son, captured by the Germans, for a number of German officers captive in Russia. His son died in a Nazi camp. In his personal life Stalin was, rather like Peter the Great, as hard on himself as he was on others, expecting maximum effort at all times. It would be rash to assume that Stalin lacked physical courage. If stories of his early life have any truth in them, it appears he was ready to die for the cause, and his civil war experiences back this up. True, his courage was not put to the test later in life though he did gain respect by remaining in Moscow in 1941 when the rest of the government had been evacuated and German bombs were raining down on the city. It was certainly assumed that a decent Bolshevik would be prepared to die for the cause.

In this there may have been something of the second additional ingredient Stalin gave to Bolshevik morality – the culture of the Caucasus. Roughly speaking, the code in which Stalin had been brought up was still based on dominant masculine values of honour and the feud. Insults had to be avenged and were never forgotten. Honour had to be satisfied even unto the death not only of an enemy, but also of a friend or family member who might face exile, even execution for bringing dishonour. In extreme circumstances, suicide might be expected of someone who had been in any way dishonourable. In this rough, frontier, mountain ethic one had to be prepared to kill and to die. Stalin shows many such characteristics and brought something of the culture of the mafia, of the 'honourable' gangster, into the Kremlin (where, it should be added, it had not been unknown in earlier centuries!).

It may sound odd, but the obverse of the culture of the feud was the culture of hospitality. Happily, as anyone who has visited Georgia will know, the 'totalitarian' hospitality of enforced giant drinking bouts is more prominent than that of the feud. Stalin, too, appears to have picked up this culture. Some of the most vivid descriptions we have of Stalin[6] show him presiding over Georgian-style banquets in which his guests – though rarely Stalin himself – were forced to down excessive quantities of alcohol (not that this is not also something of a traditional Russian characteristic). In his earlier years, however, all the evidence suggests that Stalin was a sociable and even charming man who enlivened those around him with his presence. Certainly, in 1917, at the age of 38, he charmed the young teenager Nadezhda Alliluieva sufficiently for her to agree to become his second wife. Although the marriage ended fifteen years later in her tragic suicide, Stalin seems to have maintained his friendship with the Alliluiev family. Indeed, he remained strangely loyal to many of his close friends – Voroshilov, Budenny, Molotov – throughout his life, though he was brutally prepared to let others die, like Bukharin, who was never so personally close to him, even though he was part of the Kremlin social round of dacha visiting and attending parties to celebrate birthdays and so on. According to some sources, Trotsky never paid a social visit to Stalin's dacha.[7] It is one of the darker speculations to try to fathom what was in Stalin's mind when he sentenced former close colleagues, like Bukharin, to death. However, it is part of the paradox of Stalin's personality that it could embrace the extremes of friendship and sociability and of hardened cruelty. The answer, perhaps, is to be found in the fact that these are integral features of mafia-type cultures. One act of dishonour and the pat on the back could hide a stiletto to the heart.

The Contradictions of Stalinism

A Reduction of Tempo

In December 1932 the First Five-Year Plan was declared to have been fulfilled 'by and large' in four and a quarter years. While the 'fulfilment' was fictional, or perhaps symbolic, from one point of view the situation at that moment appeared to be on the verge of improvement.

Perhaps most significantly the initial hits of rapid collectivisation and full-scale industrialisation were giving way to a reduced tempo of change. In the countryside the change can be dated back to the dramatic impact of one of Stalin's craftiest ruses by which he wriggled out of a dangerous situation. In his letter 'Dizzy with Success', published in *Pravda* on 2 March 1930, he denounced the collectivisation squads who had, he claimed, been unjustifiably overzealous. Indeed, as we have seen, up to that moment many collectivisation brigades composed of enthusiastic young worker-volunteers backed up by militia, secret police and even military units had been behaving both ignorantly and cruelly. In true Stalinist manner they had been sacrificing the niceties of means to the all-encompassing ends. Stalin's letter completely undercut the authority even of more reasonable brigades. In the letter Stalin claimed that the squads had exceeded their brief and it was not the intention of the government that the establishment of collective farms should be anything other than voluntary. 'The success of our collective-farm policy is due … to the voluntary character of the collective-farm

movement … . Collective farms cannot be set up by force.'[8] Certain comrades had become 'dizzy with success'. Stalin's gross hypocrisy and
betrayal of his own ardent agents worked. From a critical situation, in
which army chiefs warned they could not guarantee the loyalty of troops
to put down peasant rebellions, Stalin's retreat reduced the pressure
before a complete meltdown could take place. Official figures for the
number of collectives formed show the impact graphically. On 1 March
1930 supposedly 55 per cent of peasant households had been collectivised. By 1 June the figure had fallen to a more realistic 23 per cent.
The massive initial drop shows how many 'collective farms' had existed
only on paper. But could it be called a retreat? In no sense was it an
abandonment of the goal, rather a change of timetable for its completion. In any case, the initial hit, in which some one million 'kulak' families had been uprooted and deported, had rendered prolonged,
organised resistance impossible. By July 1936, collectivisation was virtually complete. In this respect, collectivisation is typical of Stalin's proce-
dures. What appeared to be 'concessions' were often only tactical
manoeuvres to expedite achievement of the main goal.

A similar case could be made out for industrialisation. While the ultra-
utopian madness of the early stages was abandoned by 1932 it had,
nonetheless, done its job of shocking the country into radical change.
From that time the Soviet Union was setting off in a completely
new direction. Though the wilder extremes were abandoned, the major
changes were not undone. Industrialisation remained the number one
productionist priority and it was still pushed ahead as rapidly as possible.

The term 'Great Retreat' was initially coined to describe developments occurring in the fields of culture and values. Here it appears to
fit more readily than elsewhere. The utopian cultural revolution which
accompanied the Stalin revolution was certainly constrained by 1931–2.
In place of radical proposals for sexual 'liberation' and free love, and for
the replacement of the family, with the state playing an ever-growing
role in childcare, and local organisations taking over housekeeping tasks
like providing meals and laundry facilities, a more 'conservative' set of
values began to be proclaimed. Motherhood and childbearing brought
honours and bonuses for 'heroines' who produced numerous children.
Abortion became more difficult to obtain. Curiously, in an attitude
which resembled that of its arch-enemy, the Roman Catholic Church,
the party frowned on divorce. No Soviet leader was ever divorced. Divorce
was deemed to be a sign of revolutionary weakness, of an unreliable
character who put personal happiness ahead of revolutionary duty.

Right the way through to the 1980s divorce remained a handicap to a party career.

While the return to certain supposedly traditional values has frequently been remarked upon, a second major aspect of cultural retrenchment has been less frequently looked at. The formation of the Writers' Union in 1932–4 has attracted considerable comment and much has been made of Stalin's intervention in the field of history,[9] as has the fact that, as we have seen, a number of those initially imprisoned through the action of radicals were released. However, it has been less commonly noted that the organisations across the whole spectrum of creative and professional intelligentsia life were transformed in this period. While intellectuals were released from prison, the institutions to which they returned had much less independence and authority than the ones from which they had been ousted. In the 1920s, cultural institutions, though they lacked the wider freedom of the chaotic civil war years, were still semi-independent of the authorities even though the latter were ever encroaching on their remaining rights. Many organisations disappeared under the assault of radical leftists unleashed by the party leadership, before they, in their turn, were toppled when the time came for the leaders to turn the tap off again. But they had done the centre's job for it. They had sown complete chaos in many fields and had atomised large parts of the intelligentsia, and undermined its authority on the grounds that it was largely composed of lukewarm, pre-revolutionary specialists and fellow-travellers. This enabled the party to step in to build new institutions which it could more readily supervise. A similar model came to be applied in many intellectual and professional areas. First, one had to belong to the institution, most of which were called 'unions' (*soiuzy*), before one could practise in one's field. Once accepted, the union often provided support and privileges in the form of a stipend, a well-supplied club, foreign travel, access to information from abroad via the overseas press and academic publications, not to mention above-average accommodation. For this mess of pottage the intellectuals only had to give up their freedom and toe the line! It was often the case that members thrived through making large gestures of loyalty while producing very little actual output (a phenomenon not unknown among administrative careerists in overmanaged intellectual institutions elsewhere). At the head of each union stood a board dominated by the party and supervised by the Central Committee. Not only was there state censorship but projects had to be approved by the union beforehand, every step of the way. Excessive confrontation could lead to a reduction of privileges, for instance, preventing foreign travel, and, eventually, expulsion into the oblivion of not being able to practise one's specialism. Curiously unions were often protective of their more wayward members despite extensive party supervision. While details differed, the crucial feature of all of them was a closer link with the party than had been the case with their predecessors.

Other intellectual institutions were also pulled closer into line. While university autonomy had been overthrown by 1922, the venerable Academy of Sciences had been left more to its own devices right up to 1928. In a typical development of the period, it was at first attacked by the radicals to break up the old guard and then 'moderate' party mediators stepped in to control it more fully in the name of the leadership. Once again, the Central Committee became the instrument of supervision and the Academy, which was vastly expanded – particularly in, but not confined to, the areas of scientific research, of interest to the party in connection with its productionist industrial and military aims – became a kind of superunion for the academic elite in all disciplines. Better food, housing, information and travel were the reward for many of its members. Above all, the elite within the elite was given large amounts of resources for projects in the fields of aerospace, communications and nuclear technologies. Within this framework, brilliant work was produced and, despite extensive party supervision, something of the atmosphere of the pre-revolutionary intelligentsia was preserved. Even so, the academic disciplines were closely tied in to leadership goals and priorities, including the detailed elaboration of specifically Marxist (by now Marxist–Leninist) approaches to intellectual problems. History, as an obvious example, was supposed to prove the basic theses of the founding fathers. A prestigious Institute of Marxism–Leninism was set up in the mid 1920s as the jewel in the crown of the intellectual apparatus. Its task, apart from its close links with policy formulation, was to provide an orthodox basis for all intellectual disciplines, including science. It became the major source of approved party ideology.

Here was the quintessence of totalitarianism. The party and its leaders dominated every aspect of intellectual life in a closer relationship than ever before. Intellectual independence was driven to the margins of society and into emigration. But it would be a mistake to see the pyramid being built to exercise control for its own sake as so many interpretations of the Stalin period suggest. The system was driven by the belief, in Stalin's ringing phrase, that intellectuals (he was speaking of writers) were 'engineers of the human soul'. In other words, the vast apparatus was driven by the desire to harness the intelligentsia to the task of social-ist construction. They were to be the cultural outriders of the party, tweaking and tuning human values and knowledge to fit the new soci-ety. They were to be in the forefront of constructing the ultimate of all Stalinist constructs, the 'New Soviet Person'. Can such developments be thought of as a 'Great Retreat'? Hardly. As elsewhere, the tempo was reduced but the direction and dynamism were maintained. After an ini-tial sprint, the pace had to be moderated for the long haul.

Paradoxically, it is perhaps in the vital political field that the reduc-tion of tempo came closest to a real 'thaw'. From 1932 to the 1934 Party Congress, a fragile atmosphere of 'reconciliation' can be detected. While Stalin's response to a catalogue of criticisms of his action from within the party, the so-called Riutin platform named after its author, hardly promised 'thaw' – he seems to have demanded that Riutin should be shot – he was unable to get his way and Riutin was imprisoned instead. Nonetheless, a little openness did begin to appear. At the Seventeenth Party Congress in 1934, disgraced oppositionists Kamenev and Zinoviev were allowed to make public recantation of their offences and retain some of their privileges. Bukharin continued to carry out important party tasks including representing it abroad. In fact, one of the centre-pieces of the 'thaw', the constitution adopted in 1936 which, if it had been applied even in its flawed form of legitimising the party monop-oly, might have transformed the fate of the Soviet Union, was closely associated with Bukharin. The constitution proclaimed the end of class war in the Soviet Union and the establishment of socialism. A wide range of civil rights and democratic freedoms was promised. However, all was permitted only 'in conformity with the interests of the working people and for the purpose of strengthening the socialist system'. It also recognised the party as 'the leading core of all organisations of the work-ing people, governmental and non-governmental'.

In fact, the process of drawing up the constitution outlived the brief moment of slight openness in which it had been initially mooted. Its promulgation took place against a much more sinister background. The ambiguous amelioration had not, in any case, signalled any slackening in the leadership's mobilising drive for the construction of socialism. Rather, it was a change of tactics brought about in part by the failure of the initial extremism, in part by the impossibility of maintaining all-out effort indefinitely, and in part by the success of the initial shocks in breaking up opposition so that the desired goals could be achieved with less force. In these respects it was a little like the early history of the

Soviet system – all-out effort in the civil war, a step back in the form of NEP brought about in part by opposition but a step back which consolidated a more stable foothold for steady further advance in the 1920s. However, the contradictions of Stalinism were such that the limited improvements noted here were increasingly overshadowed by three of the greatest human tragedies of the century, indeed of any century – famine (1932–3), terror (1936–8) and, worst of all, Nazi occupation and its costly overthrow (1941–5).

Into the Whirlwind: Famine and Terror

In terms of loss of life, the famine of 1932–3 was the greater of the tragedies of the 1930s. It has been a focus of controversy from the time it took place. The Soviet authorities tried to prevent the full picture from being known at the time, not only because it contradicted official propaganda about the successes of socialism à la Russe but also because of the strategic implications. An internal food crisis could trigger attack by an enemy who saw the weakened state of an opponent. However, the basic information could not be entirely suppressed and rumours quickly circulated abroad. Journalists and writers like Malcolm Muggeridge and Ewald Ammende wrote about a vast famine, although they were often not taken seriously, not least because their reports were vigorously denied by the Soviet authorities who went to considerable lengths to fool visitors into thinking all was well.[10] The controversy has continued ever since. It took a particularly acute turn during the 'second cold war' of the Reagan period. In the early 1980s astronomical figures for the number of victims of both the famine and the terror were dreamed up. More careful calculations were somehow deemed to be a sign of being a Stalinist apologist. One of the most extreme theories linked the famine with Stalinist terror and asserted it had been deliberately inflicted on Ukraine by the authorities as punishment for its lack of enthusiasm for Stalinist policies.[11] Even though the obvious flaw in the argument – that the famine deeply affected south Russia and the Caucasus as well as Ukraine – was quickly pointed out, the theory, nonetheless, gained considerable credibility in the hostile atmosphere of the time. Only recently have more convincing analyses, based on archive materials not available in the early 1980s, begun to appear.

As far as the cost in lives is concerned the widely accepted figure now is that there were 5–6 million deaths. This comes at the higher end of earlier estimates though it is lower than the highest figures which gained currency.[12] Harrowing accounts of the suffering have given graphic and emotional impetus to this horrendous figure. Whole villages died from exhaustion. Rumours of cannibalism have surrounded the controversy from its origin.

Why did it happen? Of course, like most famines, it was triggered by climatic conditions but, as with the much less extensive famine of 1891–2, that was not the point. The issue was that, under normal circumstances, traditional safety valves – stored grain, market transfers, relief organisations – can alleviate the worst effects. In this case (as in 1921), human agency, witting and unwitting, had added to the crisis. In 1922, the general state of chaos had worsened the famine in the Central Volga region brought about by drought. In 1932–3, chaos also played its part. However, post-Soviet research has highlighted the role of the central authorities. According to this interpretation, the centre did not believe there was a serious famine until it was too late. Instead, it continued to scour the regions affected (and elsewhere, of course) for further grain procurements after the harvest of 1932 over the protests of peasants and some local officials. These protests were dismissed as 'kulak sabotage' intended to dissuade the authorities from seeking out 'hoarded' grain. In the late 1980s a BBC TV programme interviewed surviving local officials and peasants from a village in the Ukraine affected by the famine and their testimony bore witness to this. One official, who had requisitioned grain from the village, still asserted his conviction that he fully believed at the time that the peasants were hiding enough grain to enable them to survive and that the increasing exactions he was ordered to make by his superiors could have been met by the peasants. However, once it became clear to the authorities (in police reports of early 1933 to which historians only gained access in the early/mid-1990s) that the peasants did not have hidden reserves, they had already disposed of much of the requisitioned grain through exports to pay for industrial imports. It also appears that the strategic grain reserve – deemed to have been sufficient to feed the affected population had it not been deliberately held back by the authorities, according to the terror–famine theory – was, in fact, much lower, not least because recalculations of the 1932 harvest suggest it was lower than had earlier been assumed. In addition, such as it was, a substantial reserve was potentially required by the state because of the menacing situation in the Far East, where Japanese aggression was building up and the grain store might be needed to feed an army defending Soviet territory from attack. The reduction of grain procurement targets in the years following the famine might also suggest that the authorities had recognised their error in setting them far too high. Thus, if this theory is correct (and it does depend on a number of assumptions and calculations which could be subjected to revision) we have a much more likely interpretation than any of its predecessors. The central authorities still bear responsibility but the incompetence and revolutionary brutality and crudity associated with Stalin are more prominent than deliberate intent.[13]

Similar factors of criminal incompetence and the vagaries of revolutionary 'morality' mentioned earlier – namely that one might, as in war, have to accept the sacrifice of innocent lives to gain the main objective – also have a bearing on explanations of the terror. Here, too, massive controversy has surrounded the events since they happened and, once again, it is only fairly recently that interpretations based on archival evidence rather than rumour and folklore have enabled a more convincing set of analyses to emerge, with respect to both extent and motivation.

As far as the number of victims is concerned, the numbers have begun to settle at much lower figures than some of the more improbable estimates widely circulated in the early 1980s.[14] Even so, they are horrible enough. It has been confirmed that, between 1936 and 1941 inclusive, almost one million people were executed. Figures for camps, prisons and similar places of detention suggest there were about four million prisoners in the late 1930s, including common criminals who were probably in the majority.[15] The death rate in the camps has been calculated at about 7 per cent of inmates per year to give annual death rates in the purge years of about 55–75 000. Deaths in camps appear to have peaked at around 250 000 in 1942 – dreadful enough, though nowhere near the astronomical figures often quoted and still widely believed in Russia today.[16] One point still to be resolved about the numbers is that the peak years for camp deaths fall outside the purge years, and the number of executions also is not differentiated into purge years and prewar years. Thus, while it is easy to explain why so many prisoners died in 1942 during the worst period of the war when shortages prevailed throughout Soviet society and prisoners had the lowest priority, it is not yet entirely clear how many of those executed and imprisoned were victims of the terror and how many died or were imprisoned as a result of the ruthless sweep the secret police made in the territories of eastern Poland and the Baltic States acquired through the Nazi–Soviet treaty of 1939. Soviet action here in 1939–41 was particularly vicious as the newly occupied areas were far 'behind' in the construction of socialism, that is, they were more feudal or capitalist than socialist. This meant they were full of the social groups that Stalinism had swept aside – landowners, priests, bankers, factory owners and a professional middle class. From the Soviet point of view, with war inevitable sooner or later, these areas had to be secured and dubious class elements uprooted without delay. It goes without saying that this piece of typically cruel Stalinist clumsiness immediately cancelled out the not inconsiderable support the arrival of Soviet troops initially had in areas threatened by Nazism.

While the implications of the suppression of opposition in newly acquired territories have yet to be clarified, the reasons for it are fairly obvious. With the terror itself, however, the reasons are still to be satisfactorily explained. In the past, many theories were put forward, not least by the victims themselves who, being thrown together with masses of other innocent people, could only speculate on why such a disaster had happened. It has often been pointed out that most of those arrested initially thought they had been picked up in error. It was also a widespread belief among victims at various levels that Stalin did not know what was happening. The most widespread academic interpretation has been the 'totalitarian' one that the purge was a deliberate attempt to silence society and to break it up into state and party-dominated groups, to atomise it. A revisionist challenge to this was mounted in the 1980s which showed, convincingly, that there was no generalised pall of terror which fell across the whole of society. The impact, it was argued, fell more heavily on particular groups, notably educated state and party officials in cities, especially Moscow and Leningrad. Ordinary workers and even peasants got on with their lives without being completely dominated by fear of the authorities. While one weakness of the extreme totalitarian view was that it seemed to propose an almost supernaturally all-seeing, all-knowing, powerful state, the revisionists rightly pointed out that the state apparatus was not deadly efficient but was still a ramshackle, arbitrary and shambolic structure (and perhaps all the more deadly for that). The all-embracing state of the postwar years had not yet appeared. In any case, by and large, a well-established state has no need to resort to extraordinary measures to preserve itself. Contrary to what we sometimes assume, terror is often the sign of a weak state trying to assert itself whether it be Stalin's Soviet state, the Nazi state or a more traditional Middle-Eastern, Asian or African dictatorship. It has become a little easier, since 1991, to find out about what was happening at the centre during the terror, and we can piece together more fragments of an interpretation than has been possible hitherto. Aspects of both totalitarian and revisionist theories can help us to do so. But first, bearing in mind that our main focus is to study the formation and dissolution of the Soviet system – the forces bringing it together and the contradictions which eventually blew it apart – rather than to provide a comprehensive history of the Soviet Union, we need to look briefly at the nature of the purges before trying to understand why they happened and how they fit in as an element in the Soviet system.

The terror took place on two levels. One, the tip of the iceberg, was not only public but put up on a pedestal and illuminated for all the world to see. The other was entirely secret in that no systematic information about it was ever published. (There was also an intermediate level of shadowy trials which were not publicised but whose verdicts had to be made known because the victims were so prominent. The main example is the purge of military leaders such as Tukhachevsky and Yakir.) At all levels an odd format of legality was laid over what were, in practice, highly arbitrary and totally unjustified acts. No doubt the veneer of legality was, in part, necessary window-dressing but it also made those carrying out such ghastly policies feel justified in their work. One of the curious features of prisoner narratives is that the interrogators and guards never seemed to doubt what they were doing. The bizarre prominence of confessions obtained under extreme duress including torture, threats to the victim's family and so on, sprang from the same roots. Confessions also gave the process a bogus legitimacy. Apart from that, the public and secret terrors were rather different and the relationship between them in the past – when the very limited public terror of the show trials was much more widely known than the vast, unacknowledged secret terror – has confused interpretations. For example, one could readily understand the show trials of prominent Bolsheviks as a consequence of power struggles within the party.[17] However, the arrest of millions could hardly fit into the same, narrow framework.

There were three main show trials. The first, in August 1936, saw Kamenev and Zinoviev as principal defendants. The second, in January 1937, featured lesser-known party leaders like Piatakov and Radek who, nonetheless, had been close associates of Lenin. In the third trial, in March 1938, Bukharin was put on trial with others. In all cases the charges were a strange concoction of 'anti-Soviet' political offences, notably being Trotskyists, foreign spies, wreckers and saboteurs. In all cases the defendants, who had all been forced to confess – sometimes on the basis of false promises of clemency – were summarily executed with a shot to the back of the head very shortly after the end of the trial. The proceedings were broadcast and filmed and widely shown. In the fearful atmosphere of the time even some foreign observers were led to believe the charges were justified. Very few people were ready to denounce the Soviet Union at a time when the rise of Nazism and the Spanish Civil War were more pressing preoccupations for West Europeans, especially those on the left. In a time of darkness many were reluctant to abandon the illusory light of the false dawn they saw in the east. However, it was not the international audience that was uppermost in Stalin's mind at the time. The trials were mainly for internal consumption. The Soviet population was put on guard against alien influences and an explanation for the difficulties of the time was provided which exculpated the country's leaders. Indeed, they were portrayed as the vigilant guardians of socialism and protectors of the ordinary Soviet people.

The show trials also made mass arrests seem more believable. If great leaders could stoop to treachery then their accomplices at lower levels had to be rooted out. The same bizarre cocktail of imaginary offences was thrown at the mass of those arrested. Confessions were also the order of the day. Fear of the knock on the door in the middle of the night led people who thought themselves vulnerable to sleep with suitcases ready packed. Arrests often followed on from one another in grizzly chains. The arrest of a boss would be followed by that of his deputy, the deputy's deputy and so on. One arrest in a family often led to others. Arrests tore through the fabric of Soviet society like, in the term used by one of its victims, Evgeniia Ginzburg, a whirlwind. The horror for those caught up in it has been epically recorded by Alexander Solzhenitsyn in the three volumes of *The Gulag Archipelago*. A vast number of accounts have come down to us. Some of the most politically observant have come from imprisoned supporters of the system like Ginsburg or Lev Kopelev and foreign communists like Joseph Berger and Karlo Stajner.[18] Can we make any more sense of these unbelievable experiences than those who underwent them?

Many, many aspects of the terror remain murky but thanks to the work of Russian and foreign historians who have had unprecedented – though, as yet, far from complete – access to the archives and the publication of remarkable sources like the unexpurgated memoirs of members of the elite, with Molotov in the forefront, we can begin to discern some of its main features. We can also, tentatively, assess its place in Soviet evolution and dissolution.

In the first place important background influences have to be considered. On 1 December 1934 a single gunshot ended what remained of the thaw and unleashed Stalin's more vindictive instincts. The victim of the assassin was Stalin's close associate Sergei Kirov, head of the Leningrad party apparatus. While there is no doubt that the actual killer was a deranged admirer of nineteenth-century terrorist groups with links to the party and the opposition, the real issue, as it so often is, has been whether the murderer acted alone or whether there was a conspiracy. As is also often the case, absence of evidence of conspiracy is often taken to be proof of its effectiveness, especially given the coincidental deaths of one or two minor figures. For many, the finger of suspicion pointed at Stalin. If he was responsible, he did a brilliant job in concealing it, not least through his actions at the time. On hearing the news he rushed to Leningrad by train (he did not trust aircraft) and personally interviewed the suspect at length. He then set up an investigative commission and, on his return to Moscow, drew up draconian emergency legislation. Meanwhile, trainloads of suspects were deported from Leningrad. Stalin, it seemed, also had an ill-founded conspiracy theory based on lack of evidence. His was that the opposition was behind it. Kirov himself was buried with full honours and his name was given to a major avenue and bridge in Leningrad as well as to its world-famous opera and ballet company. If he was a victim of Stalin, no other was treated with such honour. Usually, every effort was made to obliterate their name and destroy their reputation though there were a number of other ambiguous and unproven cases – such as the death of Ordzhonikidze by his own hand and Gorky through natural causes perhaps precipitated by criminal medical intervention – where the possible victim retained his reputation.

Stalin's complicity has never been proved despite extensive efforts during the first de-Stalinisation campaign of 1956 and by a commission set up during the *perestroika* period in the late 1980s. Why Stalin should have killed Kirov is unclear as Kirov shows every sign of having been entirely loyal to Stalin and vice versa. Rumours of extensive opposition to Stalin and support for Kirov at the 1934 Party Congress appear to have been exaggerated. If we assume Stalin did not order Kirov's murder it would fit better into the pattern of events in that it could be seen as a trigger to Stalin's obsession over the next five years to root out the remnants of the opposition. If, as he may have thought, they could penetrate Kirov's security in his own headquarters surrounded by secret police then they could strike at anyone, including the beloved leader of the world proletariat himself. However, one can only speculate, especially about what might have been going on in a mind as secretive and labyrinthine as Stalin's.

Two further background factors also heightened the potential for paranoia. One was the rise of Nazism and its sweeping takeover of Germany which left the world's second largest communist party in shreds. The second was continued criticism from Trotsky himself culminating, in 1936, with *The Revolution Betrayed*, his most eloquent and sustained attack on Stalinism.

Like almost everyone else, Stalin, Comintern and the Soviet leadership underestimated the Nazis. It seemed completely impossible that such a ragbag of hooligans and misfits with absurd and chaotic ideas of Nordic blood and Teutonic supremacy should come to power in a civilised country like Germany, especially since it had a well-organised working class. The shock of its success was perhaps more profound in Moscow than anywhere else in Europe outside Germany itself. By 1934 it had brought about a complete reorganisation of Soviet policy. The 'class against class' line of the initial years of the Stalin revolution was abandoned for a more conciliatory approach leading to the formation of popular fronts and a new foreign policy orientation which, amazingly, put hostility to the old imperialisms like Britain and France on the back burner in the face of the new and more threatening enemy. While the international implications of this, particularly the apparently weak resolve of Britain to do anything about it, and the almost equally important emergence of Japanese aggression in the form of its invasion of Manchuria in 1931 and China in 1937, will be considered in the next chapter, the internal repercussions need to be noted here. Above all, anti-Fascism became the centrepiece of all ideology and fear of infiltration became obsessive. Paranoia there certainly was but there were also real and dangerous enemies abroad.

In such a context, it is little wonder that Trotsky's irritating attacks should take on a greater prominence than they deserved. From his exile in France and eventually in Mexico, he launched a fusillade of what were, in reality, only pinpricks in the tough hide of Stalinism. However, both Trotsky and Stalin were, because of their deep-rooted and long-lasting enmity, inclined to rub salt into each other's wounds in a way that no one else could. Above all, Trotsky boasted incessantly about his influence over a vast opposition within the Soviet Union which, he said, would soon take over from the defunct, arthritic Stalinist regime. In the final pages of *The Revolution Betrayed* Trotsky vaunts the potential of 'twenty or thirty thousand Oppositionists' to conduct an inevitable 'new revolution' based on the fact that 'the vast majority of the Soviet workers are even now hostile to the bureaucracy. The peasant masses hate them with their healthy plebian hatred.'[19] Indeed, there were many potential enemies of Stalin, mostly of his own making – dispossessed peasants by the million; disgruntled workers; 'former people' of the pre-revolutionary educated and propertied classes; disillusioned party members; repressed nationalists; former members of other political parties and so on. One can only agree with one historian who has argued that Stalinism 'had a genius for making enemies'.[20] Even so, despite the existence of some minor links, for instance between Trotsky's son and some of the purged opposition leaders, the notion that substantial numbers of people looked to Trotsky for guidance was pure fantasy. It is hardly an exaggeration to say that only two people really believed in the Trotsky conspiracy, one being Stalin, the other Trotsky. But that was enough to help precipitate disaster for millions, including Trotsky himself who was finally silenced by Stalin in 1940.

Not surprisingly, some of the most recent theories of the terror have come to revolve around ideas of an assault on internal enemies. Some of the earliest theories of the purges also put forward the view that it was aimed at real enemies and that it might have been connected with preparation for inevitable war against Nazism. However, such theories seemed to have been outweighed by the obvious objections that obliterating one's own leading military talents and arresting half the officer corps could hardly be seen as a sensible way to prepare for war, or that there could not be so many millions of enemies. However, such reasonable objections overlook the unreasonableness of Stalinism, with its vindictive incompetence and brutal determination that not one guilty person should escape even though many innocents might be punished. In some ways, the most surprising and hardest thing to believe about recent revelations is that the leadership really seems to have thought that it was surrounded by enemies and traitors and that many of its victims were guilty of real crimes against the revolution.

Oleg Khlevnyuk, one of the younger Russian scholars who has had extensive access to archives of the period, has talked about the search for a 'fifth column' or, in effect, several fifth columns. He also notes that the term itself was coined in the period by the Francoite General Mola explaining how he would take Madrid.[21] He points out that the leadership swept systematically through what it considered to be suspect groups – the party, the economic ministries, the military, the Communist International, minority nationalities, notably Poles, Germans, Turks, Koreans, and others who, it was thought, might harbour dual loyalties to their national states outside the Soviet Union. In accordance with the perverted principle that it was better to punish the innocent than that one guilty person should escape, collective guilt was imposed on vast numbers of people.[22] In other words, the terror was not, as some of the totalitarian school had argued, a purely arbitrary device for repression of all, rather it was, at least in the eyes of the leadership, targeted at what were believed to be enemies or potential enemies.

Certainly the guilt of those arrested was widely accepted in Soviet society, not least by, as we have noted, those responsible for establishing it and guarding those condemned. In many cases, it was only when someone was arrested that they realised the awful truth. It is also the case that the purges tended to hit groups all at once. Also, for whatever reason, certain groups were protected. There were no American or British prisoners in the Gulag and very few French. This could not be explained if the process were purely arbitrary. Many of the often-quoted snatches of Stalin's remarks suggest he thought the bulk of victims were guilty. Nowhere is there any indication that he admitted it was a cynical exercise whose victims were innocent.[23]

But can one actually believe the leadership thought their victims, including former close comrades, were actually guilty? Though it is far from definitive one of the most remarkable *perestroika*-era documents suggests this may be so. The last survivor who could have unlocked the mystery was Viacheslav Molotov. He had a remarkable career. As a very young Bolshevik he was a member of the Petrograd Soviet in 1917 even before Lenin returned from exile in April. He remained at the top and for many crucial years he was a member of Stalin's inner circle. He was eventually removed by Khrushchev in 1957. Thereafter he could be seen pursuing research and studies in the Lenin Library. From the late 1970s almost until his death in 1986 at the age of 96 he had a series of informal conversations with a sympathetic journalist named Feliks Chuev. In 1991 Chuev published the substance of his conversations.[24] Throughout, Molotov maintains the purges were necessary. The revolution was surrounded by enemies and had to be defended. A few innocent people might have been caught up in it, including Molotov's wife who served four years in the camps (1949–53) after being accused of links with Zionists including the Israeli Ambassador Golda Meir, but that was a price that had to be paid in any war (remembering that for Bolsheviks class war was conducted according to the rules of any other war, not according to the happier standards of peacetime). Although the issue is far from fully resolved, at the moment the weight of evidence suggests that, after all, the most obvious explanation, namely that the pursuit

of internal enemies was a prime motivation of the purges, seems the
most likely.

One obvious objection to this view is that the terror went far beyond
real 'enemies of the people' even by the most elastic definition of that
much-abused term. Here, some of the findings of revisionist research
are helpful in putting the picture together. Pointing to the disorganised
nature of the Stalinist state, J. A. Getty has argued that the terror was
magnified by irresponsible local officials using the situation to settle
their own scores against their local and regional enemies. They may
even have pressed for purges to achieve this. Getty calls such people
'little Stalins'. From what we now know of the mechanism of the terror,
there may be an important element of truth in this insight. Once the
centre had decided by 1936 that there were enemies to be rounded up,
its method of doing so was to order local authorities, notably the secret
police working in conjunction with other state bodies, to make arrests.
Such bodies were given *limity* (in Russian) on the number of arrests to be
made. We have to note here that there is a crucial ambiguity in the
Russian term. *Limity* means not only a maximum or ceiling, as its simi-
larity to the word 'limit' suggests to us, it also means 'quota' which can,
in some respects, be the opposite of a ceiling. Quotas are often taken to
be minimum targets. We do not know for sure which of these meanings
was uppermost in the leadership's mind. It is not impossible that, predicting unrestricted chaos if they gave local authorities a free hand, they
wanted to keep the process within bounds, and intended the figures to
be maxima. However, in the atmosphere of the time, once they were
received by those who were to carry them out, the orders were seen as
'quotas', as targets to be fulfilled and, if one were really zealous, to be
overfulfilled. Clearly, there was fear that those who did not arrest
enough people might themselves be arrested for negligence. Even leading secret policemen were threatened. Iagoda, the head of the political
police, was accused, in September 1936, of 'being incapable of exposing
the Trotskyist–Zinovievist bloc', and of allowing the OGPU to fall 'four
years behind in the matter'.[25] He was replaced by Ezhov and found himself in the dock in 1938. In the event the centre was flooded with
requests for permission to make additional arrests which may, in turn,
have led the centre to believe the problem was even wider than they
had expected. In most cases such requests were granted even though
those making them often had no idea how they could fulfil them.
As Solzhenitsyn chronicles in *The Gulag Archipelago* they often just
hauled in those whose arrest would cause least disruption – he gives the

example of a group of gypsies rolling into a small town at the wrong moment. Anyone with a record might have it brought up. Class origin might reemerge. People would sometimes be arrested without thought of the consequences. Again Solzhenitsyn gives examples of parents being arrested, leaving unattended babies and children in their homes. The torrent of arrests spread in other well-known ways. Denunciation spread 'guilt' rapidly. Association with an arrested person might be tantamount to contamination by that person and so on. In this way the arrests turned into a snowball. Only when they had created unbearable chaos (like the famine) did the centre see the need to rein it in.

Examples of how the decision-making proceeded in the government apparatus in the 1930s have been collected in a recent study.[26] In particular, it shows that there was a tendency within economic decision-making to move from stability to chaotic mobilisation which had to be abandoned because it was causing too much damage. Once stability returned the cycle was prone to repeat itself as happened in the years 1929–32 and 1936–8. Something very similar happened, as we have seen, with the cultural revolution of 1928–32 and it seems to be the case that the administration of the Great Terror fits into a similar cycle with a centrally instigated campaign getting out of control and having to be rapidly scaled down because of the damage it was doing to production.

The findings of this careful study put the terror into the same framework as other elements of Stalin's revolution from above in that all of them had to be stopped after they had incurred extensive costs. True, each had also achieved key objectives but the terrible cost came to frighten the leadership into changing tempo once this had been done. The same is true of the terror. Having broken any possible opposition, it was brought to a halt because of the economic, administrative and military disruption it was causing. Terror, of course, remained an integral part of the Stalin system. Arrests and executions for anti-Soviet activities, wrecking and sabotage continued but, with the massive exception of the sweep through the newly occupied territories between 1939 and 1941, the levels were much lower and remained lower in the war years when camp inmates were often released, some into senior military command positions – a quite incredible transition – or straight into the ranks of the military, others into punishment battalions and given near-suicidal missions. Survival could mean rehabilitation.

While the totalitarian theory appears to have been wrong in positing a cynical exercise of massacre of the innocent in order to silence the rest, and to have underestimated local augmentation of the process, there are other key areas in which they have the advantage over their opponents. It is now unchallengeable that, while the centre did not fully control the process, it did initiate it and bring it to a halt when the damage it was doing was all too apparent. Important questions of detail remain, notably which individuals have what responsibilities for the course of events. While there is no possibility of a 'Stalin didn't know' interpretation comparable to Hitler revisionism, it may be that Ezhov hid aspects of the terror and misled the leadership. There is also the question of bogus evidence fabricated against some of the show trial defendants which originated with the Gestapo and with White émigré organisations. Who exactly designed it to pull the wool over whose eyes? Answers will not alter the fact that Stalin's responsibility looms large. Molotov, in his conversations, never hid central responsibility, indeed, he asserted it was a necessary and unavoidable part of building socialism. In this sense, the purges fit into the political dimension of the Stalin revolution we have already remarked on. Each aspect was motivated by the desire to mobilise the population and to construct a stronger central apparatus to make this possible and overcome opposition. The terror completed the process. By the time it was over, the longest-lasting 'Soviet system' – that built in Stalin's image – had emerged. Economic control was in the hands of the central planners. Culture and the generation and dissemination of ideas was a near-monopoly of the centre (although even dictators cannot stop people from thinking, only from widely distributing and discussing their thoughts). The party had been smashed and turned into a body of social, cultural and economic managers looking to the centre instead of a politically active and faction-ridden organisation of convinced revolutionaries. Revolutionary 'inspiration', henceforth, was provided ready-made by the grey men of the Central Committee Propaganda Department. The party's job was to implement, not to originate, policies; the latter task was to be left to the centre, to the all-wise leader. Productionist policies flourished as never before. The Five-Year Plan became the centrepiece of Soviet life. Party cells became plan fulfilment supervisors as much as anything else. Since every institution – from heavy industrial factories to corner shops and kiosks, from power stations to schools and hospitals – had its own plan and almost everyone was an employee of the state, that supervision spread deeply into everyday life and a network of informers built up. To progress in almost any career one had to progress in the party. To progress in the party one had to be loyal to the current line and give up one's independence of thought. The ensuing consequences also justify one other aspect of the traditional view of the Soviet Union. There is no better term to describe the model on which it was built and the expectations of the leadership about it than the word 'totalitarian'. But did the model fit the actual realities of life in the Soviet Union in the 1930s?

Living Through the 1930s: State, Society and High Stalinism

One of the chief fracture lines, eventually bringing down the Soviet system, was the conflict between leadership aspirations to construct socialism and the real priorities of the people who were supposed to construct it. How far was Soviet society 'on message' with its leaders in these formative years? Not surprisingly, scholarly controversy has raged over the issue. Although they still represented the vast bulk of the population, the peasantry-turned-collective farmers have, until recently, aroused relatively little interest from scholars who have been content to write them out of socialist construction and simply allow them to fade away. The other two classes of Soviet society, the workers and the intelligentsia, have attracted considerably more attention. From our own perspective of looking for the main lines of construction and deconstruction of the Soviet system, can we evaluate signs of success and failure among the ordinary Soviet people at this crucial time?

'Life', Stalin informed his people in 1935, 'has become better, life has become more joyful.' Officially, every effort was made to prove it in the 1930s. Newsreels showed a happy, enthusiastic population of builders of socialism in factory and field. They depicted the spread of new cultural, sporting and recreational possibilities – films, stadia, parks and palaces of culture, holiday centres. The new working class, according to the official line, was moving into ever-better equipped cities with decent homes, well-supplied shops, cheap and efficient transport with the Moscow metro taking pride of place. A booming country was also depicted with ever-expanding production, an explosion of educational opportunity and an elite of artists, musicians, sportsmen and women, not to mention daring explorers and pioneers of aviation whose exploits held the country in thrall.

As is often the case with successful propaganda, the picture presented was not so much out-and-out lies as a concoction of half-truths. Aspects of Soviet life that did not fit the picture – the hardship of workers on far-flung construction sites; the long delays in completion of major projects; the low wages and, in reality, undersupplied shops; the chaos often encountered in trying to set up an 'ordinary' family life – were ignored. There was, of course, no reference to mass terror or to the vast labour camp and exile system. The unmasking of enemies and wreckers was often announced, but the vast scale of the operation was never alluded to. Everything that was optimistic was exaggerated, everything pessimistic was hidden from view,

Nonetheless, there were some grains of truth in the official image. The Soviet Union was on a path of rapid urbanisation along which it was to continue during all the peacetime years of Stalinism. By the time of Stalin's death, the country had transformed itself from being overwhelmingly rural to about half-urban, half-rural. Transport within and between cities was vastly extended, although only rarely did it meet demand and many areas were overlooked by the planners, but the Soviet Union became a highly mobile society. Rural migrants flooded into the new towns and young men and women workers chased better employment prospects around the country, or departed for volunteer work in farms and factories organised by the Komsomol (Young Communist League). Eventually, internal exiles also joined in the drift to towns. It was also the case that the years of high Stalinism saw an enormous expansion of education. The number of school pupils increased from 14 million in 1929 to over 20 million in 1931. By 1939 there were a million university graduates in the country, about one-third of whom were engineers. This was more than ten times the figure in pre-revolutionary Russia. Early on, acute observers such as Isaac Deutscher saw this as the Achilles heel of Stalinism, writing in his biography of Stalin that 'there have been many positive, valuable elements in the educational influence of Stalinism, elements that are in the long run likely to turn against its worst features'.[27] The system was, he argued, building up a class of educated people whom it vitally needed, but in so doing it was building up among such people knowledge, expectations and a requirement for liberty which were incompatible with official values. Even so, immense progress was made and the leadership's boasts of catching up with capitalist countries – most of which were languishing as a result of the Great Depression – seemed less hollow than usual. The sense of a country on the move was captured in the memoirs of foreigners, many of whom were working for western companies on contract during the early and mid-1930s. In particular, John Scott, an American engineer, wrote eloquently about his experiences in the Urals and the long-time resident American journalist and historian of the revolution and civil war William Chamberlin wrote of what he called Russia's iron age. Every effort was made to project Moscow as a bustling metropolis of gargantuan building projects to rival the skyscrapers of New York. True, the most ambitious proposal – to build a massive congress centre topped by an immense statue of Lenin to be built on the site of a large, ugly late nineteenth-century church vandalistically blown up to make way for it – failed. The vast hole created ended up as an open-air swimming pool. Eventually, in post-Soviet times, the church was rebuilt so that its great bulk once again dwarfs the central Moscow skyline along with the infinitely more beautiful cathedrals of the Kremlin. However, vast numbers of old buildings were swept away and massive construction began with huge new buildings like the Ministry of Defence or the Red Army Theatre, and continued into the postwar years when the characteristic 'Stalin wedding cake' skyscrapers were built. A memorable painting of the time by Yuri Pimenov depicted a *New Moscow* (1937) seen from the back of an open-top motorcar, a Moscow of colourful bustling boulevards, fashionable hairstyles and bright clothing. Ironically, near the centre of the painting is the House of Columns in which the show trials were held.

Nonetheless, for many people it was an exciting time of unprecedented opportunity. Talking to people of that generation over the years in the Soviet Union, many visiting scholars have been surprised how little impact the terror has had on many people's memories of the 1930s. Instead they talk of opportunities, of stability, of discipline in a positive sense, and of hope. For instance, people I have known for many years talk about their life working for the medical branch of the transport ministry. In this capacity they followed the course of the Trans-Siberian railway setting up medical posts every hundred kilometres or so. They would pass on elementary training to local people – some of whom were just abandoning the nomadic way of life and many of whom had had no formal education – and, once the enterprise was self-sufficient, move down the line and do the same again. They saw themselves as lucky people able to bring tangible improvements into the lives of others. Their story could be multiplied millions of times among the increasing flood of teachers, medical workers and engineers who, in a sense, were fulfilling romantic populist dreams of transforming the lives of the peasantry (from whom most of them sprang) by a flood of 'small deeds' of education, medicine, mechanisation and electrification. The dark side of Soviet life seems barely to have impinged on them.[28]

Whether these experiences had much to do with the construction of socialism as understood by the leaders, or whether it may have been a major step to undermine it as proposed by Deutscher, is a matter of some controversy. Consensual views tend to portray an intelligentsia in which only hacks actively supported the regime and a working class over which there is fierce controversy about their commitment to Stalin-style socialism as opposed to simply getting on with their lives as best they could under the circumstances. About the peasantry there has been very little, bar an assumption that they were outside the process and simply withering away, although, since the advent of *perestroika*, scholarship has updated these assumptions, especially in the direction of depicting peasant opposition to collectivisation and its consequences.

Certainly there were enthusiasts for Soviet construction. Many, particularly younger, men and women were enlisted in its service. Every party initiative brought forth a flood of Komsomol volunteers. Among established workers, the picture has been controversial. Some scholars have detected extensive support for Stalinist objectives among workers from the time of the Five-Year Plan and have posited a kind of generational and class struggle within the working class between older, artisanal workers, often former Mensheviks, and trade unionists, who were sceptical of Bolshevik aims, and younger workers who had acquired the newer skilled and semi-skilled practices of mass, mechanised production in factories and mines.[29] Others have portrayed a cowed and sceptical working class whose enthusiasm and support for Stalin were purely synthetic and tokenistic, the result of enforced obeisance to a resented system which they passively subverted through frequent job changes, absences and poor-quality workmanship. In this view, workers mainly tried to live out their lives as comfortably as possible against a background of planners' incompetence and lack of concern for individuals and for their personal lives.[30] Even studies of the undoubted enthusiasts of the time – those who participated in the extraordinary Stakhanovite movement of massive norm-busting – are ambiguous.[31] Genuine Stakhanovites seem to have been few and far between, and ordinary workers were more likely to hate them than to imitate them. By and large, material incentives (wages, bonuses, living standards) rather than moral incentives (socialist enthusiasm, patriotic construction) seem to have motivated most workers. One of the most detailed regional studies reveals a workforce at Magnitogorsk which showed only superficial support for regime goals and which lived its own life avoiding, as much as it could, the restrictions put on it by the authorities and ignoring its own contractual obligations. For instance, having had enough of the shortages and difficulties of a primitive outpost in which, in the early years, only tents were available to them for habitation, often workers simply packed up and left the site before their agreed term of service was completed. The continuous inflow and outflow of workers was one of the managers' biggest headaches (as it was in many other enterprises). Even the introduction of an internal passport system in December 1932 did not solve the problem. Workers were now supposed to have papers and permits to move to and reside in new areas. However, the system took many years to settle down and was, at first, more of a challenge to the ingenuity of workers who could obtain documents through forgery, theft or illegal purchase. When a settled population emerged at the showpiece project of Magnitogorsk, it was not so much through the eventual success of the controls attempted by the planners, as through 'a new society coming into being' where workers 'were able to find a niche for themselves: a job, a place to live, perhaps a family and some sense of self-worth'.[32] Magnitogorsk shows little evidence of the emergence of a 'New Soviet Person' among the working class.

Perhaps the nearest equivalent to a new class came from among the emerging managerial cadres but, by and large, they were far from being 'New Soviet People'. Their separation from workers was envisaged, at Magnitogorsk, by the planned construction of a managers' suburb, initially intended for visiting American engineers, made up of detached houses with gardens and landscaping to make the area more attractive.[33] A pioneering study based on literature has shown definitively how the managerial groups were already in the grip of 'petit-bourgeois' values of a 'nice' house with lace curtains and pot plants.[34] The intelligentsia proper shows little sign of greater socialist involvement. As in other spheres, those who did support regime values, genuinely or careeristically, tended to drift up into administration and interfere extensively in the lives of the rest through control over research funds for scientists; publishing contracts and commissions for writers, artists and filmmakers; engagements for performers; and special goodies like trips abroad for many categories. Ultimately, there was the sanction of censorship and even of the police, some major artists such as the poet Osip Mandel'stam and the theatre producer Meierhol'd falling victim to the terror. Once again, the picture is one of a regime-orientated apparatus dominating a mass that was partly enthusiastic, partly indifferent and partly sullenly hostile. While many intellectuals, like workers and some managers, could be motivated by the populist/patriotic, 'small deeds' aspect of their work to improve the lives of their fellow humans, extensive Marxist enthusiasm remained a minority characteristic.

Needless to say, in a countryside often portrayed in films at this time as teeming with happy peasants joyously gathering in the harvest and delightedly admiring their new tractors and combine harvesters, the post-collectivisation, post-famine reality was even grimmer from the regime's point of view with the rancour aroused in the Stalin revolution simmering on through the decade.[35]

Even a cursory survey, therefore, shows that little headway was being made in the crucial Leninist process of raising the consciousness of the masses. Instead, Lenin's practice of revolution from above was being continued in that a mass of socialist institutions was being built – the party; publicly owned industrial, agrarian and transport enterprises; communally provided healthcare and education and so on – but there was little evidence of a rapidly rising socialist consciousness to give them life. Instead, 'petit-bourgeois' values of prioritising personal and family life and comfort, the glimmerings of consumerism and so on are much easier to find. The majority of the Soviet population lived through the 1930s rather like canoeists negotiating rapids. They tried, as best they could, to pick their way around the rocks of the system and to utilise the currents to their advantage, though a false move could lead to disaster. There was little feeling among the majority that it was their system, though they were happy enough to pick up whatever advantages they could from it – education, employment, cinema, electricity and so on. In this way, the mobilising state apparatus was an alien entity for most of its citizens who preferred to keep it at a distance. Unless the gap was filled the Soviet system would lose its battle for the soul of the Soviet population and its whole project would be endangered. A temporary solution to the problem came in the most unlikely form of Nazi invasion.

6

FROM WORLD WAR TO COLD WAR

From the first day of its existence Soviet Russia had been at odds with the outside world. Its revolutionary challenge was not going to be quietly ignored by capitalist-dominated powers. Wars of intervention had crippled the new state from the beginning. Fear of invasion in 1927 had helped to precipitate Stalin's revolution from above. The emergence of Nazism provided a baleful background to and partial motivation for the terror. None of these, however, had a fraction of the effect of the great convulsions that lay ahead. From 1920 to 1941 Soviet Russia had been relatively isolated, a world apart which was going its own way. From 1941 to its demise in 1991 Soviet history was closely entwined with that of the outside world. Invasion obviously had this effect but from the American point of view, the Cold War, too, was designed to severely hamper Soviet development. Its last prophets even proclaimed that, through the arms race, they had succeeded in bringing the Soviet system down. Although there is little to support such a claim, external security considerations in a nuclear age and the ever-widening cultural, social and economic threads of globalisation meant isolation was no longer an option. Indeed, the Soviet Union's enforced arousal from isolation was often seen, by western cold warriors above all, as a tendency to expand. From the Soviet point of view such actions, from the counter-invasion of Germany to the attempt to prop up the revolutionary government in Afghanistan, were seen as largely defensive. In this sense, Hitler was the founder of the Soviet Union's eastern empire. Prior to 1941 the Soviet Union had shown no signs of expansionism though the quarrel began even here. The Nazi–Soviet Pact of 1939 transferred, as we have already mentioned, substantial border territories, formerly part of the tsarist empire, back to Moscow's control. A war was fought against Finland to push the frontier further away from Leningrad which would surely have fallen in 1941 had this not been done. Aggression or defence? The argument was already up and running. The main aspect to note from our point of view, however, is that the period when the Soviet system could operate in a relatively enclosed environment had passed. Like it or not, the Soviet Union was becoming enmeshed in world politics in a much bigger way.

The process had begun to speed up even before 1941. The Nazi takeover of Germany (1933) and the Japanese invasion of Manchuria (1931) were its twin precipitants. Soviet acceptance in the League of Nations (as Germany was expelled) and the United States' recognition of the USSR in 1933–4 were clear signals of the change. How did the Soviet Union pick its way through the minefield of international relations? How did it end up fighting the war? And, the main questions from our point of view, what do the experiences tell us about the strengths and weaknesses of the Soviet system and what changes did they bring about?

Nazi Occupation and its Overthrow

The Soviet Union was not prepared for war when it came in June 1941. But even so, it could have given a much better account of itself than it actually did. The war opened with massive initial defeats and astronomical losses. Stalin and the Stalin system were, in large part, responsible. But, it has to be said, they were also instrumental in engineering recovery from the depths of defeat. Let us look at each aspect in turn – Soviet unpreparedness; the initial disasters; the long, costly haul to eventual overwhelming victory.

The Road to War

The complex threads of Soviet international relations have been capably untangled by numerous writers in recent years.[1] Though many disagreements continue, we know enough to make a number of observations relevant to our theme.

There can be no doubt that, once it was clear that Nazism was more than a flash in the pan, Soviet policy went through a major revolution. At the state level of foreign relations and the party level of the Communist International, radically new instructions went out. Diplomats were told to bring about the previously unthinkable, in the form of treaties, including military alliances, with capitalist powers. In pursuit of its goals of collective security, such treaties were signed in 1935 with Czechoslovakia and France and they became the bedrock of Soviet diplomacy up to the outbreak of war. Party militants in the international communist movement were instructed, in 1935, to join broad coalitions known as popular fronts. These were wider than their predecessors, the so-called united fronts of the 1920s. The latter were supposed to be coalitions with other radical forces for the common goal of revolution against imperialism. Popular fronts put revolution and even anti-imperialism on the back burner and set up anti-Fascism and peace through collective security as the prime focus. This went so far as to turn policy on armaments around completely. From being a party which denounced imperialist militarism, communists were urged to become advocates of rapid rearmament on the part of anti-Fascist countries. In France in particular, where a popular front came to power for twelve months in 1936–7, the turnaround brought severe tensions and put the communists more into line with the centrist Radical Party than with the French Socialist Party which was reluctant to rearm. The French Communist Party began a long and relatively successful phase of its life during which it wrapped the republican flag around itself, and claimed to be the heir of the Jacobins in a sort of French equivalent of Soviet patriotism.

However, it was in Spain that affairs came to a head. In the face of a Fascist military rebellion, a very broad popular front stretching from anarchists through Trotskyists to socialists, radicals and liberals, was formed to defend Spanish democracy. Although an international non-intervention agreement was signed, the reality was that the Fascist allies of the rebellion, Germany and Italy, gave extensive assistance to General Franco. Only the Soviet Union and Mexico came to the help of the republic. France was restrained by Britain from helping. The United States also simply looked on. The sad story of the Spanish Civil War is well-known. Gradually, superior weapons and assistance brought the Fascists to victory. The republican cause was badly undermined by Stalinist intransigence. It was unthinkable for Soviet Russia to be pursuing Trotskyite enemies throughout the highways and byways of the Soviet Union and, at the same time, fighting a war alongside them in Spain. Tragically, the purges spread to Spain, as Comintern chiefs, who were themselves facing arrest, imposed Moscow's values on the left of the popular front. This internal fight seriously weakened resistance.

However, it was not just the internal political dynamics of the war which were of concern to Moscow. It also highlighted the international relations arena. Central to any successful policy of collective security was an agreement with Britain. The war showed that the British government, far from being instinctively anti-Fascist, was prepared to turn a blind eye to a Nazi-backed assault on Spanish democracy. Its reason for so doing was that it wanted to avoid pushing Italy entirely into the hands of Germany. This was not a negligible consideration. Britain wanted to come to an agreement with Italy to ease tensions in the Mediterranean which, at the territorial height of its empire, Britain considered to be its vital sphere of interest since it and the Suez Canal were the main artery of that empire. From Moscow, however, it looked more like a none-too-cleverly concealed preference for Berlin over Moscow. Britain remained the stumbling block to a policy of collective security, despite French urging that the German threat be taken more seriously. In truth, Britain was more worried about Far Eastern developments, notably Japan's invasion of China in 1937, which threatened its key imperial outposts of Singapore and Hong Kong.

The outcome was, of course, one of the most topsy-turvy and tragic series of blunders in European diplomatic history. Britain followed appeasement to the last minute, only deciding to make a stand over Poland in 1939 after handing Czechoslovakia to Germany on a plate at Munich in 1938. As a consequence of Munich, the Soviet Union gave up its attempts at collective security and adopted its own version of appeasement in the form of the Nazi–Soviet Pact of August 1939. Britain had dragged its feet over negotiations with the USSR until the very end. It seems hard to see how and why it should make a stand over Poland, which it could not defend and which could not defend itself, when the more defensible Czechoslovakia had been given away. In addition, unlike the Soviet Union's ally Czechoslovakia, Poland had a deep distrust of the Soviet Union which prevented the two countries from coming to an agreement, since Poland would have had to open its borders to Soviet troops if the Soviet Union were to engage the Germans. Poland was completely unprepared to do so, not only because of distrust of Stalin but because of its experiences with Russia since the eighteenth-century partitions.

From Moscow's point of view, Britain's policy seemed to be clear – turn Hitler east and embroil him in war with the USSR which would weaken both powers and solve two problems at once, the communist and Nazi threats. As war loomed, Stalin was concerned that the Soviet Union might be isolated in this scenario since he, too, failed to see how Britain's guarantee to Poland could ever be enforced by anyone other than Soviet troops. Indeed, the 'phoney war' seemed to bear him out and did nothing to persuade Stalin of Britain's anti-Fascist credentials. At the last minute, he pulled off the agreement with Hitler which, he hoped, would give the Soviet Union a breathing space until 1942 so that it could prepare more fully for war. Despite its glowing terms, neither side saw it as more than a cynical ploy which did nothing to blunt the deep hostility between them.

Even so, the pact has been the object of much speculation. Some have even suggested that it was Stalin's preferred policy and that the drive for collective security and popular fronts was a diversion. While such an argument was always hard to sustain, it seems at the time of writing, to have little merit. No serious evidence has come to light to support it. Like any other state, the USSR had contingency plans – a plan B if plan A should fail. In this case, an agreement with Germany seems very much to have been plan B. Backdoor channels of communication had existed between the two countries before the pact. In the early days of Nazi takeover, there was some continuing confusion since Germany was the USSR's main ally prior to it. However, there is now no doubt that Stalin continued to think war with Nazi Germany was inevitable, despite the pact.

At the beginning of the twenty-first century, Stalin's policies are open to a much more soundly-based and equally devastating set of criticisms. In the first place, the horrendously repressive nature of the regime made it difficult for liberal democratic states to ally with it. Its protestations of abandonment of immediate revolutionary objectives also failed to ring true. Its ally, France, had great difficulties in sustaining the relationship against this background, and it was only the national trauma of the First World War which convinced the country that it was a lesser evil. Britain did not have quite the same experience, nor did it have Germany as an immediate neighbour. That, plus its imperial interest, gave it less incentive to turn a blind eye to the nature of the Soviet system. Interestingly, the United States was more prepared to deal with Soviet Russia, which it recognised in 1933. It was represented by the controversial ambassador, Joseph Davies, who is on record as believing the show trial defendants were guilty. Whatever one thinks of Davies, American interest was driven by the search for an ally against resurgent Japan. Even so, the relationship was very uncomfortable. Incidentally, it should be borne in mind that, contrary to the disaster in the west, Soviet deterrence of Japan worked out much better. A series of often overlooked direct military encounters dissuaded Japan from taking on the Soviet Union. In 1938 some 15 000 Red Army troops fought off the Japanese at Lake Khasan and there was a further major battle in May 1939 at Khalkin-Gol in Mongolia. As a result of its defeats Japan never joined the German assault on the USSR. Instead a truce was signed on 15 September 1939. Stalin was spared the nightmare of a two-front war, although he had to remain watchful in the east where an army of over 100 000 remained on the alert.

Second, Stalin's purge of the military was well-known and led almost all foreign observers to downgrade Soviet military capability. For the anti-Nazi powers this meant the USSR was worth less as a potential ally. For potential enemies the effect was to encourage them to attack what appeared to be a seriously weakened enemy.

Third, Stalin's diplomacy clearly blundered, as did Britain's. There is some tragic irony here and incompetence rather than conspiracy, but both sides must take responsibility. At the time of Munich the USSR had over one hundred divisions on alert. This was the time to have resisted Hitler. So deep was the conviction in Moscow after Munich that Britain would never stand up to Hitler, that plan B moved up the agenda, though it was never the dominant one until it seemed clear that Britain still was not prepared to act. Tragically, Soviet policy turned around in a desperate bid to stay out of the war just when Britain was about to stand, if not entirely firm given the nature of the phoney war, at least firmer. Only the German invasion of France and the Battle of Britain in 1940 convinced Stalin that Britain really was in the war. Even so, the pact was a bad miscalculation on his part. The cost of Moscow's breathing space was a relatively free hand for Hitler in the form of a one-front war with a rapid mopping up of Poland and a campaign in France that would have delighted German military planners in 1914. By the end of 1940, Nazi Germany was immensely stronger. It dominated the Continent from the Soviet border to the Atlantic, had concluded a firm alliance with Italy – which had opportunistically joined the war to grab territory from France as it collapsed – and there were sympathetic neutrals in the Iberian peninsula. Britain and the Balkans were the only areas of significance not subdued. Having made his bed, Stalin had to lie on it. The rapid fall of France had upset all calculations. Stalin was desperate to postpone war until 1942 and went to great lengths to ensure it. Above all, he wanted to avoid any 'provocation' of Germany. As a result, he stuck to the letter of agreements which included the dirty business of handing over German communists to Nazi 'justice'. In the twisted morality of Stalinism, the greater goal outweighed the fate of a few unfortunate individuals. It should be recalled that this harsh morality of everything being subject to the immediate ends – preparing for war in this case – was behind the unspeakable sweep for 'enemies of the people' through the newly acquired border areas and the execution of 20 000 captured Polish officers at Katyn and elsewhere in 1940. Stalin, to avoid any appearance of provocation, also stuck to economic and trade agreements to such an extent that trainloads of materials were on their way to Germany even as the invasion began. However, this is not so surprising. Economic and cultural relations between Britain, France and Germany also continued up to the last minute.

More astonishing, however, is Stalin's blindness to the build-up of the war. Intelligence reports were flooding in which all told the same story. Germany would attack in 1941. Some even provided the exact date. Moscow did go so far as to ask Germany why it was building up its forces in Poland, and was given the disingenuous answer that it was to get them out of range of British bombers. This answer appears to have satisfied the usually immensely suspicious Stalin. Intelligence reports were deemed to have been British plans to try to embroil the USSR with Germany in order to pull Britain's chestnuts out of the fire. Even information from defecting German troops, and interrogation of pilots of German spotter planes brought down over Soviet territory, which pointed to imminent attack, was also ignored as German 'provocation'. In order to deprive Germany of a cause of war Soviet units were not given permission to open fire even after the invasion began and were sometimes overwhelmed before they were permitted to fire back. In these respects, Stalin's obsession with postponing the war another year was disastrous. How can we explain it? Only by the fact that he deeply believed the Soviet Union could not stand alone against Nazi Germany and its allies in the conditions of 1941. If so, the words attributed to him at this time – 'Lenin left us a great inheritance and we, his heirs, have fucked it all up' – take on a real significance. Apocryphal or not, as the war began, the sentiment appeared to be all too true.

The Course of the War

Nazi Attack   In terms of casualties, prisoners, ground occupied and war materials captured or destroyed, history had known nothing like the Nazi invasion of the Soviet Union which began in June 1941. The bare figures are beyond imagination. The assault force was made up of 5.5 million troops, 2800 tanks, 5000 aircraft and 47 000 artillery pieces.

It advanced in three major directions. In the north-west they advanced 450 kilometres in two weeks. By 10 July Soviet troops had fallen back 500 kilometres on the western front. Sitting in Moscow, Stalin and the high command received nothing but appalling news. In the first three weeks some thirty Soviet divisions had been destroyed, another seventy reduced to half strength; 3500 planes and half of their fuel had been destroyed. Lithuania fell in hours. On 1 July Riga was captured followed by Tallin in late August. Leningrad was cut off by September with Finns invading from the north and Germans from the south. On the road to Moscow Minsk was captured on 9 July, Smolensk on 16 July. Moscow itself was threatened. In Ukraine, Kiev was captured on 18 September. In the first six months some three million prisoners of war were in German hands. By the end of 1941 about four million Soviet citizens had been killed. Some 40 per cent of the Soviet population of 1941 and up to half of its material resources were under German control. All this masked the fact that two key objectives, Moscow and Leningrad, had not been taken by the assault force but it appeared to be only a matter of time. Some Soviet government departments and foreign embassies began to be evacuated to Kuibyshev in the Urals but Stalin remained in the Kremlin in a symbolic gesture of defiance. The November parades even went ahead with troops and equipment leaving Red Square to head directly to the front.

Even so, the Germans were far from a spent force and victory was by no means beyond them. Failure in the northern and central arms of the assault was balanced by success in the south, and the capture of Kiev. While the Germans never quite repeated the shock of the initial campaigns, they still made advances in 1942. Moscow and Leningrad continued to hold out but the focus of Hitler's attention turned south, drawn to the grain supplies of Ukraine and south Russia and the more distant prospect of oil in the Caucasus, notably the Baku oilfields of the Caspian where Stalin's career as a grassroots revolutionary had begun. They made further massive advances in this direction. After absorbing premature Soviet offensives, the Germans and their allies advanced via the Crimea and Rostov to the Caucasus. They also took Voronezh and nine-tenths of the city of Stalingrad. But once again they missed their key targets. They failed to reach the oil of the Caspian and they were cut off at Stalingrad.

Nonetheless, the Nazis, at the height of the campaign, occupied over 50 per cent of European Russia. The rest of the Soviet Union was cut off from some of its most productive food-producing areas, and 1942 was a year of terrible shortages. Famines struck cities and rural areas. Industries ground to a halt. Death rates rose. There were massive losses of life among remaining labour camp occupants, and war prisoners could expect little priority in the desperate nationwide queue for food. On the second day of the war, prisoners' already meagre rations were cut, discipline was tightened further and the pace of executions was speeded up.[2]

Desperate as conditions were in the unoccupied areas, those in the occupied areas were infinitely worse. Slavs, like Jews, were classified as subhuman in Nazi ideology, and communism was interpreted as part of the Jewish conspiracy for world domination. Jews, who were mostly to be found in eastern Poland, Lithuania and western Ukraine, much of which had come under Soviet control in 1939, were destined to be removed from the 1000-year Reich. Plans for this, of course, evolved from expulsion (which, curiously, led Hitler to sponsor a sort of Zionism for a time) to the unspeakable attempt at extermination. Slavs were too numerous to be expelled or exterminated so they were to be 'hewers of wood and drawers of water' for the superior Aryans. In other words, they were to be its slaves. Although the average German in the occupying army probably thought little about such matters, the ideology was imposed by specially fanatical forces such as the SS, Gestapo and Einsatzgruppen (Extermination Squads). The ideological determination of the occupiers cannot be discounted. Largely because of it, the Polish and Soviet peoples were subjected to infinitely harsher conditions than most of the occupied areas of Western Europe. No population has suffered a scourge to compare with it. Immediately behind advancing Nazi troops came Einsatzgruppen charged with cleansing the captured areas of Jews and communists. Then forced deportations would begin. Although calculation of numbers, apart from being distasteful in appearing to be a clinical, statistical measure of infinite human tragedy, is extremely difficult in the swirl of border changes, troop advances and retreats, floods of refugees and forced population movements, it appears that the human costs of occupation were even beyond those of the 1930s. Some two million prisoners and forced labourers are thought to have died in German labour camps. What proportion of the six million holocaust victims considered themselves Russian or Soviet as much as Jewish we will never know. We do know that 5.5 million Jews were resident in the prewar Soviet Union of whom some 2.2 million were killed. Mass exterminations took place in Ukraine. The main sites of death camps were in the Polish/Ukrainian/Belarussian region.

The Nazi attack on, and occupation of, the Soviet Union remains one of the blackest pages of human history, outweighing even the disasters inflicted on the USSR by its own leaders. Memory of its savagery lingers on among those still alive who survived. Take one personal anecdotal example. Talking, in the mid-1990s, with elderly inhabitants of a village near the Moscow–Kiev railway line between Kaluga and Sukhinichi and Briansk, I asked what they could remember of victims of the various traumas inflicted on the village. They could recall that one, out of some forty to fifty households in the village at the time, was evicted as *kulaks* in the collectivisation drive. One of the sons came back after the war having achieved officer status in the army. The terror brought memories of 'Black Crows' (secret police and their prison vans) being everywhere but, when pressed for specific examples, one arrest in the village was recalled. The village, was occupied by the Germans for four weeks or so as they advanced along the railway towards Moscow in late November/December 1941 and fell back again to Briansk at the turn of the year. That, however, was long enough for them to execute 17 people in a ravine near the village. After the invaders had been driven back Soviet militia came to the village, showing captured documents with the names of further victims down for execution as communists, including one of the people to whom I was talking and members of her family. The Germans had been acting on information supplied by 'a malicious person' known to the villagers, whose fate I never discovered. While this is only a single example it is not unique. In its barbarism and brutality, Nazi occupation was second to none. It has been calculated that eleven million Soviet citizens died under German occupation, including about five million who died in captivity.[3]

Soviet Fightback   Conventionally, the battle of Stalingrad is seen as the turning point of the war. However, the Soviet fightback had begun earlier. In some respects, the battle of Moscow, in 1941, was at least as important. In the face of the enormous losses of the first weeks Soviet desperation was evident. Stalin was even prepared to contemplate the deployment of British troops on Soviet soil. There was no remaining military screen of any significance between the advancing Germans and Moscow. Given time, the Soviet Union could, perhaps, deploy its dormant strengths. The problem was, how could they gain that necessary time? There was only one option. It was a gamble which had to be taken. As we have seen, Soviet armies had been engaged in the country's Far Eastern provinces in substantial battles against Japan. Despite the risk of a recurrence of danger from that quarter, it was more important to defend the heartland of European Russia. Troops were transported as quickly as possible and, under their commander Georgi Zhukov, they were deployed against the advancing Nazi divisions. On 5 December 1941, 700 000 Soviet troops counter-attacked along a 900-kilometre front before Moscow, and threw the invaders back hundreds of kilometres. The threat to Moscow was lifted.

Although the Nazi advance remained spectacular and the German army groups were suffering from over-extended communication lines and an inexplicable lack of preparedness for winter war, the Soviet victory before Moscow was vital. Not only did it rally the country, it also, for the first time, put the Nazi war machine into reverse. Along with the defence of Leningrad, which remained under siege for two and a half years, the check imposed on the German army was crucial. Given the nature of German blitzkrieg tactics, which presupposed rapid campaigns rather than sustained wars of attrition, failure to achieve a key objective was fatal. The longer the war threatened to go on, the more the initiative was likely to pass to the Soviet Union which had a much larger population and a vast, uninvadable, or at least unconquerable, territory. For the Germans, the fall of Moscow and Leningrad was supposed to have led to rapid capitulation and liquidation of the Soviet Union. Even if Moscow had fallen there is little chance that the war would have ended, but since it did not fall, German plans were in turmoil. In that sense, one could argue that the war had already begun to turn by the end of 1941.

Be that as it may, it was another year before the Soviet Union was able to celebrate a second major victory, at Stalingrad. While, to some extent, the battle was seen as symbolic by both sides, since the city bore Stalin's own name and was a showpiece of 1930s development, it was also strategically important. Situated on the Volga, it was the hinge around which the Soviet front turned. Collapse here would not only open the road to the Caucasus, but also threatened an eventual encirclement of Moscow. On the other hand, defeat for the German forces would expose their southern salient. While senior generals urged Hitler to make a strategic withdrawal from the area which would enable them to hold their key positions elsewhere, the Führer would not hear of it. His heroic army would hold out and prevail. After nearly four months of the most unbelievable fighting at close quarters, in which local positions might change hands several times in one day, the Soviet army managed to complete its encirclement of the city on 24 November and doom its occupying army of 250 000. Hitler was sure his commander von Paulus would fight to the end but he did not. He surrendered his remaining force of about 92 000 on 31 January 1943. Hitler's forces in south Russia had no option but to stream back as fast as possible before they, too, were cut off.

Hitler, however, was still not finished. Rather, he was determined to wreak his revenge over the impudent, subhuman Slavs who had so humiliated him. He planned it by means of an overwhelming assault, code-named Operation Zitadelle. The target was a supposed weak point on the Soviet central front, the Kursk salient. A concerted pincer movement might incise it and get German troops through Soviet lines. In order not to make any mistake, Hitler brought together the elite of his armed forces including the Waffen SS. Nothing was to be left to chance. Nothing was to go wrong. However, the situation went badly wrong. In the first place, Soviet intelligence, backed up by British Enigma intercepts, presented Soviet commanders with the complete German order of battle. The Soviets, too, were making their provisions in the form of the most complex web of defensive lines the world had ever seen. In some cases they were 200 kilometres deep. They also concentrated their vast number of T-34 tanks. The German assault was held, even though in many respects the Germans had military superiority. They were able to attack fairly freely from the air and their Panzers, on a one-to-one basis, were superior to the T-34 (though not to the less well-known KV tank) but they were unable to deal with the vast number of tanks unleashed. In the words of one German soldier, 'We found ourselves taking on a seemingly inexhaustible mass of enemy armour – never have I received such an overwhelming impression of Russian strength and numbers as on that day. The clouds of dust made it difficult to get help from the Luftwaffe, and soon many of the T-34s had broken past our screen and were streaming like rats all over the battlefield.'[4]

It was the apparently inexhaustible resources of the country which were beginning to tell. While the German army held, and even gained ground, it did not break through. The immense array of forces had failed. Germany was unable to sustain the losses of men and equipment this failure entailed. The Soviet army was now making massive advances. Kharkov was retaken on 23 August, Smolensk on 25 September and Kiev on 6 November.

For two years the Soviet Union had borne the brunt of the fighting against Hitler. Allied landings in Italy in 1943 were dismissed as an imperialist sideshow designed to re-establish British power in the vital Mediterranean region without confronting Germany directly. However, the American–Japanese war had safeguarded the Soviet Union against a resurgence of Japanese attacks in the east. Nonetheless, Stalin wanted a serious second front to be opened in the vital European theatre. Nowhere were growing Soviet linkages with the rest of the world more apparent than in the growing diplomacy of the war years. Churchill's visit to Moscow in 1942 was followed by the Tehrān Conference of 1943 at which a second front was agreed for 1944 and unconditional surrender of Germany was to be demanded. Economic and military aid, in the form of lend-lease, was also stepped up. In return for the second front, the Soviet Union promised a major assault in the east within twelve days of the proposed Allied landings.

In the western mind, the Soviet campaigns of 1944 have been blotted out by the cult of D-Day. However, they far outweighed the efforts of the Allies. Hitler spent more and more time at his eastern HQ, the Wolf's Lair at Rastenburg, where he pondered how he might halt the hordes about to pour down on the Reich from the steppes. Formerly loyal nationalist officers were doing the same and came to the conclusion that the removal of Hitler would enable Germany to get American help in halting the impending catastrophe. The conspirators, who did set off a bomb at Rastenburg which Hitler miraculously survived, should, perhaps, be thought of as premature progenitors of NATO, but their failure shut off any hope of achieving their aims.

No wonder senior Germans were wondering what was about to hit them, not from the west but from the east. For once, the fabled 'Russian steamroller' was cranking into action. An immense force of some 160 divisions was gathered, backed up by 375 000 partisans behind German lines. Germany's last hope, Army Group Centre, was annihilated within a month. The Soviets advanced at a speed comparable to that at which their enemies had advanced on them in 1941. By autumn they were crossing their 1920 border and their 1939 border was in range. The advance brought a whole host of political problems. What would become of the Baltic States? How should Poland be dealt with? What were the Soviet Union's legitimate security interests? What would be done with Germany once it was defeated? However, the Allies were equally worried about what might happen if the Soviet Union were to halt at its 1939 borders. Then the boot would be on the other foot and it would be the Allies who would have to face what was left of the German army. The impact would have been considerable since, as it was, only some 20 per cent of German forces at the peak were fighting in the west, compared to the 80 per cent facing the Soviet army. However, there was little chance of Stalin slowing up. As he said to the young Yugoslav communist Milovan

Djilas at this time, 'This war is not as in the past; whoever occupies a territory also imposes his own social system on it. Everyone imposes his own
system as far as his army can reach.'[5] Soviet security would not be served
by waiting for the Americans and their allies to slog through to Warsaw.
Instead, the race for Berlin was on.

From the beginning of its 1944 campaigns, cities fell to the advancing
Soviet army like ninepins. The siege of Leningrad was lifted in January
1944. Minsk was liberated on 3 July. On 1 August the Soviet army
reached Warsaw. Controversy surrounds its assault on Warsaw where it
failed to support an internal rising within the city as its troops
approached. Given the complexities that would have been involved in
crossing the Vistula and fighting in a vast city like Warsaw at the end of
a rapid, long advance, and the fact that the aim of the uprising was to
thwart Soviet aims in Poland, it was unlikely that Stalin would take risks
to help it, as its inaugurators probably knew (or at least should have
done). In the end, it was one more tragic episode, along with the 1939
partition and the Katyn massacre, which made any accommodation
between Stalin and the Poles even more remote. It was only on 17
January that Soviet troops were able to take Warsaw. Soviet troops also
reached Auschwitz and Birkenau around this time. Even veterans of
Soviet camps could hardly believe their eyes.[6]

The complexity and cost of the final struggle, the battle for Berlin,
shows that taking a large city is no easy matter. It was also a much bigger battle than is generally realised. Soviet forces of 3.8 million were
involved including 2.5 million who took part in the final assault. Some
300 000 Soviets and 200 000 Germans died in the final battle. Berlin fell
on 21 April. The war in Europe was over. Soviet troops hoisted the red
flag over the Reichstag. All known and many previously unknown intox-
icating substances were consumed. Special units started removing industrial equipment from Germany as part of reparations. Soviet troops in
the streets relieved everyone in sight of their wrist watches. More serious
looting, assault, murder and rape were only gradually brought under
control by the authorities. Very few Soviet troops were punished. A
German–Soviet Friendship Society was set up in the ruins of Berlin.
Stalin's Russia had arrived at the heart of Europe.

The Soviet System and Soviet Society at War

For many observers, war was the test of Stalin's system. Victory seemed
to suggest that it had passed successfully. However, the conclusion is not

so clear. Alec Nove reported two views. One, from an old German communist, was that 'The result of the battle of Stalingrad proves the basic correctness of Stalin's policies', while another Soviet observer argued that 'Perhaps, if it were not for Stalin's policies, the Germans would not have got as far as Stalingrad.'[7] Can we solve the riddle?

The first direction in which those who say victory depended on Stalin and, in some way, made sense of the sacrifices of the late 1920s and 1930s tend to look is towards the advantages of centralisation. By having a military-style chain of command (and, as we have seen, even a military-style morality) in the economic, social and cultural fields as well as in the military sphere proper, the centre had power the other combatant governments strove to achieve but which even the enemy dictatorships could not match. Of prime importance, so the argument goes, was the formidable control exercised over the nation's economic resources. This enabled extensive mobilisation of scarce resources. Where Britain relied, for example, on voluntary, patriotic donations of unnecessary metals to augment war production and encouraged people to grow food for victory, in the Soviet Union railway tracks in Irkutsk were simply ripped up and transferred to Stalingrad during the battle and city squares, for instance St Isaac's in Leningrad, were dug up and turned into vegetable gardens. The authorities' power of decision reached into every industrial, service and agricultural enterprise. War production became an overriding priority from educational arrangements to labour camps. An all-powerful State Defence Committee was set up shortly after the invasion to supervise the transition of all institutions onto a war footing. It was chaired by Stalin, and its members were Molotov as Deputy Chair, Malenkov as Senior Party Secretary, Kaganovich and Mikoyan as Politburo members, Voznesensky as head of the State Planning Apparatus, Beria as Security Police Chief and Voroshilov representing the armed forces. Its success can be measured by the fact that, according to some calculations, the Soviet Union was able to devote some 50 per cent of its GDP to the war where other countries, held back by trying to balance private economic and other interests, were held at about 20 per cent maximum.

The centralised system had also enabled war planning to be readily incorporated into the economic decision-making process. Indeed, as we have seen, it may have been a main source of Stalinist transformation from the beginning. In any case, non-market and non-optimal decisions (from the purely economic point of view) had been taken which enabled the country to survive. In the front rank was the decision to set up industries, at enormous cost, in remote areas of the Urals, Western Siberia and Central Asia. These factories and the crude and fragile infrastructure around them became the key platforms of weapons production and were beyond enemy reach. They expanded considerably during the war.

It was also the case, though its exact significance is argued about, that Soviet planning included provision for rapid switching from peacetime to wartime production. The legendary capability of the Cheliabinsk tractor factory in the Urals, to switch the majority of its production lines from producing tractors to producing tanks, is often quoted. Closer studies have revealed difficulties which made the concept easier to implement in theory than practice but, nonetheless, an impressive number of factories soon switched to armaments.

However, we should remember that the Stalinist economic system has not become renowned for its overall efficiency. Endemic problems did not disappear. Shortages had always been the bane of the system, opening up a cycle of bottlenecks appearing, resources being transferred to break them and thereby shifting the bottleneck elsewhere. While Soviet plans were neat enough on paper, in reality they were often crude and open to interpretations which might lead to waste of output. Even where precise specifications and blueprints of output were provided, fulfilment often relied on ignoring the exact plans at times in favour of working round them, setting up informal contacts, even bribing key suppliers and managers and persuading blind eyes to be turned on numerous occasions. Often local short-cutting could cause problems for the standardisation of military equipment because, while on paper, the war machines would be identical, in practice, factories, working on a semi-artisanal basis in many cases, would use up whatever supplies they could get to complete a job even though the specification might not be identical to that required. While, obviously, this would not apply to key components like the gun barrels of tanks it could apply to, say, their radiators, frame-bolts and so on which would cause severe problems later in repair and maintenance shops.

All this added up to an immense quality control problem. It was part of the folklore of the Soviet Union, right down to its last days, that standards of military production were higher than those of civilian production. In late Cold War times, one sometimes got the impression that some observers thought there were two Soviet economies operating, a very low quality civilian sector and a secret, deadly efficient military and space economy, much vaunted by American politicians when the time came to vote massive military expenditures through Congress. While a division of this nature remains in the realms of myth there was, indeed, a significant difference in quality control for military and civilian output. In most cases, civilian quality controllers were employed by the factories in which they worked. This made it easier to pressure them into accepting shoddy output because, if the plan was not fulfilled, they would suffer along with everyone else. By comparison, military quality controllers were more independent. Post-Soviet research has shown that in key enterprises there could be several hundred military quality inspectors. Having such a vast number, made it very difficult for the factory to put pressure on them and extremely dangerous to contemplate bribing them. While this undoubtedly improved the situation, it was not a complete solution to the problem and many Soviet weapons remained of doubtful quality. Certain aircraft had a reputation as death traps, and munitions could be relatively unstable causing tragic accidents in supply dumps, a tendency added to by undisciplined, not to mention intoxicated, handling of equipment. In an interview for a BBC TV documentary in the late 1980s, a veteran of the battle of Kursk said he and his team of sappers preferred to locate, dig up and relay German mines on the battlefield rather than handle Soviet-made mines which they feared would explode at any moment.

Despite these endemic problems, the achievements of Soviet weapons construction have to be acknowledged. In key areas they produced formidable weapons in massive quantities. T-34 and KV tanks outnumbered and, eventually, outperformed the best Panzers. Lorry-mounted Katiusha rockets – known as Stalin organs because of the number of launch pipes – were devastating. Cheap, effective fighter aircraft eventually pushed the Luftwaffe out of the skies. Light weapons were perfected. Prototypes of the Kalashnikov rifle – still the weapon of choice of many who need such things – appeared in 1942 though the design was not perfected until after the war. The strength of the system lay in choosing a key weapon and then producing it in overwhelming quantities. Even where it was outperformed, like early T-34s, the sheer weight of numbers made up for the deficiency. Through enormous efforts of this kind, including authorised and unauthorised imitation of foreign designs, the Soviet war economy began to outproduce Germany in key weapons by the end of 1942. By the time that point was reached, there was little short of a miracle which could win the war for Germany. Of course, in a sense, that miracle was closer than we might like to think in that, in some areas, Soviet decisions to concentrate on what was produced meant setting aside other projects which might have been more effective. Most famously radar, jet propulsion and rocketry were initially considered unrealistic by Stalin, and some of their proponents, like the rocket scientist Kurchatov and the jet propulsion specialist A. I. Shakurin, were imprisoned.[8] What might have happened had German scientists been the first to produce atomic weapons also does not bear thinking about. Soviet efforts in this direction, which produced weapons much earlier than outsiders expected, were aided by information from spies without which Stalin's decisions might have been fatal in the postwar years. As it was, however, the war economy was, undoubtedly, the backbone of Soviet recovery and victory.

The second area to which those advocating the advantages of centralisation look, is to Stalin's control over the military and, by extension, over civilian society. In this area there has long been a relatively substantial picture of Stalin's command style thanks to a profusion of military memoirs, especially from the Khrushchev period, as well as accounts by many western diplomats and politicians who met Stalin at the various inter-Allied meetings during the war. More recent studies which have had access to wider sources, like that of Dmitri Volkogonov who was himself a general who knew a number of those who worked closely with Stalin during the war, have tended to confirm the picture. Although Stalin was clearly a forbidding figure and a dangerous person to cross, the idea that he made all decisions and kept everyone around him in a constant state of terror is far from the truth. He was, unlike Hitler to whom he is often compared, very much a hands-on participant in command discussions and had a great grasp of detail as well as of the larger picture. This is hardly surprising since, as we have seen, it was his practical ability which brought him to Lenin's side in the first place. He tended to listen to a variety of points of view on strategic issues before choosing an option. Where Hitler, whose self-delusion included the belief that he was a grand strategist, often made sweeping decisions in the face of professional advice from his high command, Stalin tended to work within the framework of professional military discussion. There is no record of any senior commander suffering sanctions for putting forward a point of view in military councils. Disobeying decisions once taken, however, could be fatal as could disobedience to any order, no matter how absurd it might look in the particular circumstances of those who were supposed to carry it out. Senior officers were dismissed for incompetence, particularly after the initial disasters. These included some of Stalin's longest-lasting and closest associates such as the civil war hero and cavalry general Budenny and, in May 1940, the Defence Commissar, Kliment Voroshilov. Friendship with Stalin alone did not protect one from reprisals but in these cases the purged generals remained honoured figures. Budenny kept a large ranch on which he bred the Soviet Union's best racehorses and one of the finest tanks of the war, the KV, was named after Voroshilov. Other officers also came and went according to their ability but, by and large, military leadership showed Stalin at his most competent and most pragmatic. Where he trusted someone, notably the main architect of victory, General Georgii Zhukov, he tended to let them have their head. This tendency was not, however, continued into peacetime when some of the war heroes appeared to be a political threat to the ageing Stalin.

Stalin's diplomatic activity was formed in the same mould. While he was undoubtedly aware of the irony of his cooperation with the wily, imperialist fox, Churchill, the pragmatic near cynicism of both men struck a mutual chord. By comparison, Roosevelt and the Americans were often treated as though they were exceedingly naive. Most foreigners, whether horrified or impressed by Stalin, acknowledged that he was shrewd, sometimes with a kind of peasant craftiness, and well-informed. There are no grounds in such memoirs for any of the psychopathic monster theories of Stalin's personality. Rather, he had his wits about him, knew what he was doing and, though he made major mistakes from time to time like all politicians, often pursued his country's best interests. He might have been tough, cynical, totally contemptuous of liberalism which he (following his mentor Lenin) saw as sickeningly hypocritical, but he was not crazy.

Stalin's style of control was deeply reflected at lower levels of the army. Duty and discipline were, in theory, absolutely paramount. The soldiers' vow included a commitment to die rather than surrender. It was not just rhetoric. Many soldiers, particularly commanders, who did surrender were imprisoned when they returned from enemy prison camps. Disobedience to orders also brought the security police to a commander's door. The idea was to impose the strictest discipline over the military. The result, as usual in Stalin's Russia, was arbitrariness. Some got away with it, others paid the supreme penalty. The overall mixture of anarchy and inflexibility could be found throughout the war years. The latter tended to dominate. Orders had to be obeyed to the letter. There are many examples of German officers hardly believing their senses when hopeless Soviet attacks were continued with wave after wave of assaults which simply cost more lives. But a Soviet officer ordered to take a position knew that failure could lead to court-martial. It has often been remarked that Soviet tactics of this nature were wasteful of human life. Once again the grim Bolshevik morality of ends justifying means, of sacrificing the present for the sake of the future, came into play. Defeat would have cost even more lives. End of story.

If anything, Stalin's grip over society also tightened during the war but, paradoxically, it was in part the abandonment of extreme methods that allowed this to happen. There were many minor modifications to the system which allowed better relations between state and society to build up. Terror wound down from its pre-war levels though it was still very much present. Concessions to national, especially Russian, traditions were made. The Orthodox Church was allowed to emerge from the shadows and it became a major supporter of the war, collecting money for supplementary war supplies and encouraging the defence of the country. Pre-revolutionary military heroes – Alexander Nevsky, who was saint and tsar; Suvorov and Kutuzov, who resisted Napoleon – were commemorated in monuments, street names and film. There was a very limited 'thaw' in relations with the west. Some western literature was published and slightly warmer rhetoric prevailed in the press. Tragically, many of those who had contacts with foreigners in this period were made to suffer heavily for it in the post-war years when the Cold War built up Stalin's always active suspiciousness to new, ever more disastrous, heights.[9]

For the moment, however, the gap between state and society was closed to some extent by the shared effort of national defence. There was no resistance to the draft. Sons of peasants flooded into the armed forces even though their parents had been treated so cruelly by Stalin. Around 17 million people are thought to have passed through the armed forces during the war, some 7–8 million being killed and a further 2–3 million imprisoned and/or enslaved in Nazi Germany, most of whom also did not survive. While Stalin might have protected his troops better, the prime responsibility for the terrible toll lay with the invaders, not the tactics of the defenders. Massive sacrifices brought the country together. The army became, as it had been in the revolutionary years, a prime point of contact between the leadership and the masses though, in a sign of the times, the once all-important role of the political commissar was downgraded in the war years. The now inert Communist International was officially shut down on 23 May 1943. Clearly, the building of socialism was secondary to victory alongside the imperialists over the common enemy.

The growth of party institutions reflected the new relationships. For the first time in Soviet history they became mass institutions. Party membership grew from 1.9 million in 1938 to 3.4 million in 1940 and peaked at 3.8 million in 1942.[10] But it was the Komsomol, the Communist

Youth League, which showed the greatest growth. At the height of the war it had five million members. Although, again reflecting the mood of the moment, these figures fell rapidly after the war, they nonetheless foreshadowed the post-Stalin roles of party institutions.

The nature of this new conjuncture raises questions about the argument that the Soviet Union's key advantages lay in its centralisation. Are there not signs that Lenin's old bugbear, spontaneity, might be raising its head? Do the Soviet people not deserve at least as much credit as their leaders for the part they played in the victory? A number of areas of activity help to show the nature of the relationship between state and society during the war.

One of the most extraordinary aspects of the war occurred in the first few months when 1500 factories were transferred out of the war zone and re-established in safer areas such as the Urals, Western Siberia and Central Asia. For anyone who has even moved house the experience is usually traumatic enough; moving a factory defies the imagination. If one then throws in the vast distances, the underdevelopment of the receiving areas and the pressures of war, especially on the transport system, the whole affair seems to be something of a miracle. At one time, central control of the process seemed to be the key. Factories had contingency plans to up sticks and go. New sites were allocated centrally, labour power and transport facilities were laid on. However, memoirs of the period have modified such views. In particular, the role of the factory workers and the local officials appears to be vital. It was the latter who often had to scout for sites in the absence of, or in contradiction to, official orders. They had to use all their Soviet-style managerial skills to cajole others and scrounge trucks, locomotives and schedule slots for trains. Massive efforts had to be made by the labour force to pack and unpack the crates of equipment and reassemble the machinery in working order. The destination sites were often little more than building shells. It was not unusual to have to extend the electricity supply system or add tens of kilometres of railtrack to reach them. Some sort of housing had to be provided and supply lines for food and raw materials and finished product had to be established. In some cases the results are hard to believe. For instance, there are examples of factories being down for only three months. Considering the train journey could take two or three weeks in war conditions, this is truly amazing.

There was no way such tasks could have been achieved simply by pressing buttons at the centre. Immense hard work, dangerous and slow railway journeys, painful reassembly of unloaded crates had to be accomplished by those on the ground. In particular, the crucial role of local and regional party secretaries, at the source and destination ends of the process, and of transport, factory and trade union managers has been emphasised by more recent accounts. But at the same time, the centre provided an overall framework and crucial information, such as the location of construction sites and other likely recipient zones to which factories could be sent. Thus, while a balance between centre and periphery was crucial one cannot help but stress the immense real efforts of those untold thousands who had to strain every fibre to get the actual job done.

One could say something similar about the military. Without the divisional and junior officers and the fighting spirit of the troops, which still shines out from a dwindling band of veterans for whom victory was the achievement of a lifetime and who are confused about what it now means in the ex-Soviet Union, victory would not have been possible. For a generation the war was the centrepiece of national life. It came to eclipse the revolution itself as the legitimating event of Soviet history. The massive memorial in Moscow, built to commemorate the fiftieth anniversary of victory, shows it still retains much of its significance even in post-communist times. Traditionally, the authorities absorbed much of the glory for themselves and even the first de-Stalinising reformers were slow to criticise Stalin for his military activities. However, the immense determination of the ordinary soldier and officer were the sinews of victory. They put up with immense hardship. The case of one soldier illustrates the fate of millions. Signing up for the military when his region of southern Russia was overrun in 1941–2 he fought with his unit across Russia for three years, losing touch with his family for most of that time. In his first battle, at Rostov in November–December 1941, 1100 members of his brigade were killed or missing. He fought at Kursk and was decorated for improvising rafts and ferryboats to transport mortars across the Dnepr under relentless bombardment and gunfire. He fought at Kiev and was decorated twice more. Once again, in the Carpathians, his division lost 461 dead and 1500 wounded. After a long silence, in 1944 his family was, wrongly, informed he had been killed during a battle in the Carpathians. Fortunately, he had only been wounded. He eventually recovered but it was the end of his war. How do we know this? The soldier was called Sergei Gorbachev and his son Mikhail became world-famous and tells the tale in his memoirs.[11]

One crucial area which has yet to be clarified involves the issue of partisans. In the war mythology of many countries, the role of resistance has been built up for the obvious purpose of salving the national conscience and concealing the ugly realities of collaboration. More objective research has, however, blown many such myths apart. Careful, well-established research on Soviet partisan movements is only in its infancy. Some things can, however, be said. Partisans were always ambiguous in the Stalin leadership's eyes because the difficulties of controlling them left them open to dreaded spontaneity. The majority of partisans were party officials and Soviet troops stranded behind enemy lines by the break-up of their units during German offensives. Some of the latter simply turned into bandit groups scavenging ruthlessly off the land and terrorising fellow Soviet citizens as well as the occupying forces. Genuine partisans were at their most effective in the deeply-wooded areas of western Russia and Belarus, but even so their military effectiveness has been questioned. There are also doubts about their numbers and the degree of support they got from the local population. Latest research, not surprisingly, tends to show that recruitment and support were low when the Germans had the upper hand but increased as the Soviet army got closer. As has become apparent from research into the French resistance, the picture of a heroic population backing the partisans is completely mythical. The murky question of collaboration remains largely unstudied. While it is no longer believed that German troops were welcomed with open arms in the early days of the war (at least, no more than any sensible person 'welcomes' an occupying army they can do nothing about), there were many cases of collaboration. Some of the border nationalities – Lithuanians and Ukrainians – have often been accused of wholesale anti-Semitic collaboration. However, there are no more grounds for seeing collaboration as a popular cause than there are for resistance. Once the realities of the occupation came to bear on populations it was, in any case, usually too late because the devastating sweeps of the Einsatzgruppen had put the occupying forces in control of the situation. In the end, the ordinary population appear to have done what they had done for centuries – endure incredible hardship as best they could.

While there is little ground for seeing either mass support for, or mass rebellion against, Stalinism, the profound antipathy for the occupiers, even though much of it remained passive, was obvious enough. When the time came, returning Soviet troops were genuinely welcomed by the Russian and Belarussian populations. The further west they went the less enthusiasm they engendered, but among groups persecuted by the Nazis, with surviving Jews in the forefront, the Soviet army was certainly the lesser of two evils. Victory was a great national festival and, for the time being at least, the gap between state and society had been filled. But would it last?

The Final Years of Stalin

Stalin lived for another eight years after the end of the war. They are among the bleakest. They were dominated by the Cold War and recovery from wartime devastation. Together, these two great shaping forces blotted out any hopes for post-war relaxation of the system. Instead, austerity and shortages were imposed. Contacts with the outside world became more controlled than ever. Political repression returned in systematic and chilling forms. Labour camps were filled with people who had fought to the limit for the Soviet Union. Crude attacks were made on leading intellectuals. The cult of Stalin's personality reached grotesque depths. These grim circumstances put the final touches to the political, social, economic and cultural system Stalin was to bequeath to his successors.

More than at any previous peacetime moment Soviet policies in general were deeply affected by outside events, in the front rank the onset of Cold War. Its origins have become a *locus classicus* of historical debate – the first major discussion in which the term 'revisionism' (initially adopted tongue-in-cheek from Chinese denunciations of the Khrushchev leadership) was widely used. As is often the case, heat rather than light was often the chief product. While it is not our prime concern to follow the threads of the argument we need to consider certain aspects of the Cold War since its impact was so pervasive.

The groundwork for the post-war world was laid at a conference held in mid-February 1945 in the Soviet Union, in the tsars' holiday palace at Livadia in the Crimea. Essentially, it divided Europe up into military occupation zones but left many details vague. Stalin, however, had, as we have already seen, got the point, judging by his comment recorded by Djilas, about armies pushing the limit to claim control of territory. When the war ended a few adjustments were made on the ground, the most significant being American withdrawal from Prague in deference to the Soviet army. The main reason for American concessions to the Soviet Union at the time is often forgotten. The United States believed it was in for a long and bloody campaign to subdue Japan in its home islands and it wanted to recruit the Soviet army to share the sacrifice. Exactly on schedule the Soviet Union declared war on Japan on 8 August and an army of half a million advanced into Manchuria. By then, however, the situation had changed radically in that the Manhattan Project had produced the world's first atomic weapons. It has often been pointed out that their use, on 6 August at Hiroshima and 9 August at Nagasaki, bracketed the Soviet declaration of war. Many historians argue that their use was in part determined by a desire to impress the Soviet Union and in part to preempt its move into Japan. More controversially, some have even argued that Japanese surrender on 2 September owed as much to the desire to make peace with the Americans before Soviet power could be brought to bear on them as it did to the terrible effect of nuclear weapons (after all, the fire-bombing of Tokyo had been more destructive). The Soviets were close to landing troops on Hokkaido, the main northern island of Japan, but, although the Americans could have done nothing about it militarily, Stalin decided not to go ahead, in order to avoid complicating the situation. Nonetheless, it is clear that, in American eyes, Soviet Russia was no longer an ally but was once again the enemy. This was not a promising background against which a multitude of thorny issues had to be solved. Did Stalin also assume that the old adversarial relationships would be resumed once hostilities ended?

In many ways, Soviet policy on key issues required at least a period of continued cooperation with the western allies. Soviet concerns were twofold. One, it should be protected from a third German invasion. Second, Germany and its allies should pay for the cost of the enormous destruction visited on the Soviet Union. The key to all other questions here was the future of Germany. Soviet policy was driven, for obvious reasons, by the desire to keep Germany united so that all powers, despite the military zones, would have access to all parts of the country. In other words, the Soviets wanted Germany as a whole, and especially the industries of the Ruhr, to be available to pay reparations. American planners debated this[12] but came down in favour of a 'spheres of influence' solution, that is, each power had its own area of activity and promised not to interfere excessively in other areas. The reasons for this, too, are fairly obvious. Europe's richest countries – Britain, France, the wealthiest sectors of Germany, Italy, Spain and Scandinavia – would be in the American sphere of influence. Its poorest countries – notably the Balkans – would be in the Soviet sphere. Poland was a particular problem. It was, of course, Polish independence which had been the cause for which Britain and France had gone to war in the first place. The Poles themselves, especially after Katyn and the failed Warsaw uprising, were deeply hostile to Stalin. Yet Soviet security could only be achieved by access to Germany, which put Poland in the way. In another world perhaps Poland could have been 'Finlandised'. In Finland, itself a place of great geopolitical importance to the Soviet Union and a former German ally to boot, a compromise agreement was reached based on Finnish neutrality and acceptance of Soviet bases in return for pledges

of non-interference in Finland's internal affairs. However, Polish intransigence came into sharp conflict with Soviet determination that it could
not permit a hostile government to emerge in Poland. The outcome
was, of course, the establishment of a Moscow-dependent communist-
dominated regime. As the Cold War developed this, rather than the
Finnish model, spread across Eastern Europe. By 1949 almost the whole
Soviet-liberated zone had communist regimes though there were interesting differences in the degree to which the Soviet model was applied.
While economic planning was de rigueur, collectivisation on the Soviet
model was not imitated. Germany and Austria were divided. It is hard
to know if these were Stalin's preferred options, as cold warriors insist.
Certainly, Soviet interests would have been better served by greater
access to Germany and, officially, Soviet policy supported reunification
for decades afterwards. But, in many ways, the iron curtain was being
shut down by the west on Soviet encroachment as much as the Soviets
were pulling it down to keep the west out. We now know the Marshall
Plan was never intended to be available to the Soviet Union and western initiatives, like setting up a separate West German state in 1947 and
forming NATO in 1949, were the crucial steps which established the
separation. Indeed, even as the war was being fought, the Soviet Union
had, in what it considered to be a violation of agreements, been
excluded from discussion of the future of territories liberated by the west
from the first, Oran in 1942, to more important areas like Italy and,
more crucially for the Soviet Union since it sat across its Arctic sea lanes,
Norway. Along with the long delay in setting up the second front,
Stalin's ever-acute suspiciousness had been given plenty of material to
feed on. However, by 1949, particularly if we take into account the success of the Chinese revolution and the unexpectedly early explosion of
a first Soviet atomic bomb, a new world situation had congealed.
Ironically, the man denounced by Trotsky as the betrayer of international revolution was the actual head of communist regimes across a
third of Europe and was a revered figure in Mao's China. The dangerous atomic imbalance had been broken down within four years. The
Soviet Union was a force to be reckoned with everywhere in the Eurasian
land mass and was the only power on earth able to mount even a partial
counterweight to the massive global dominance of the United States.
How did such momentous changes affect the Soviet system itself?

One might expect such a massive expansion of Soviet power and
status to alleviate some of Stalin's sense of insecurity and lead to the
emergence of some degree of relaxation in the regime. Sadly for the

Soviet people who had sacrificed so much to fight for the survival of their country and its state, the exact opposite was the case. Ideological and political shutters came slamming down. One of Stalin's chief agents in this was Andrei Zhdanov who became the centrepiece of a campaign to exclude western influences and reestablish the values of Soviet patriotism. The country's greatest poet, Anna Akhmatova, was denounced as 'half nun, half whore'. Writers were silenced. The film-maker Eisenstein was severely criticised as was the composer Shostakovich. Zhdanov's death from a heart attack in 1948 did not halt the process. Indeed, it had already got much wider. Anyone who had had contact with a foreigner might be suspect. Soviet officers who had made friends with British or American counterparts were jailed for receiving letters from them. The camps, far from emptying, were filling up, perhaps most tragically with returned war prisoners who were screened by the security services on their return. Many innocent people fell victim to the usual dread principle of imprisoning the blameless to ensure that none of the guilty should get away. Political repression also returned at the highest level. In the still-murky 'Leningrad affair', Politburo member and key Soviet war planner Nikolai Voznesensky and others were executed without public trial. At the time of Stalin's death a campaign around a supposed 'Doctors' Plot' based in the Kremlin was getting under way. This was particularly disturbing in that many, though by no means all, of those under suspicion were Jewish. Ironically, the Soviet Union had been one of the first supporters of the state of Israel because they thought it might prove a thorn in the side of British imperialism in the Middle East. However, Soviet policy changed quickly when Israel was seen more as an outpost of the rapidly growing American informal empire and switched instead to the support of radical Arab nationalists in the area. From this moment on, 'Zionist' became a part of the vocabulary of Soviet demonology along with '*kulak*', 'bourgeois', 'imperialist' and all the rest.

Closely associated with the repression was the ever more grotesque development of the cult of Stalin's personality. The cult itself had begun before the war but it reached much greater proportions in Stalin's declining years, driven by the sycophantic attention of his lickspittle courtiers using it to establish their own positions through currying favour with the leader. Like the process of terror where people denounced others to preempt being denounced themselves, it became necessary to find ever more enthusiastic ways to praise Stalin in case faint-hearted praise was interpreted as concealed opposition. A grotesque farce surrounded his seventieth birthday celebrations in 1949. Members of his entourage tried to outdo one another in inventing super-honours for Stalin. He was already Marshal of the Soviet Union and had been presented with a Victory Order of the highest rank. A second Victory Order was pressed upon him but the invention of the title Generalissimo and the inauguration of the Stalin Prize and an international Stalin Peace Prize topped the lot. Stalin feigned anger and reluctance but accepted most of them anyway. A gala was held at the Bolshoi Theatre. Mao Zedong described him as great. Other speakers called him 'genius', 'thinker and leader of genius', 'teacher of genius', 'war leader of genius' and 'object of the people's love'. An article by Poskrebyshev in *Pravda* entitled 'Beloved Father and Great Teacher' celebrated Stalin's great achievements in the cultivation and study of citrus fruits and scientific innovation in the form of introducing eucalyptus trees to the Black Sea coast and melons to the Moscow region.[13]

In this atmosphere, Stalin's power came as close as ever to being absolute. It was, perhaps, constrained by some dependence on supporters and some cultural and rhetorical limits still held out in that the name of socialism still had to be invoked and Stalin, as ever, saw himself in the heroic revolutionary light. But the wisdom of the great leader began to impose itself in unexpected areas. In particular, the case of the biologist Trofim Lysenko is illustrative. He put forward an unfounded theory that improvements through hybridisation and breeding could be passed on by natural genetic modification. The promise of the theory was that it provided a rapid way to improve Soviet grain production – develop a superhybrid and the advantages could be passed on to the next generation. It was also deduced that, in human terms, if the elusive 'New Soviet Person' emerged, his or her values could also become genetically encoded. Competent scientists who stood out against this nonsense had their careers ruined. The atmosphere had degenerated so far that wishful thinking dominated logic, reason and science.

However, Stalinism had lost none of its ambiguity. While quacks and charlatans emerged in science and hacks dominated the creative arts, major achievements in the form of economic recovery and the rapid development of atomic weapons were recorded.

The devastation left by the war was unimaginable. The generally accepted headline figures are 27 million dead; US $128 billion in damage; 1700 towns and 17 000 villages destroyed; 25 million people homeless; 31 000 industrial enterprises destroyed; 65 000 kilometres of railway track destroyed; 40 per cent of agricultural output lost.[14]

In demographic and material terms no other country had had to face up to such damage. Only Yugoslavia had suffered comparably in the war. At the time, the figures were secret, less, as was suggested in the Cold War, because they had to be concealed from the population since they revealed apparent carelessness of life in the war victory, than for the obvious reason that, in the growing atmosphere of hostility, it would, rather like the figures for the military purge in the late 1930s, have encouraged foreign adventurism if the weak state of the country and economy had become known abroad. Similarly, preconditions for the Marshall Plan were, correctly, assumed by their promoters to be unacceptable to the Soviet Union in that the country would have to hand over on a plate critical information about its military and industrial capacity which foreign intelligence services were straining every sinew to discover.

The consequences were felt across the whole of society. Like France after the First World War, the Soviet Union had lost a generation of males. The productionist ideology rolled on so women were called in to take the place of men in numerous areas of labour. It was this pressure rather than any ideological promptings which brought more women into the workforce. On the whole they got the worst of all worlds. Family care was immensely time-consuming in the Soviet urban context of perennial queuing for food and other goods and services in short supply. Time-consuming bureaucratic entanglements surrounded many aspects of everyday life. At work, women were generally poorly paid second-class citizens. Occupations in which women predominated, especially services like education and medical care, were at the bottom of the Soviet salary scale, a teacher earning typically about half the wage of a bus driver. Senior posts within those professions were mainly occupied by the members of the male minority. The informal hierarchy was visible to every visitor. Motor bus drivers earned more than trolleybus drivers who, in turn earned more than tram drivers. Bus drivers were almost exclusively male, tram drivers mainly female and trolleybus drivers more or less evenly split. 'Token women' airline pilots and, eventually, cosmonauts, did not alter the fundamental inequality.

The drafting of women into the labour force and their retention in factories in which they had been employed during the war was one aspect of the reawakening productionist juggernaut that was the Soviet system. Planning returned with full force. Priority areas of heavy industry and defence meant the austerity of war continued into peacetime. Soviet consumers had to wait for Stalin's death before their needs were addressed. Within this framework, however, Soviet recovery was surprisingly rapid. The extraordinary story of the atomic and hydrogen bombs, involving information from spy rings, scientists working in enclosed prison conditions, immense concentration of material resources and the brilliance of project leaders such as Kurchatov and younger scientists like Sakharov, later to become a leading critic of the Soviet system, illustrates the bizarre complexities of the period. So does the opposite story of critical failure. Stalin dismissed rocketry as fantasy and broke up the scientific team working on it, executing leading members as traitors. It was only after the development of V-1s and V-2s that the error became obvious. Thanks to Stalin's mistake the Soviet Union (not the United States as Kennedy falsely claimed in his election campaign) suffered from a dangerous 'missile gap' which was not plugged until the mid-1960s and which had led to the near-catastrophic adventure of the Cuban missile crisis.

By the early 1950s the cult of Stalin was more grotesque than ever, whereas the reality of old age taking its toll, produced a more unpredictable and dangerous Stalin than ever. His writings became ever more pretentious, even establishing claims to linguistic expertise in *Marxism and Linguistics*, which concludes with the rather un-Stalinist thought that 'Marxism is the enemy of all dogmatism'. His last work was devoted to *The Economic Problems of Socialism*. It was as though, in his final years, Stalin was trying to round out his image as a universal genius by presenting himself as a sage.

On 1 March 1953 Stalin had not emerged from his room in his dacha by midday. Anxiety grew by the early evening but the staff, including secret police guards, were too scared to disturb him. At 11.30 in the evening they eventually did so, finding the great leader sprawled over his sofa in a semi-coma resulting, it turned out, from a stroke. Politburo colleagues were called from Moscow. Beria could not be tracked down and only arrived at 3.00 a.m. on 2 March. He dismissed the fears of the entourage saying that Stalin was simply sleeping soundly. He returned at 9.00 a.m. and only on his arrival were doctors allowed to see Stalin. While there may have been an element of calculation in this, in that colleagues were glad to be rid of the ogre, it is more likely that Stalin himself had become a victim of his own tyranny. He had created such an inflexible system that he could not even get the medical help he needed at the crucial moment. For once, at 9.50 p.m. on 5 March, it was around Stalin that the darkness closed in.[15]

Part II: Breaking the System

'It's easy to make fish soup out of an aquarium but who can make an aquarium from fish soup?'

(A saying frequently heard during *perestroika*)

7

SUCCEEDING STALIN

Stalin's Legacy

Stalin died in March 1953, but the system he had created lived on. His successors had to deal with it. The fact that they were, themselves, in large part its products did not make the need for change any less imperative. The problem was whether alterations could be made without endangering the stability of the country as a whole. From 1953 until the system's collapse in 1991 there was a strong lobby opposed to any change, because they feared collapse. On the other hand, a variety of reformers argued that leaving things as they were was the more risky course, that the system itself was ultimately unstable.

In a sense, the division between the two schools of thought reflected the ambiguities of the Stalin legacy. Stalin's achievements were captured in a well-known phrase from Isaac Deutscher. Stalin, he wrote in 1953, 'drove a nation of 160–200 million people to jump the chasm which separated the epoch of the wooden plough from that of the atomic pile'.[1] The Soviet Union was, indeed, a very different place from what it had been in the 1920s. A form of modernisation was being experienced in every sphere. For a start, it was on the verge of becoming a predominantly urban society. The growth of industry and services associated with such a change had been colossal. There did not appear to be any reason why growth at a high level should not continue into the foreseeable future. The engine room of change remained productionism, which, in Stalin's later years, had become more prominent than ever and remained the main defining characteristic of the Soviet system. In other words, ideological and revolutionary goals were transformed into a battle for production in order to catch up and overtake capitalism and lay the foundations of future communism on a basis of material abundance. Social and political life were focused on this end. As we have seen, the party had become, above all else, a supervisory, managerial and cheerleading organisation devoted to ensuring the fulfilment of the plan at all levels. Social duty focused around plan fulfilment. Not playing a part – that is, not having a job – was, at times, illegal. Services and leisure activities were often utilitarian in nature in that they encouraged better work practices. Continuing the Leninist tradition, work itself became a leisure-time activity with the continued institutionalisation of the *subbotnik* or voluntary Saturday labour devoted either to an unpaid day of regular labour – for example, to produce extra railway locomotives or rolling-stock for less well-off 'fraternal' countries – or social tasks in the town or enterprise such as tidying up the site of the workplace or a town square. Much social policy and legislation focused on keeping citizens fit for work. For instance, attempts were made to restrict vodka supplies on working days and make it more readily available at holiday weekends. Wherever one looked, work and production were at the heart of the Soviet system.

As we have seen, Isaac Deutscher also made a prescient point in his comments on Stalin, that the chief weakness of the system was its need for and extensive encouragement of education. The better educated the population, the more it would resent the restraints associated with the system. At first sight this might not seem to be obvious, in that education, at least as much as and probably more than most other areas, was heavily imprinted with productionism. Utilitarian subjects – various forms of engineering, science, medicine, mathematics, languages – dominated the curriculum. The rapidly expanding higher education system was geared to turning out producers. Officially, there was little room in the system for purely reflective and critical subjects. Literature at tertiary level was taught primarily to those who were expected to teach it in schools. Philosophy and history served the political purpose of establishing the correctness of the Marxist (or, more accurately, Marxist–Leninist–Stalinist, soon to become Marxist–Leninist) view of the world. However, even within the forbiddingly 'practical' and utilitarian ethos of the system critical thought could not be completely suppressed. By various means unofficial ideas – from theories of basic science to social and political criticism – continued to circulate by various devious channels. No matter how carefully geared to productionism the educational plans were, at the end of the day people were not robots, and expansion of official education led ineluctably to the expansion of unofficial education. Official and unofficial education produced criticism.

Deutscher had pointed to a fundamental contradiction of the system. Like its tsarist predecessor, the Stalin system wanted to educate its citizens in order to encourage economic growth. Unlike hard-line tsarism, the Soviet aim was not the absurdity of preventing change but the equally illusory hope of controlling and channelling it into the shining future prescribed by the system's 'true' theory of history. However, what Soviet citizens saw around them was not always what they were supposed to see. As well as achievements the population became increasingly aware of shortcomings and came into conflict with the increasingly disliked containment systems of Stalinism.

Since productionism was at the heart of the system it is not surprising that its shortcomings were central to the dissatisfaction of the population. As we have seen, the command economy had developed along with a command society under Stalin. Both aspects were under strain. The two chief counterproductive elements of the economic system were the overrigid, excessively bureaucratic nature of the planning system and the relatively moribund state of agriculture.

Looked at from the perspective of the twenty-first century, the notion that the whole of a modern economy, every product – from airliners to tiepins – and every service – from surgical operations to ice-cream stands – could be centrally planned seems hopelessly optimistic. Even with the much less variegated inventory of products and services characteristic of the mid-twentieth century the enterprise still seems quixotic. In some ways, it is remarkable that the system was able to have as much success as it did in that the country did, to some degree, feed, house, employ, entertain, equip and defend itself and provide increasing living standards. However, the difficulties were multiplying, particularly in the consumer sphere which was very much secondary in the Stalinist way of thinking. The system was at its best in focusing vast resources on a relatively narrow range of options – war production, for instance, or basic post-war recovery – and at its worst in providing quality consumer goods. Stories of grotesque waste surfaced in the first post-Stalin years. 'Pairs' of shoes both of which were left-footed; coats all in one extremely small size because it was economical with material; uneven availability of goods so that one would never know what might be on sale in a given place at a given time: these and myriad other problems plagued the Soviet consumer in the mid-1950s. Crude plan targets meant many products were unusable in that the specification of what was produced did not always match that which was required. Enterprise success was often measured by sheer bulk so they would produce whatever they could most easily make in vast quantities. If that did not suit their 'customers' that was not their problem. The pressure in the system was on input and, where capitalist enterprises tended to spend vast resources on marketing to persuade people that they wanted to buy the output at the highest possible price, Soviet enterprises employed key personnel, known as *tolkachi*, whose job was to scout around to find the best input available for the enterprise whether it be high-grade coal or steel, leather, glass or whatever. Diversion of loads, bribery and undercover contracts were common in the pursuit of raw materials. As far as output was concerned, demand was usually so high that even a consignment of left-footed shoes could be disposed of. The problem of plan targets even surfaced in the official press, one of the most famous examples being a cartoon depicting a factory joyfully unveiling a completely useless two million-watt light bulb with the caption 'Plan fulfilled'.

Agriculture was also the butt of official and unofficial humour and of serious concern at the top level. With typical Stalinist ambiguity the countryside had fed the army during the war and the workers after it. But it had not always fed the village itself and famines could still occur, notably in 1947, though not on the same scale as between the wars. Shortages were endemic. Only basic staples like potatoes and bread could be relied on. Milk, butter, cheese and eggs came and went. Meat and meat products never fully met demand. Those with a little more money had extensive recourse to the collective farm markets which were severely controlled on ideological grounds in the Stalin years.

Finally, planning rigidity meant innovation was becoming an increasingly serious problem, particularly since technical development was increasingly a matter of life and death in the growing age of the arms race. Massive concentration of resources had produced the Soviet atomic and hydrogen bombs but Stalin's opposition to rocketry meant there were no suitable delivery systems in the pipeline. While individual gaps could be plugged in Stalinist fashion as priority sectors, the world was on the verge of rapid product and technological development with which, as we shall see, the centrally planned system was ill-equipped to cope.

Given its mobilising nature, the system also exerted command from the centre over society itself. The authorities unashamedly set up constraints on everyone in the name of building socialism. Its main agents in this were, of course, the party and the political police. By the time of Stalin's death the party had become the medium through which what is now called civil society in democratic states interacted. Almost every aspect of public life had to go through the party. It obviously supervised politics and encouraged people to take part in public meetings and campaigns and organised voting on election days. These, however, were largely symbolic roles. More important, party membership had become essential for career promotion in almost all fields, especially business and administration. It was absolutely essential for the highest posts, the so-called *nomenklatura*. Membership of the Communist Youth League (Komsomol) was a prerequisite for higher education although most Young Communists did not go on directly to the party proper. Social and sporting life was also mediated by the party. While skilled performers did not have to be party members to represent their country they did have to conform to required norms of behaviour. All delegations were led by party members. Within the country it was impossible to set up any kind of club or even to hold a large meeting without party participation. A cycling club, rambling group or chess organisation had to be officially constituted via the party or a party-controlled organisation. The fact that many semi-military sports, especially motor sports, came under the military umbrella of an organisation called Dosaaf, a voluntary society for supporting the armed services, was hardly a mitigation of party control. Every social and cultural step had to be taken under the watchful eye of the party.

Party control was informal in that it had no right to formally sanction non-members. However, its enforcer was the political police descended from Lenin's Cheka. Through its party contacts and a network of direct informants it permeated Stalinist society. It had, since the 1930s, even become instrumental in disciplining and punishing the party itself on a wide scale. As well as party supervision the political police also had offices in major enterprises, including universities, and was particularly active in areas of economic and cultural contact with foreigners. It had become the direct instrument of Stalin's dictatorship and, at the time of his death, was headed by his fellow-Georgian associate, Lavrentii Beria, who had held the post since the end of 1938. As well as the police, the censorship system had become ubiquitous in the Stalin years and it was impossible to print even a bus ticket or product label without official approval.

Political control had also led to cold war and international isolation. True, by 1953 the Soviet Union was no longer a single country standing alone but a socialist camp of formidable size in terms of population and area since it included China and much of Eastern Europe. However, it was much less impressive in terms of prestige, influence and weaponry, where the United States still reigned supreme. In the late Stalin years, following the Berlin crisis, relations with the capitalist powers were about as bad as they could be and diplomatic, economic and cultural contact remained limited. The Soviet Union did not, for example, participate in the 1948 London Olympics though it did already have some sporting contacts, the famous visit of the Moscow Dynamo soccer team to Britain in 1945, for example.[2] Helsinki 1952 was the first Summer Olympics in which they competed and it was only in 1956 that the first Soviet team appeared at the Winter Olympics, held in Cortina, Italy.

In sum, then, Stalin's legacy reflected the ambiguities of his rule. A rudimentary welfare state with full employment existed. Healthcare and education were available free of charge for all citizens at all levels, though there were considerable inequalities in take-up of these services and in the quality provided across the vast geographical area of the Soviet Union. Living standards were also slowly rising and the economy was expanding. The country also appeared to be united and, beyond the grumbling of a few intellectuals, there was no apparent nationality problem. These were no mean achievements. However, there were many economic bottlenecks and cultural constraints on personal well-being. Formal ownership of immovable property tended to remain with the state and private cars were frowned upon for ideological reasons. Official restraints exercised through the party and the political police were so extensive that, at least in terms of aspiration to control, the word 'totalitarian' still does not seem out of place, and no better one has been found to point out the distinctive nature of a ubiquitous, mobilising system of the Stalinist kind. However, even before Stalin's death the zeal which had brought about the particular forms of the Soviet system was already flagging and the exhortatory institutions had themselves become devoid of revolutionary energy and were being filled instead with the old bugbear of 'careerist' aspirations. Combined with the vast scope of central control, the system was spawning an immense bureaucracy in all fields. There was an ever-increasing tendency for those who belonged to it to look for their own comfort and privileges and to pay less and less attention to the ideological drive of building socialism. This was the complex legacy with which Stalin's successors had to deal.

Immediate Steps

Correcting the problems left by Stalin, in a word, de-Stalinisation, was at the heart of the strategic orientation of every post-Stalin Soviet government. Under Khrushchev and Gorbachev, changes – reforms – were actively pursued. Under Brezhnev much less spectacular, but in many ways equally influential, policies were followed which, unwittingly, did a great deal to undermine the Stalin system. However, the process of change did not begin with Khrushchev's famous 'secret' speech in February 1956. It began almost as soon as Stalin died. Three momentous changes, unthinkable under Stalin himself, took place even before Khrushchev had secured himself in power.

The most pressing problem was that Stalin's demise left a crucial, Stalin-shaped hole at the centre of the system, a gap made much more significant by the vast cult of personality, which had become a central prop of national politics. How would the gap be filled? For many years, from Khrushchev's own memoirs, we have been able to glimpse the difficulties and dangers facing the leadership at that crucial moment. The wrong word in the wrong ear could have meant arrest and possible execution. The problem was that Beria, Stalin's police chief and a man of appalling degeneracy according to the stories about him circulated later, seemed to be in the best position to take over Stalin's mantle and, most probably, intimidate and even terrorise his fellow-leaders. Whatever differences the rest of the Politburo had with each other, a common bond of survival linked Khrushchev with Molotov, Malenkov and the rest. Secret conversations in the Kremlin gardens, out of earshot of Beria's microphones, led to a dramatic coup. With the assistance of Zhukov and the army leadership – needed to counter any attempt by Beria to manoeuvre his own security forces – the trap was sprung. On 26 June Beria was arrested at a Politburo meeting at which several members were carrying guns in case things got out of hand. Zhukov remained outside the meeting with a squad of armed troops. Beria was successfully arrested and carried away to the cells. He was secretly tried and executed on 24 December, the last political execution in Soviet history. Already the bloodiest page of Stalin's misrule had been turned.

If Stalin-style terror was now off the agenda what about its millions of surviving victims languishing in camps? Here, too, dramatic events were in the offing. News of Stalin's death had caused riots in many camps as political prisoners collectively protested their innocence.[3] To the surprise of many, releases began quickly. At first they were only a trickle but within three or four years millions of inmates were allowed back into mainstream society. To prevent them from flooding out the major cities they were only allowed to reside in smaller towns and rural areas – one of the most famous of them, Solzhenitsyn, winding up in a village called

Turf (meaning peat) in Riazan province – but it was a return to much greater freedom and a vast improvement on camp life. From that time onward the number of political prisoners was probably in the range of 10–25 000, in itself bad enough but certainly not comparable to the Stalin years. Many of the post-Stalin internees were actually imprisoned for religious reasons. The largest categories were pacifists who refused to do national service and spent a term in the camps instead and Jehovah's Witnesses who obstructed medical treatment for their children on grounds of conscience. Significantly, a number of, initially, lone voices spreading nationalist ideals among the larger minorities of the Caucasus, Ukraine and Baltic States also found themselves in camps.

Dramatic change was not confined to internal politics. Believing that, in many respects, the Cold War had been encouraged by Stalin's intransigence, the new government made a number of extraordinary gestures in response to the new American President Eisenhower's call for the opening of a new era of post-Stalin international relations. A truce was declared in Korea. Israel and West Germany were recognised. Yugoslavia was gradually recognised as a socialist state. The Soviet armed forces gave up their base at Porkkala in Finland, strengthening the view that 'Finlandisation' might have been a viable alternative to Sovietisation in Eastern Europe and Germany. A further indication of this came with the negotiation of the Austrian State Treaty (1955) under which, in return for a guarantee of its neutrality, the control of Austria between the four great powers was ended and Soviet, American, British and French occupation forces withdrew. Vienna was liberated six years before the Berlin Wall was even built. Soviet policy claimed it would accept the same model for Germany – withdrawal and reunification in exchange for neutrality. Incidentally, even in 1990 the same formula reappeared. Western ideologists of the Cold War claimed that Soviet policy on reunification was bluff throughout but it was cruelly negligent that the option was never seriously put to the test. Instead, western policy, dominated by the arch-hawk John Foster Dulles rather than the more pragmatic Eisenhower, favoured a vastly expensive and dangerous arms race, the nuclear consequences of which still cast a giant shadow over international affairs as the bad example of the first nuclear powers is followed by more and more countries around the globe. Instead of offering a basis for a new relationship with the outside world, the Austrian State Treaty was interpreted by the west, deep in the grip of McCarthyite cold warriors, as a sign of uncertainty, confusion and weakness in the post-Stalin Soviet leadership. If the new Soviet leaders did believe Stalin had worsened the Cold War, the rude reaction of the United States over the Austrian State Treaty disabused them and made them much harsher in their future dealings with such an apparently implacable foe.

One other international development confirmed the tone. At Geneva in 1954 a conference drew up a 'post-war' settlement for Vietnam as the French withdrew after defeat at Dien Bien Phu. It entailed temporary division of the country into northern and southern military zones to be followed by reunification elections in the whole country in 1956. The United States refused to recognise the treaty and tore it up in 1956 by refusing to allow elections in the south, which it was certain would be won by the nationalist communists of Ho Chi Minh. The United States also approved German rearmament in 1955, a move which led to Moscow taking the initiative in forming the Warsaw Pact as a means for coordinating the military policies of the Soviet bloc countries, a kind of eastern NATO. If 1954 had offered a moment of reconciliation by 1955/6 it was fast disappearing, and the legacy of Stalin in international affairs was proving more obdurate than it had at first appeared to the new leaders.

Khrushchev and the First *Perestroika*

Khrushchev's emergence as Soviet leader can be attributed to three factors above all. First, he had undoubtedly stolen a march on the apparently more powerful Malenkov by leading the risky campaign against Beria while Malenkov was still supporting him. Malenkov's second mistake was to opt for a leading role in the state institutions, since Stalin had used them rather than the party to impose his rule, and Malenkov expected the same system to continue. Stalin, however, had also set out as General Secretary of the party and it was Khrushchev who presciently took up the equivalent role of First Secretary. From this position he set out to regenerate the party and, in so doing, develop his own career. This was the second factor. He was able to label opponents of this correction of one of Stalin's abuses as the 'anti-party group', making them appear to be opposed to the revival of the party. The third factor was the much more widely-known speech he made to the closed session of the Twentieth Party Congress, a speech somewhat misleadingly called the secret speech because, although it was not published in the Soviet Union at the time, it did circulate throughout the medium levels of the party and its contents quickly became known and were acted on. It was published in its entirety abroad from copies distributed to foreign communists and from the copy thoughtfully provided for the American CIA by the KGB.

The speech was the main rallying cry of Khrushchev's campaigning rule. In it he denounced certain aspects of Stalin's governance of the Soviet Union. The careful way Khrushchev dealt with the thorny issue illustrates the delicacy of the moment and, even though Khrushchev did not write the speech, most of the text apparently coming from a draft report of a commission on Stalin set up by the Central Committee of the party, it did show the line of his attack. The speech was by no means a root-and-branch denunciation of Stalin. In the first place he was only said to have diverged from 'Leninist norms' in the early 1930s, thus there was no question of revising the issue of collectivisation, nor was the issue of the famine raised. Stalin was also praised for his war leadership though Khrushchev did, for the first time, raise the question of Stalin's inactivity in the face of the invasion, implying he had had a breakdown, something which has not been fully confirmed by documentary evidence. The main line of attack, however, was over Stalin's abuse of the party rather than the country. Here, too, Khrushchev raised a spectre which has haunted historiography ever since and has also to be confirmed. He accused Stalin of complicity in Kirov's murder. This was a particularly appropriate accusation for Khrushchev to make since Kirov was still a revered figure. To imply Stalin had been involved in his death was truly shocking to Khrushchev's listeners. By and large, Khrushchev concentrated on similar, loyal party figures who had become Stalin's victims. There was no attack on the show trials as such, nor was there any attempt to rehabilitate the leading victims. While one might have imagined that Bukharin at least might be declared innocent, Khrushchev passed over that can of worms which would have led to the trickier cases of Kamenev and Zinoviev and ultimately to Trotsky who remained the arch-enemy and chief renegade. However, it can be seen that the main thrust of criticism fitted in with Khrushchev's wider policy of restoring the party. Stalin's chief crime was to have abused it and to have brought about the death of masses of innocent, hard-working, loyal communists of whom Kirov was the role model. In place of party rule by decent, ordinary communists, Khrushchev asserted that Stalin had established state – that is, direct secret police – rule and a personal dictatorship encased in the cult of his personality. Tactically, too, the ploy suited Khrushchev because, by implication, he could accuse his chief rivals of complicity by not having denounced Stalin's crimes and establish himself, in the eyes of the party members before whom he made his speech, as the champion of its restoration to primacy.

Limited though it was in scope, the speech was a start and as such it had a profound and well-known impact not only in the Soviet Union but in Eastern Europe and the world in general. There were disturbances in East Germany, a full-scale uprising in Hungary and convulsions in the western parties, leading many communists to resign and to set up alternative 'new left' organisations and journals. It is not without irony that it was the moment the party began to come to grips with Stalin's crimes that it should suffer such a crisis of confidence around the world from the anti-Stalinist elements it appeared to be supporting. But it has to be remembered that, for many communists, Stalin's reputation, particularly as the chief cause of the downfall of Nazism and Fascism, was high, albeit not unblemished by his 'mistakes'. To turn the debate from mistakes to crimes was an enormous shock. On the other hand, less critical admirers of Stalin were shocked by Khrushchev's betrayal of their leader, none more so than Mao Zedong and the Chinese leadership which eventually denounced Khrushchev as a 'revisionist' watering down the tough revolutionary doctrine of Bolshevism. In China, Stalin remained a revered figure and, as the cult rapidly wound down in the USSR, so, in Beijing, Stalin's works, posters of him and so on continued to be produced. At the other extreme, Tito's communist movement, which had been banished from the ranks of orthodoxy by Stalin, was welcomed back as a member with a status quite different from that of the Soviet 'bloc' proper. This was signified by its non-adherence to the Warsaw Pact and together, eventually, with that other independent communist gadfly Castro's Cuba, its association with the non-aligned movement. True to form, whatever Yugoslavia did Albania did the opposite, setting itself up, under Enver Hoxha, as the world's last hard-line Stalinist enclave.

It is clear from the above that 1956 was a major watershed for international communism. One of the bedrocks of Stalinism, not to mention Leninism with its 21 conditions for admittance to the Comintern which were intended to turn it into a worldwide Bolshevik party, had been broken down. Communist unity had shattered. Beijing (and Tiranë) increasingly denounced Soviet revisionism. Yugoslavia and later Cuba went their own way. Western communists, notably the Italians, talked of different roads to socialism, and even within the puppet regimes of Eastern Europe national characteristics and idiosyncrasies began to emerge. Although the more determined cold warriors tended to dismiss the obvious evidence as a vast game of bluff and deliberate deception on the part of Moscow which was still seen by them as having an iron grip over the world communist movement, the term 'polycentrism' became current among foreign observers to describe the emerging situation. World communism had clearly gone beyond Moscow's control and the last, vestigial internationalist coordinating body, Cominform, was wound up in 1956. Moscow had to find its way in a much more complicated world than that of Stalin's imperialist and socialist camps. In particular, Moscow no longer had a monopoly on producing orthodox doctrine. Foreign communists, and even left-wing dissidents, proved more dynamic than Moscow in developing Marxist ideas culminating in events like the Prague Spring and movements like Eurocommunism, the principles of which were reflected back into the Soviet Union itself and had a profound effect.[4]

Ironically, the immediate effect of the speech in the Soviet Union was muted but it did begin important processes. The cult of Stalin's personality wound down more and more rapidly. His image, words and statues began to disappear. Towns, factories, farms, hospitals, schools and all the rest were renamed, most notably Stalingrad itself which became Volgograd in 1961 at the same time as the most symbolic blow fell with Stalin's body being removed from the mausoleum in Red Square and buried, reportedly under a thick layer of concrete, alongside other prominent revolutionary figures in the Kremlin wall. To this day, however, his bust remains in the garden at the back of the mausoleum.

Khrushchev was serious about revival of the party. It already, as we have seen, had a hand in every aspect of Soviet life and Khrushchev had no intention of changing that. He did, however, foster important developments. In the first place the party was practically doubled in size to over 11 million members. The change was intended to strengthen it by giving it much wider representation through society and to enable it to penetrate ever deeper into workplaces and enterprises. Party membership was still a badge of conformity, conservatism, loyalty, leadership and, frequently, achievement rather than a political commitment in the more widely accepted sense. Second, the party was elevated to first place among Soviet institutions. Leninist subordination of state posts to party ones was restored. Under Khrushchev, however, the state was put in its place. The secret police was reorganised, went through its last Soviet change of acronym to become the KGB (State Security Commission) in April 1954 and was placed under firm party leadership. The key central institution of the party, its Central Committee, was revived. Its membership came to include key figures from local party organisations in the large towns, key *oblasts* (counties or provinces) and the non-Russian republics as well as controllers of the military, police, censorship and cultural apparatuses and so on. It was expanded in size to cover these fields and it met on a more regular basis. In 1952 it had 233 members, in 1961, 330. By 1966 it had 360 members, by 1981 a massive 470. In 1958 it met six times but an average of around two or three times per year became more typical. While the Presidium (formerly Politburo) remained the main, cabinet-like, decision-making body, the Central Committee's importance grew to the extent that it became the legitimating base for the Presidium itself. In an irony of ironies it was eventually the Central Committee, which owed everything to Khrushchev, that voted him out of office. Khrushchev was, in his own way, proud of this outcome. In the early years, however, the changes worked very much in his favour as, once again, they had a tactical impact in removing the power from his rivals with leading state rather than party positions, notably Malenkov as 'Prime Minister'. For this and other reasons, Khrushchev was finally able to dismiss his 'anti-party group' rivals in 1957 and govern unchallenged for seven years before having the unique experience for a Soviet leader of being voted out of office in 1964. Until its ultimate collapse, posts in the Soviet state remained secondary to those in the party and the secretaryship of the party was the main power base of subsequent Soviet leaders. In this respect, the first *perestroika* differed significantly from that of the late 1980s when Gorbachev attempted to restore independent life to state institutions and personally divested himself of his party roles and took up, instead, the Soviet presidency which had been a purely formal post until that moment.

Khrushchev's reforming zeal was not confined to the party and spread to many other areas of apparent Stalinist dysfunctionality. Most of the attempted reforms of the period were associated with perceived problems of the Stalin legacy. In the forefront, we have already identified overrigid, overcentralised planning as key problems holding back productive efficiency and economic growth. While he remained firmly within the productionist mentality, Khrushchev attempted to achieve its ends in a less directly controlled fashion. As far as industry was concerned he made two major changes. First, most economic ministries were broken down into over 100 regional economic councils (*sovnarkhozy*) and, second, he diverted a larger proportion of investment towards the needs of ordinary citizens in the form of increased expenditure on housing and consumer goods, notably fridges and televisions which

began to appear in Soviet homes. The economic space for this investment was partly created by reducing military expenditure. The number
of military personnel fell considerably but, as sceptics pointed out, much
of the reduction was the consequence of switching to a nuclear-based
strategy.

Neither of these initiatives was a notable success. The new regional
planners fought with each other over resources and overlapping responsibilities since large enterprises required inputs from, and distributed
their products to, several of the new economic regions. Each region
tended to hang on to its raw materials and outputs, further complicating
nationwide exchanges and thereby putting pressure on economic growth
rates. While the idea of bringing planners closer to producers was not in
itself a bad one, the form of implementation was disastrous and was abandoned quickly after Khrushchev's downfall. Token gestures also failed to
satisfy consumers. The housing provided was of poor quality, notably,
apartments thrown up were small and the accommodation cramped.
They were soon dubbed 'Khrushchev slums', which was rather harsh, but
the solution to the housing problem certainly lay far in the future.

Agriculture also showed the same kind of approach – potentially good
ideas unsupported by serious ancillary measures. Opening up virgin
lands and expelling the Agricultural Ministry from Moscow to a collective farm were the most striking measures. Khrushchev was also known
for his faddish enthusiasms, none more than his infatuation with maize
after seeing the extent of its cultivation during a prolonged visit to the
United States. There was also a brief return to Lysenkoism – the scientific quackery that promised miracle results for agricultural production.

Once again, token gestures failed to work. The virgin land scheme was
pushed too far, upsetting the delicately balanced ecology of the steppes
and creating barren dust bowls. Harvests fluctuated wildly in the Khrushchev years. His political career was boosted by the excellence of the 1954
harvest in the virgin lands, and finally undermined by poor results and
declining returns in the early 1960s. However, the fluctuations showed that
no stable solution to agricultural problems had yet been arrived at.

The Khrushchev years were also noted as a period of cultural 'thaw'.
Indeed, the cultural monotony of the post-war Stalin years was modified. In literature, Dudintsev and Solzhenitsyn focused attention on the
camps. Voznesensky and Evtushenko declaimed their anti-Stalin verses
to halls, even stadia, crowded with thousands of listeners. A wider
repertoire was permitted in theatre, opera and ballet. In academic life
socially analytical subjects like history gained a slightly wider space for

interpretation through the works of Zaionchkovsky on late tsarism and the controversial publications of Burdzhalov on the February revolution, published in 1956, and Nekrich on the crisis of 1941, published in the mid-1960s. Sociology began to emerge as a separate discipline.

What, at the end of the day, did Khrushchev's reforms amount to? Did they constitute a new direction for the Soviet system? Khrushchev's greatest strength was that he had identified the most dysfunctional features of Stalinism – the cult of the leader, the power of the political police, the eclipse of the party, the rigidity of the command economy, the stultifying cultural monotony, the dangers of the cold war. However, he did not find suitable solutions nor did he move out of the strategic framework of Stalinism. His reforms were tinkerings within the system he inherited rather than radical alterations. Khrushchev remained within the 'Stalinist' mentality in numerous ways. He did not waver in his commitment to the Soviet version of socialism, nor did he doubt the well-entrenched method of building it from above through extensive cultural manipulation and productionism. He constantly proclaimed that the USSR would outproduce the capitalist world, indeed, that it would 'bury' capitalism. A perspective 20-year programme was introduced in 1961 which promised the achievement of the basic essentials of communism. His cultural 'thaw' was aimed at centrally determined goals, notably the anti-Stalin campaign. It was, therefore, as instrumentalist as any previous Soviet cultural policy. There was no room for real toleration, nor any sense that art and literature were mature enough to look after themselves. The blundering refusal to allow Pasternak to receive the Nobel prize for *Doctor Zhivago* and the continuing refusal to publish it in the USSR, showed the narrow limitations of the thaw. Even though certain of Solzhenitsyn's works were published, notably *A Day in the Life of Ivan Denisovich* and *Matryona's Home*, his great novels *The First Circle* and *Cancer Ward* never quite made it into print.

Elsewhere, Khrushchev's reforms bore the mark of apparently crafty, low-cost short cuts which had not been really thought through, for instance the reorganisation of the economic and agricultural apparatuses and the virgin lands scheme. Nothing shows these characteristics better than the decision to base nuclear missiles in Cuba. Inspired by the proximity of American missiles in Turkey to key areas of the Soviet Union, Khrushchev thought he could overcome the real problem of delivering Soviet missiles to American targets by stationing them equally close to the United States and seeing how they liked it. Unfortunately for him, US intelligence revealed the scheme before the installation was complete and, after a well-known and well-documented brush with nuclear war, the crisis was defused and Khrushchev withdrew the missiles, gaining in exchange withdrawal of Turkish-based missiles and a guarantee not to invade Cuba, which has held up to the present moment.

Khrushchev's reforms remained very limited. He did not have the radical imagination to question fundamentally deeper assumptions of the system. He refused, for example, to acknowledge any democratic deficit in Soviet society and certainly did not intend to allow the leadership to lose its grip. He, himself, never had the same personal power as Stalin at his peak, but power still remained within a very narrow elite. The leader depended on the Presidium and, as Khrushchev showed in 1957 when he outsmarted Malenkov and as his own opponents showed in 1964 when they outsmarted him, the Central Committee could be a vital arbiter of disputes. But politics in any real sense never extended beyond these circles. Khrushchev, like his model, Lenin, believed his mandate came from possession of perfect historical vision and ownership of the key to the future of the human race. There was no need for mandates to be provided by a fickle and easily swayed electorate other than in the form of 99.9 per cent voting in support of the leadership. He was fully convinced that the rights of Soviet citizens were greater than those of American and Western European citizens, whose hypocritical democracies were colonised by millionaires and major financial interests and who were subject to ruthless 'market' pressures of unemployment and economic insecurity engineered by those at the top. In the west, Soviet ideologists argued, democracy stopped at the gates of the enterprise. In the Soviet Union, workers' councils supposedly gave voice to workers' concerns and they could criticise their management without fear of dismissal. Khrushchev also expected communism to outproduce capitalism economically and it was against this background of expected success that 'peaceful coexistence' – seen in Moscow as the context for the economic obliteration of capitalism – came to dominate international relations. While, in the 1950s, growth rates appeared to show that there was some catching up taking place, it soon came to nothing in the technological explosion of later decades, replication of which, as we shall see, was quite beyond the Soviet Union.

Khrushchev's commitment to socialism and his distance from any form of liberalism is shown in one of his most deeply implemented policies. Between 1959 and 1964 over 50 per cent of Soviet churches were shut down. At first sight such a policy seems to make little sense against the background of reforms intended to ease the lot of Soviet citizens and to go against the grain of any supposed cultural thaw. However, it could be seen to fit in with aspects of Khrushchev's policy. It demonstrated his unwavering commitment to traditional Soviet values of replacing religion with scientific thought (Gagarin, the first man in space, supposedly helping the cause by saying that he had not seen God on his travels) and 'protecting' Soviet citizens from the wily influence of priests who played on popular emotions, beliefs and superstitions. It could even be seen, in part, as anti-Stalinist since Stalin had improved relations with the church during the war and allowed it greater freedoms. Khrushchev claimed he was, as in other respects, returning to Leninist rectitude and correcting Stalinist aberration. He never doubted he was doing Soviet citizens a service. As a result of the closures, churches virtually disappeared from rural areas.

Limited though the reforms were by the persistence of the cultural dimension of revolution and the all-pervasive mentality of productionism, nonetheless Khrushchev did have important credits to his name. The primacy of the party lasted for another generation and held the system together. The Central Committee remained powerful. There were no more blood purges or political executions after 1953. Fallen politicians like Molotov and Khrushchev himself could live out their lives in comfort and security, even producing their historically invaluable reminiscences on the quiet. The police-informer network remained ubiquitous but not all-powerful. Soviet consumers remained hard-pressed but, undeniably, had never had it so good. The Soviet Union was a force to be reckoned with around the globe and was the only significant point of resistance to American domination. Under Khrushchev, a new balance had come about within the system. The worst aspects of Stalinism had been eliminated, but the fundamental system remained – a command economy, a narrow political leadership, a claim to control all areas of life, the goal of building socialism from above, productionism as the day-to-day focus of policy-making and a continuing commitment to mass education, health service and full employment. Could the balance be maintained?

8

DE-STALINISATION HALTED

Curiously, what were to become key features of the Brezhnev period were captured in a wartime report of August 1942 by a regimental Political Commissar on the activities of Brezhnev and other political officers in the 18th Army. The report concluded presciently that they were 'incapable of bringing about the desired improvement in mood and behaviour' and that the group of cronies to which Brezhnev belonged was 'a negligent, complacent, familiar, mutually-backscratching bunch of boozers'.[1] If the Khrushchev era was characterised by often ill-thought-out experiments, the Brezhnev years were characterised by stagnation, stifling repression, corruption and complacency. Yet under this unappealing shell, vital changes were continuing in Soviet society which made it fit less and less easily into the role assigned to it by the leadership.

The early Brezhnev years are noteworthy mainly for the reversal of certain of Khrushchev's most unpopular changes – the division of the party into agrarian and industrial sections was abolished; the regional economic councils were reintegrated under the centre; the Ministry of Agriculture was reinstated; routine rotation of posts was abandoned; the central planning agency (Gosplan) and the economic ministries were restored to primacy. There was also an eventual refusal to grant enterprises more independence to fulfil their plan targets, despite the promptings of the second most influential person in the leadership, Alexei Kosygin. There were rumours that, at the 1966 Party Congress, steps would be taken to rehabilitate Stalin. In the end, nothing substantial was said. The congress did restore the name Politburo in place of Presidium to give the impression of a return to revolutionary, and Stalinist, roots but nothing more significant emerged. In 1965, two writers, Andrei Siniavsky and Iulii Daniel, were arrested and eventually sentenced to terms in the camps for their 'anti-Soviet' activities. Already the Brezhnev hallmarks were apparent. The organisational changes showed a new policy of appeasing the *apparatchiki*; the refusal to reform emphasised conservatism and timidity; the arrest of writers spoke of narrow philistinism with anti-Semitic overtones; and the name change showed a desire to give an appearance of change rather than its substance. So the Brezhnev reign was to go on.

The core of Brezhnev's approach to the system was what has become known as 'stability of cadres'. In reality, this bland title was the cover for a series of obnoxious and, eventually, self-defeating characteristics. A blind eye was turned to nest-feathering and corruption by senior administrators and managers. Acceptance into the upper levels of society – the party-approved *nomenklatura* – opened the way to a comfortable job for life, lubricated by privileged access to imported goods, better apartments and state-owned dachas in select, unobtrusive areas. Where Khrushchev had made the mistake, politically at least, of undermining the security of senior bureaucrats by frequent sackings and demotions, the new rulers curried their favour by giving them almost complete security. From the Politburo and Central Committee down it was almost unknown for anyone to be sacked. The number of top jobs expanded steadily so that, for example, the Central Committee numbered 360 in 1966 and 470 in 1981 at the end of the Brezhnev period. Of these, 44 per cent had remained in post throughout the period with the result that the average age of the membership rose from 56 to 63.[2] The party itself also expanded from 12.4 to 17.4 million members.[3]

The Brezhnev leaders only had to see a problem to turn away from it. They shied away from internal controversy in almost every area. It was fear of revealing differences which led it to kick the Stalin issue around in the dust, in the hope that it would disappear rather than make a decision about it. Similarly, economic reform was watered down to virtual non-existence. Instead, the Brezhnev years became the classic age of trying to 'speed up' the system by exhortation alone.

The Brezhnev compromise did not stop at the elite. Workers, who had rioted under Khrushchev, were courted through job security, declining work discipline and controlled flows of vodka. Workers drifted from job to job. Drunkenness at the workplace became endemic. Productivity declined steadily. Farmers also benefited. In order to try to prop up food production, vast resources were invested in agriculture and rural incomes, for once, rose more quickly than urban incomes. The result?

Reliance on food imports from the west from the early 1970s onwards. Only more thorough institutional change would have helped agriculture out of its relative backwardness.

A Soviet form of 'consumerism' did continue in these years. Beginning under Khrushchev, more investment went into housing. Televisions and refrigerators became standard household items. Frowned on by Khrushchev, under Brezhnev private car ownership began to develop for the elite, a whole new city being developed to build a small saloon car, based on Fiat design and machine tools, which was still in production twenty years later. Leisure activities also developed. Parks, palaces of culture, swimming pools and sports facilities spread. Great national spectator sports evolved which became immensely popular. Soviet sports people became world-class performers in ice-skating, ice hockey, basketball, soccer, athletics, track and field and lesser Olympic disciplines, not to mention the wilder extremes such as motorcycle ice-speedway which was popular in the Urals. Weekend skiing, mushroom-picking, fishing, country walking became popular according to season, with hordes of city dwellers cramming onto the suburban *elektrichkas* in main railway stations on Saturdays and Sundays. Simple equipment for these activities was readily available and cheap. For the more intellectual and musical, books and many musical instruments were cheap as were theatre and ballet tickets, if you could get hold of them for highly-rated performances. A characteristically Brezhnevite system often operated here as elsewhere. If you wanted a ticket, it helped to have a privilege to trade in return for it, perhaps a copy of a book in short supply. Foreign currency also usually managed to do the trick. Far and away the most popular cultural activity was visiting the cinema, where a wide range of Soviet-made and a small number of officially approved, re-edited or innocuous foreign films were shown, including the 'anti-Fascist' classic *Sound of Music*. At a more material level, food prices remained stable as wages rose, thereby reducing real costs. Staples like bread were so inexpensive and became so readily available that farmers bought it as a cheap alternative to animal feeds. Meat consumption reached record highs, based on imported maize to feed the livestock. Here, too, mutual backscratching reigned supreme, the best-quality foodstuffs rarely reaching the shelves, but being put aside for customers who would pay a premium or make an exchange of some other prized product. Collective farm markets, with prices usually at least three to five times higher than in state shops where goods sold out quickly and queues were endemic, burgeoned. The price differential prompted fraud, and it was not unknown for goods delivered to state stores to be transferred, in whole or in part, to markets with the extra profit being divided among the state shop assistants and managers. Even in education and health, bribes such as undercover payments were not unknown to ensure access to better schools or to better medical treatment. An extensive black market, in part officially tolerated, greeted foreign visitors with demands for western goods, especially records, magazines, jeans and trainers and tempting but risky offers of unofficial currency exchange at five times or more the official rate. All along the line, a parallel economy or parallel system was building up.

Oddly, this growing shambles was watched over by the KGB. At times, central and regional officials promoted backlashes against the growing laxity. In the last ideological redoubt, the party agitation, propaganda and cultural departments, the icy, ascetic figure of the Stalin veteran Mikhail Suslov loomed like a ghost of the forgotten past. He was the power behind the remaining, arbitrary, ideological initiatives, such as the trial of Siniavsky and Daniel. By the early 1970s a widespread unofficial press had grown up. Leading figures such as Solzhenitsyn, Sakharov and the Leninist historian Roy Medvedev and his twin brother Zhores, a geneticist, had published important critiques of the system to which we will return. *The Chronicle of Current Events* appeared regularly with accounts of the Soviet government's violations of its own laws. A Lithuanian Catholic Chronicle did the same for instances of religious persecution and many other unofficial manuscripts circulated through the 1970s. They included banned works from abroad, Kafka and Orwell, for instance; banned Russian literature such as the poetry of Mandelstam and the prose of Mikhail Bulgakov; memoirs; political tracts from rabid right to anarchist left. It was part of the Brezhnev compromise that the underground circulation of such material among the 'harmless' circles of the intelligentsia was permitted as a safety valve and also as an energy absorber – given that many of the items, including full-length novels, circulated in typescript and it was expected that each reader would produce a new copy and pass both on. It also provided a readily available barometer of the mood of the intelligentsia, thereby helping the authorities. A joke of the time said the KGB spent half its budget on suppressing public opinion and the other half on finding out what it was. The fact that dissent was tolerated is shown not least by the fact that, when the second Cold War struck in the early 1980s, the dissident movement was shut down almost overnight. However, any attempt to spread the principles to workers was stamped on immediately.

There were, however, some issues which even the Brezhnev regime knew it could not afford to ignore. In this sense, its most important and most consequential act was the suppression of the Prague Spring in 1968.

As we have noted, since the revelations of 1956 a wave of renewal and dialogue had swept through non-Soviet Marxism. Humanistic Marxist thinkers like Adam Schaff and Leszek Kolakowski in Poland and others elsewhere in the bloc had begun to move away from the authoritarian and elitist norms of Leninism–Stalinism, though they often did it, as did Khrushchev himself and, for a while, Gorbachev later on, in the name of a more 'liberal' Lenin. Such a Lenin was largely spurious, and the manoeuvre was often tactical but nonetheless it did open up a certain amount of space for discussion. A series of Marxist–Christian dialogues, for example, were held which symbolised the parallel *aggorniamentos* of Marxism and Vatican II Catholicism taking place in the early 1960s. However, it was in Czechoslovakia that things went furthest, not least because the country was still groaning under the repressive rule of one of the least de-Stalinised parties in Eastern Europe. When change came, in early 1968, it came with a rush. Alexander Dubček was elected party leader and a democratising Action Plan was adopted and began to be implemented. Despite constant reassurances of loyalty to the Warsaw bloc and commitment to communism, surrounding regimes, notably in East Germany, feared the uncontrolled spread of the new Marxism. True to form, the Kremlin leadership hesitated. It sent troops in on manoeuvres and withdrew them again. But in August 1968 the hesitation was brutally ended and a massive Warsaw Pact military force was sent in. The Czech party leaders were unceremoniously bundled away to Moscow in what amounted to a kidnapping, and were browbeaten into acceptance of the invasion. In his memoirs *Night Frost in Prague* one of the leading reformers, Zdenek Mlynar, reported Brezhnev's appearance among the bruised and maltreated Czech leaders. In a typically long and rambling plea he made it clear that the Soviet Union would not tolerate the Czech experiment. However, it was more on the grounds of not jeopardising the Yalta agreements than on ideological grounds. The Soviet Union, Brezhnev argued with tears in his eyes, had bought its right to security with 20 million dead and had freed the Czechs from Nazi occupation. Nothing would be permitted which might reverse that outcome. In the words of Mlynar, who was a member of the Czechoslovak delegation:

Brezhnev's logic was simple:– We in the Kremlin came to the conclusion that we could not depend on you any longer. You do what you feel like in domestic policies, even things that displease us, and you are not open to positive suggestions. But your country lies on territory where the Soviet soldier trod in the Second World War. We bought that territory at the cost of enormous sacrifices and we will never leave it. The borders of that area are our borders as well.

'For us,' Brezhnev went on, 'the results of the Second World War are inviolable.'[4]

Looking back, this central episode of the Brezhnev years gains poignancy as a possible moment when communism might have revived itself. Had the new ideas been allowed to develop, a form of *perestroika* might have succeeded. The international context was much more favourable than the late 1980s when hard-line right-wing politicians dominated in the west. In 1968, the United States had its plate full with Vietnam and was reeling from the Tet offensive which, though it failed to reach the objectives set for it by Hanoi, had revealed to the American population the falsity of military claims that just one more little push would win the war. In Germany, Willy Brandt was pursuing an Ostpolitik and, in a smaller way, so was Harold Wilson's Labour government in Britain. De Gaulle was talking of European unity 'from the Atlantic to the Urals'. The ideas of the Prague Spring were shared by a vast younger generation around the world and it fed into a massive movement against the Vietnam War and the nuclear arms race. Tantalisingly, anything might have happened. The uncharacteristically resolute slamming of the door by Moscow ensured that nothing would. For the following two decades Soviet leaders appeared to lack confidence in themselves and seemed content to peep fearfully over the top of their fortress to look mistrustingly at the outside world. At times, of course, their mistrust was justified but they seemed unable to distinguish such moments from those promising a real possibility of improved relations. True, the regime moved on from 'peaceful coexistence' to 'mutually beneficial cooperation' but, though economic linkages grew apace, the Soviet leaders tried to preserve their world apart.

Curiously, the sense of insecurity of the Brezhnev leadership and its mistrust of the west reaped rich rewards. Khrushchev had attempted to come to terms with the United States and improve the atmosphere of international relations but his initiatives had been treated with contempt by American cold warriors. The Brezhnev leadership, by contrast, shipped large quantities of vital weapons and economic aid to Vietnam; built up its own nuclear arsenal including submarines which could fire missiles from positions even closer to the American coast than bases in Cuba; launched space rockets galore; constructed the world's first permanently manned space station and set endurance records for space flight. The 1970s saw a series of global advances for Soviet influence. The United States was ejected from Vietnam and its chosen successor was wiped out. Cambodia and Laos also fell to revolutionary forces. America was put on the defensive over the bloody overthrow of the democratically elected leftist government in Chile and the establishment of Pinochet's vengeful dictatorship. The collapse of Fascism in the Iberian peninsula opened up new opportunities for left-wing movements, and Spanish communism enjoyed a brief moment of influence. In Italy the communists hovered on the verge of becoming the largest party and were about to be included in government until the abduction and murder of Prime Minister Aldo Moro in 1978. They were, shortly after, to become a keystone in Mitterrand's early governments in France. The former British colony of Southern Rhodesia was taken over by left-wing guerrillas, as were the former Portuguese colonies of Angola and Mozambique, with Cuban help. Together they formed a platform against the racist regime in South Africa and sheltered militants of the eventually successful African National Congress. In 1979, America's second most important outpost in the Middle East, the Shah's Iran, fell to a revolution which saw the eventual emergence of a fundamentalist Islamic regime. In all parts of the world, imperialist forces appeared to be on the retreat. American policy-makers like Henry Kissinger were lugubriously pessimistic, famously comparing the Soviet Union to a new Sparta which would threaten the flabby Athens that was America and proclaiming, of Italy, that no country should be allowed to go communist through the irresponsibility of its own citizens. Not surprisingly, Brezhnev was upbeat in his address to the Party Congress in February 1981: 'Today, communist parties are active in 94 countries. In Western Europe alone, some 800,000 new fighters have joined their ranks in the past ten years. Isn't this evidence enough of the indomitable force of attraction of communist ideas?' Lack of imagination and immobilism appeared to have paid off handsomely.

In truth, most of the 'advances' of socialism were well beyond Moscow's control and the new relationship owed more to changes in the United States. However, détente was the order of the day in the mid-1970s. Against a background of tortuous negotiations on arms limitations and numerous political crises and setbacks, economic links with the west were inexorably increased. Soviet oil and gas exports to Western and Eastern Europe brought new dollar injections which enabled the USSR to purchase more and more foreign technology to make up for its own deficits. However, the imported technologies were seldom optimised and functioned poorly within the web of overall Soviet obsolescence. Key technologies, relating especially to computing and the developing silicon chip, were not allowed to be exported to the USSR and a shadowy office attached to the American Embassy in Paris tried to police high-tech exports to the Soviet bloc. Although the Soviet Union found little difficulty in circumventing the ban through third party imports via entrepôts like Singapore, it made little use of the new technologies, apart from in its military and space programmes. Where western societies were on the verge of a computing revolution, the Soviet system was too arthritic to absorb the new technologies and, unlike capitalism, did not have the ability to remake itself in the light of them. There was some thought that immense computing power might be harnessed to increase the efficiency of the highly centralised planning system, but even here computer application remained relatively half-hearted. In the wider Soviet world, the implications of the personal computer threatened the sacred structures of the Soviet system. In other words, central control was threatened. In a country which severely limited access to photocopiers, what hope was there for a rapid adaptation to the personal computer, with its formidable word-processing and message-carrying potential, let alone to later developments such as the Internet?

The new world continued to evolve, irrespective of the wishes of the ageing leadership of the Soviet Union. Increased trade brought increased personal contact. Artistic, cultural and sporting exchanges burgeoned. Western students began to scour Soviet libraries and, less frequently, archives in pursuit of PhD materials. Tourists began to flood into the USSR. In the mid-1970s western package tour operators added Moscow and Leningrad to their destinations and, for only £25, one could fly from Britain to spend a weekend in either one. One of the most important factors in undermining the Soviet system was its growing exposure to the outside world through steadily increasing contact and economic linkages. Even the second Cold War, ushered in by the Reagan government, did not change the underlying foundations. In fact, it restored them, in that one of the first acts of the Reagan government was to lift the embargo on grain sales to the Soviet Union imposed by President Carter in retaliation for the Soviet advance into Afghanistan. These developments had profound effects in Soviet society to which we

will return. For the moment, however, let us examine the Soviet government and its response to these developments.

Within the context of the Brezhnev approach to governance, increased
links with the outside world and especially the west provided a cascade
of patronage opportunities and a largely government-controlled bag of
sparkling privileges to be handed out. Access to scarce imports could be
dangled as a carrot in the face of many Soviet workers, especially white-
collar. Some, who dealt with foreign contacts in trade, tourism and the
like, were paid in foreign exchange certificates which could be cashed in
for goods at select, unobtrusive shops in major cities which were full of
Japanese electronic goods, Scandinavian furniture, German washing
machines, French fashions and so on. One could buy foreign cars
through such channels, Brezhnev himself leading the way with seven,
though they were mostly presented to him officially by overseas governments. The number of Soviet officials abroad in trade missions and
embassies increased enormously. Many others made short-term visits in
connection with business contracts, art shows, theatre, TV, and sporting
encounters. Millions of Soviet citizens began travelling beyond the
Soviet bloc and a *komandirovka* (assignment) or *putevka* (holiday trip) to
the west became a highly prized perk especially among the increasing
number of educated citizens. There were often absurd hoops to jump
through to enjoy such privileges. For example, party vetting was supposed to ensure that only good communists would be allowed to travel.
One of the attributes of a good communist was to profess indifference to
the outside world and a burning love for the homeland. As a consequence it was sometimes necessary to make a show of reluctance in order
to have any chance of approval for a foreign visit. Such was the absurd
world of the Brezhnev Soviet Union.

Luxuriating in its new goodies, basking in the status of 'strategic parity'
accorded in the arms negotiations and secure behind the 1975 Helsinki
Conference's ratification of the status quo in Europe, the Soviet elite
appeared to have it made. The rewards of Brezhnevite indolence and lack
of imagination appeared to be immeasurable. Looked at from another
point of view, however, the regime appeared to have been bought for a
fairly large mess of pottage.

In the crudely materialistic and deeply hypocritical atmosphere of the
Brezhnev years the Soviet system withered away. The crucial illness was
barely noticed. For the first time in Soviet history the regime had no
direction or purpose, beyond its own self-perpetuation. As we have seen,
the whole edifice, up to and including Khrushchev's reign, had been

built on justification of rule from above on ideological grounds. The Soviet system had been a mechanism for achieving the transition to socialism. While ideologists like Suslov still clung to the justificatory dogmas, Brezhnev and the Politburo as a whole showed little sign of having any regard whatsoever for building socialism. The empty rhetoric could be called into play at will, but Brezhnev even joked about the unlikelihood of anyone ever believing he would have read Marx.[5] Soviet society was declared to have achieved 'developed socialism' or, literally translated, 'actually existing socialism'. Further ideological enterprises were postponed to the indefinite future. It was Khrushchev's perspective plan for achieving communism which was buried, not the capitalist enemy. However, ideological commitment was not an optional extra for the Soviet system. Without it the whole thing had no *raison d'être*. Pragmatic day-to-day corruption and drift were no substitute. Use of existing institutions simply because they were there and fear that changing them would endanger stability was not a policy that could last forever. Having thrown away the ideological compass and charts, the regime, strong though it seemed, was in danger of heading for the rocks.

The Brezhnev regime in its last years presented a sorry sight. Brezhnev himself was clearly ill and incapable, but those around him found his survival was a convenient cover for the continuation of their own little schemes. In the end, he was wheeled round almost as a living corpse. The health of the regime was little better. In 1979 it had made its second major decision which, like its first in 1968, was a disaster. It was decided that the 'Brezhnev doctrine' (that any country's option for socialism was irreversible) should be applied to the dubious case of Afghanistan. Given the ideological lassitude of the regime this seems an unlikely burst of rectitude. In reality, the reason lay more in geopolitics. Threatened by advanced deployment of medium-range NATO missiles in Europe, the Soviet Union was very sensitive to CIA involvement in funding rebel tribes in Afghanistan which were trying to overthrow the pro-Soviet government set up in 1978. The Soviet Union had been content to see a friendly, non-aligned Afghanistan since the 1920s. It was now being sucked in against its will since it would have been glad to leave the status quo unchanged. American involvement, however, seemed to give it no choice. It could not afford to see a new American ally on its border. At little cost to itself, the United States had exploited a key Soviet vulnerability. It had also unleashed murderous instability in Afghanistan which was still in evidence two decades later and undermined any possible modernisation of one of the world's most backward countries. From Washington's point of view, confirmed by a jubilant Zbigniew Brzezinski, Carter's National Security Advisor, these were prices worth paying. Of course, it no doubt helped that it was not Americans but Afghanis that were actually paying through a prolongation of their misery. The Soviet 'invasion' of Afghanistan, as it was called even though they were trying to prop up rather than overthrow its government, had enormous effects. It became the focus for a 'Second Cold War' which started with Carter's Moscow Olympic and grain boycotts but which is largely associated with the incoming President Reagan who termed the Soviet Union the 'Evil Empire'. The same Hollywood movie also inspired the name of the main armaments initiative of the Reagan presidency, the 'Star Wars' scheme.

Architects and supporters of the second Cold War have loudly claimed that it was the pressure they applied which brought about Soviet collapse. As we have seen, the USSR was not in a particularly healthy state beforehand. If anything, the new hard line played into the hands of Soviet conservatives. The dissent movement was shut down. Jewish emigration dried up. Attempts were made, symbolised by the ambiguous figure of Brezhnev's successor, the former KGB chief Yurii Andropov, who led the country from November 1982 to February 1984, to return to some degree of ideological rectitude. These might have been a prelude to reforms of a neo-Stalinist nature; we will never know since Andropov himself became ill and died before he had a chance to promote his policies. Certainly, the Chernenko interval (February 1984 to March 1985) saw the introduction of some extremely reactionary legislation, including making it illegal for foreigners to spend the night in private Soviet homes, which was so ridiculous it was never enforced.

A System in Terminal Crisis?

The first warnings that there might be something seriously awry with the Soviet system in a way that had not been recorded before came in the late 1970s. Research showed that key indices of the vitality and sustainability of a society, its life expectancy and infant mortality rates, were going into reverse in the USSR. While some commentators explained this by the rising proportion of Muslims in the Soviet population, living in republics where infant mortality had always been higher than among the Slavic population where birth rates had fallen very low, others argued that it was a sign of a deeper malaise. Increasing vodka consumption

appeared to be behind the fall in life expectancy and that, in turn, suggested spreading demoralisation in society. These gloomy figures also
tied in with poor economic performance. Agriculture remained under-
productive. Industrial growth rates fell and no amount of exhortation by
the leadership showed any sign of reversing the trend. Key industries,
notably oil and gas which had financed a breathing space for the leadership after the OPEC price rises of 1973, showed signs of failure to
maintain the highest output rates. Less pessimistic observers argued
that falling growth rates were a sign of increasing maturity in the Soviet
economy. A relatively small, developing economy, it was argued, found
it easier to achieve high growth from a low base. Once the early growth
spurt was over growth rates would fall from spectacular figures of 7–10
per cent to the range characteristic of more advanced economies, that is
2–5 per cent.

No one, however, was saying the Soviet Union was an efficient entity.
The argument was really about how serious its economic slowdown actually was. The leadership, particularly after Brezhnev's death, took it seriously enough to try and solve it by the traditional method of instilling
discipline in the workplace and ratcheting up the planning levers.
However, these good old-fashioned methods were bringing limited
returns. There were many in the leadership who thought that more radical measures would have to be implemented to maximise economic output. But before turning to the explosion of reforms of the Gorbachev
period and the changes in Soviet society which preceded them, we need
to ask whether the system, though clearly in crisis, was actually at a
terminal stage.

The essential point here is to ask how the economic slowdown and
social malaise could have turned into political action for change or even
overthrow of the system. Politically speaking the elites were cushioned
from the crisis and were continuing to enjoy privileges of foreign travel
and foreign imports. There were very few who thought it worthwhile to
rock the boat. Workers were drowning their sorrows in vodka rather than
political action. The only attempt to set up an independent trade union
attracted only a handful of, largely, non-workers. In the countryside,
incomes were rising, an unlikely launching pad for rebellion. While
intellectuals wove schemes by the hundred they had little practical
impact before Gorbachev. In any case, the classic containment system –
party, informers, KGB – still presented a formidable obstacle to political
change. There can be no doubt, from the speed with which the dissent
movement was virtually shut down and even leading figures like

Sakharov were silenced – in his case by exile to the city of Gorky which was off-limits to foreigners and therefore he was kept out of range of foreign journalists and was not even allowed a telephone – that the will and means to maintain control, even over a sick and declining system, remained unimpaired. While the centre still had the will and the means, what hope was there of change? Where would it come from? There were no mass demonstrations, no strikes, no deep-rooted nationalist movements prepared to do anything other than dream. Certain commentators predicted doom in the form of an overspill of Islamic fundamentalism from neighbouring Iran or from Afghanistan.[6] We are still waiting for it on a mass scale. Others argued that an explosion of nationalism would sweep the Soviet Union away.[7] This did not happen either until precipitated by other changes. One can only conclude that, if the centre held together, and there was no sign that it would not, the traditional system might carry on for decades yet, increasingly moribund perhaps but immobile and unchangeable from without. After all, the twentieth century saw many corrupt dictatorships around the world stumbling on for a generation or more in, to name but a few, Paraguay, Zaire, Indonesia, Spain and Portugal, with no one able to do much about them while the military and the secret police held the initiative. There is no reason to think that the Brezhnevite 'deal' could not be maintained in the face of poor economic performance for the country as a whole. Indeed, the dead weight of the elite understood as the bureaucratic apparatus of government and industry, the overblown ministries, the central planners, the industrial managers, not to mention the (overlapping) senior party officials, were doing better than ever and showed no interest in reform and, arguably, sabotaged it to their own rather than the nation's advantage when the old system began to collapse in the 1980s. Up until then, Brezhnev's 'stability of cadres' suited them very well. They lived in comfortable homes furnished with imports and, in many cases, lived only for their next foreign posting. Compulsory pictures or busts of Lenin and editions of Marxist–Leninist classics, unconsulted and gathering dust on prominent bookshelves, were the only links such people had with 'developed socialism'. Getting tickets for the Bolshoi Ballet occupied more energy than analysis of world political and revolutionary trends. 'Careerism' had completely vanquished socialist aspirations which were left, like an established religion in a secular age, as no more than a husk of ritual and rhetoric. If we look elsewhere in society we can also see that, in the decisive cultural battle engaged in since 1917 between Bolshevik values and the 'petty-bourgeois' values of the masses, the latter had won hands down. By eschewing ideological ambitions Brezhnev had, unwittingly, removed the entire *raison d'être* of the system. Without it, the system had no legitimacy, point or purpose. Revolutionary goals had infused productionism with a sense of direction under Lenin, Stalin and Khrushchev. By abandoning them and abandoning the crucial mobilising function of the state and party which became vestigial under Brezhnev, the Soviet system became no more than the shell of a poorly functioning productionism.

Where productionism had been a means to an end for his predecessors, under Brezhnev it was virtually an end in itself. The receding chimera of economic growth became the be-all and end-all of government policy. Serious doctrinal rectitude was retreating to ever-narrower margins. Without doubt this eased the lot of many Soviet citizens and living standards did rise slowly but revolutionary ambitions were vestigial. Armed conflict broke out with the still militant China of Mao Zedong. The Chilean experiment had been applauded, but not a finger was lifted to help it. The Iranian mullahs massacred the local communists but the Soviet Union continued to try to form good relations with them. Reforming western Eurocommunist parties were held at a distance. A form of national pride rooted in the war and a perceived national interest in frustrating American globalisation replaced serious revolutionary commitment. The American arms build-up was matched though usually at a lower level, in the name of national security and at military, rather than ideological, prompting. Stalin and even Khrushchev shared the illusion that they were leading the world's workers in a crusade against capitalist imperialism. No one could accuse Brezhnev or his successors of seriously believing that they were following this path. In a sense, Brezhnev, who had held back on the anti-Stalin campaign, had, unwittingly, taken more radically de-Stalinising steps than Khrushchev. Unnoticed by himself he had removed the very heart and brain of the system. The institutions of Stalinism – command economy, secret police, a large military, censorship and cultural control – plus the Khrushchev-reinstated leading role of the party remained, but they were now empty forms. With the death of Suslov in January 1982 the last shadow of high Stalinism evaporated. For better or worse, there was no ideological fuel in the tank.

9

SOVIET SOCIETY SINCE THE LATE 1950s

Writing of the roots of revolutionary change Marx had produced a dramatic metaphor in the *Communist Manifesto*. Outdated social relations became 'so many fetters. They had to be burst asunder; they were burst asunder.' The concept fits the late Soviet system. The integument of the system fitted less and less well over the evolving society within. Although, as Marx well knew, there was nothing predetermined or inevitable about any particular form of social and political change, one could, nonetheless, identify the likelihood of certain outcomes rather than others. As we have suggested, the Soviet containment system was such that it had the capability of stifling change indefinitely, but the build-up of forces within that containment system was such that any sensible overseer would try at least to reduce or release some of the pressure. Brezhnev's 'social contract' – encapsulated in the widespread saying 'we pretend to work and they pretend to pay us' – was hardly inspiring and failed to take into account the increasing complexity of Soviet society, arising not least from the transition from a largely rural and traditional society to a largely urban and scientifically educated one.

If a person had fallen asleep in Russia around 1900 and woken up some sixty years later he or she would have had great difficulty in recognising the country. Certain historic landmarks – kremlins, cathedrals, churches, monasteries – would have remained, though much reduced in number and often radically changed in function in that many had become factories, farm dependencies, schools or storehouses. Wooden buildings would have disappeared from the centre of larger cities. Skyscrapers of various styles appeared in the metropolises, themselves vastly greater than at the turn of the century. Streets were cleaner and quieter, though motor traffic was building up. Trams would still have

178

been in evidence but trolley and motor buses had come to dominate street-level public transport. Large cities boasted (or were planning) extensive and efficient metro systems. Large factories had become the norm. At the edge of cities, *mikroraioni* (residential suburbs) of tower blocks with a few shops and cinemas but definitely no churches were developing.

Most striking perhaps would be the people in the streets. They would be much better dressed than at the turn of the century and western styles – suits, jackets and trousers for men, short dresses and cosmetics for women – would be much more widespread. The relatively high proportion of military personnel would have been familiar. Otherwise there was a much greater social uniformity. The traditional upper and middle classes had merged into a fairly homogeneous mass. The occasional official limousine hurtling along special lanes in the main roads or a discreetly curtained foreign currency shop served as a reminder of the new inequalities, but compared to the old the gap from top to bottom was now much narrower. At the bottom of the income scale 'non-productive' teachers, doctors, dentists and lawyers earned basic pay, around 1970, somewhere in the region of 100–120 roubles a month, as did a tram driver. Semi-skilled 'productive' workers earned 150 roubles or so. Skilled workers, including motor bus and train drivers, earned 200–250 roubles. Bureaucrats were paid in the same range but senior managers earned more. At the top, the official salary of admirals, generals and Brezhnev himself was around 600 roubles. Of course, privileges and bonuses made the real differential much greater but even the Soviet elite lived much more modest lives than many of their counterparts abroad, few of them even reaching the living standard of a western middle manager. Our theoretical sleeper would have been confused by the ubiquitous political posters urging plan fulfilment, honesty, sobriety, solidarity with oppressed nations, anti-imperialism and vaunting the country's achievements and praising its noble armed forces. The new name – Union of Soviet Socialist Republics – would also have been a shock but further enquiry would have shown that underneath, ideological enthusiasm was rather hollow and that traditional concerns – better incomes, housing and living standards; better jobs; promotion; shopping opportunities; educating one's children; finding vodka – were more prominent in people's everyday lives.

Should our awakened sleeper travel around the USSR and into the countryside the surprise would have continued. Central Asian towns had been transformed. Electricity was ubiquitous in urban centres and much of the countryside. A thin band of development followed the Trans-Siberian railway. A multitude of airports and cheap air travel, as well as an extensive rail network, bound the vast spaces together. Even the 'traditional' village was transformed. While the cluster of wooden buildings in which most farmers lived and the trudge to the water pump would have been familiar, the brick-built offices of collective farms and local soviets would not, nor would the ubiquitous trucks, tractors, combine harvesters and other machinery which had replaced horses and manual labour. The landscape itself would have been barely recognisable. The complex of strip holdings for peasants and larger estates for landowners had been simplified into cottage garden plots, perhaps small communal pastures and vast, often fenceless, collective farms. The manor house, which dominated the pre-revolutionary village, would, in most cases, have been demolished and its materials used for the peasants' own projects. Its garden would be overrun and neglected or incorporated into the farm. Local churches would also have fallen into disrepair, though they would be less likely to have been pillaged by the villagers. By the 1960s, outsiders from the cities were breaking into them to search for icons and other objects increasingly valued by style-conscious urban dwellers. Khrushchev's mass closures of churches ensured a supply of rich pickings for the unscrupulous. These and a multitude of other changes would have indicated that Russia had crossed a historical threshold between 1900 and 1960–70. It had become industrialised and, to an extent, 'modernised'. As we have already mentioned, around 1960 or so change had been so extensive and so rapid that the notion of 'catching up' with the advanced capitalist countries seemed less crazy than at other moments. The spectacular successes of the Soviet Union in launching the first artificial satellite – Sputnik in 1957 – and the first manned space flight – by Yuri Gagarin in 1960 – seemed to symbolise the narrowing gap. However, it was not to be. The Stalinist road to development incorporated the means of its own destruction.

Had our sleeper, exhausted and confused by his travels, decided to drop off again in the late 1960s and sleep until about 1985 he would have found, perhaps to her or his relief, that, in the meantime, relatively little had changed. If I may be allowed a personal illustration, these were years in which I travelled frequently to the Soviet Union, more often than not in the company of my students. Before departure it was possible to brief them, year on year, with practically the same information on hotel facilities; black market scams to avoid; bus fares; goods in shops; theatre ticket prices and dodges for getting into the ballet; museum admission prices and times; frequency of public transport; tolerated and less tolerated behaviour and so on. One could be 99 per cent certain that the USSR left behind the previous year would have changed little by the next. Cumulatively, the pace of change in the Brezhnev years was minimal, so much so that they came to be known as 'the years of stagnation' during the *perestroika* period.

Stalinism had been able to remake tsarist Russia but it had no mechanism to remake itself. Instead, its institutions ensured a new conservatism. Innovation was a continual problem. The containment system – the command economy and society – was geared to reproducing what was already done and preserving existing norms. The collapse of ideological aims under Brezhnev removed its only dynamic force. Happiness lay in the simplest form of plan fulfilment. Innovation was a risky headache to be avoided if at all possible. We have already mentioned the little-changing Fiat-based saloon car, the Lada, produced from the 1970s to the present. It was not unusual. For decades, Soviet cameras, motor cycles and other products were based on captured German originals from wartime. American-style trucks, copies of lend-lease materials, were produced for more than twenty years. Almost identical railway locomotives and rolling-stock were produced from one decade to the next. Indeed, there were some advantages. Long production runs and standard designs simplified maintenance and availability of spares. (These were chronic deficiencies in the system as it was. It is hard to imagine what the problem would have been like if designs had changed substantially every few years!) Also if one had a good design, why change it? We have already mentioned the Kalashnikov rifle which is still the automatic rifle of choice after fifty years in production. If there were changes they were often based on observation of foreign developments. Although many Soviet jet airliners like the Tu-104 and Tu-154 were original in design and conception, others, like the first Soviet supersonic airliner for example, came to bear an uncanny resemblance to British, French and American designs. If there were distinctive advances they were often produced as priority projects to meet military specifications. The quality of its jet fighter planes Mig-29 (Fulcrum) and Sukhoi 27 (Flanker) were second to none, testimony to the continuing genius of the Russian technical intelligentsia. The Soviet Union produced the world's largest aircraft but it was designed to carry troops and armour. It only developed wide-bodied passenger planes many years after the United States.

Against the background of world developments, Soviet economic performance showed up in a worsening light. Where, around 1960, it was, along with its neighbour Japan, one of only two countries to have broken through to large-scale industrialisation in the twentieth century, by 1985 the Asian tigers and many other places appeared to be advancing rapidly. The most advanced countries were themselves undergoing a third industrial revolution based on electronics and global capitalism was remaking itself in the light of the fastest pace of innovation the world has ever seen. The Stalinist straitjacket left the Soviet Union trailing further and further behind. It had no mechanisms for its own renewal or remaking. It was producing social and intellectual change at a rate it could not accommodate. An educated, 'modern', urban population was not going to let itself be pushed around by the KGB for ever. Incidentally, the KGB itself was evolving into a careerist rather than political and ideologically driven institution, a characteristic which, ironically, has seen it survive the collapse of the party and system of which it was supposed to be the ultimate defender. As we have already concluded, the straitjacket might have lasted for a long time but pressures were building up nonetheless.

Unofficial Pluralism

In some ways the late Soviet regime had replicated the fate of its tsarist predecessor. Economic progress was sought but the political space in which it could happen was denied by a complacent, unimaginative and incompetent leadership. Social change was happening to which the political system did not only not respond but actively resisted. The pressures, in both cases, were articulated by isolated but prophetic and, for a while later, powerful, intellectuals. While the burgeoning 'civil society' of late tsarism was more buoyant than that which existed in the interstices of the sprawling Soviet state, in the latter case dissatisfaction penetrated deep into the heart of the system.

The comparison cannot be taken too far. Tsarism was brought down by military defeat, the Soviet system was confirmed by military victory. Tsarism had always had a turbulent edge. Popular discontent, mass risings, terrorism and national uprisings frequently punctuated the tsarist epoch. After the Kronstadt rebellion of 1921 hardly any major public disturbances, certainly none of national significance, were recorded. This may be explained by the greater efficiency of the Soviet repressive/mobilising apparatus. However, there were other factors, one of which is the relative satisfaction of the population in the 1950s and 1960s. A population which is secure, has jobs, the possibility of an education, a pension, medical services, films, TV – especially the generation for which these were novelties – is less likely to be revolutionary. At a much lower level than in the west, a degree of 'affluence' was affecting the masses. Soviet national pride in the war, in space achievements, in sporting success, also blunted contestation. In addition, the central government maintained a degree of remoteness. Its concerns – foreign policy, plan priorities and other aspects of national politics – went over the heads of most of the population. They were, in Soviet conditions, undiscussable so there was no forum for public debate about them other than ritualised support of the wise decisions of the leadership. In this sense the system had abolished politics. By contrast, however, local authorities, including soviets, enterprise managements, collective farm chairs, public service administrators, enjoyed no such immunity. Indeed, it was part of the centre's self-defence mechanism to turn discontent against local rather than central targets. As a result, a modest degree of criticism was permitted. Shortages and poor services could be blamed on local officials but never on the system itself or on the central authorities. Local managers could, thus, be scapegoated for national failings. Local newspapers could and did carry local whistleblowing and fingerpointing articles which could lead to dismissal of the targets of such campaigns. Sometimes they could reach national level, as in the exceptional case of the defence of Lake Baikal on ecological grounds against the usually all-powerful military which had had an aircraft tyre factory built alongside it, which along with other industrial enterprises, was demonstrably polluting the deepest freshwater lake on the planet. However, the protest, extensive and open though it was, was unsuccessful. In less spectacular cases it was, usually, the local party which orchestrated such things and claimed the credit for defending the people against excessive bureaucracy. Of course, one could never criticise the party itself for perpetuating the unaccountable bureaucratisation which it claimed to struggle against.

The corrupt Brezhnev years saw many such local scandals. Some are quite unbelievable. An extreme case was presented by an 'invisible' factory in Central Asia, that is, one which did not officially exist but got all its raw materials, labour, equipment and finances illegally (curiously known colloquially as *nalevo* – on the left) and which had an illegal distribution chain for the luxury goods it produced. Its survival was due to the colossal profits allowing hefty pay-offs to be made at all levels. Exposure of such scams provided harmless (to the system) explanations of shortcomings. Dishonest distortion was to blame, not the system itself. Many other cases came to light, especially during Brezhnev's decline when they were used to clear away Brezhnevite officials at high levels who had taken advantage of the centre's nod and a wink at such practices. The accusatory finger approached Brezhnev himself towards the end when not only stories of his reliance on dubious clairvoyants were aired but his daughter and son-in-law were accused of using their position in the Moscow State Circus (and as highly protected members of the elite) to make money from selling passports, especially to the beautiful people of the fashionable Moscow artistic world. KGB enquiries into the affair were the clearest signal of the declining influence of Brezhnev and of the KGB positioning itself as the people's protector in connection with the rise to power of its head at this time, Yuri Andropov. At a more mundane level there were cases of the KGB cleaning up corrupt local militia (that is, ordinary police) precincts in Moscow and then calling in the victims of the militia, ostensibly to restore their property and so on stolen by the police, but also to demonstrate unequivocally that it was the friendly KGB which had protected citizens against abuse of police powers.

Local safety valves did reduce much of the pressure in the Khrushchev and Brezhnev years. However, serious flashpoints did occur. As we have seen, the Khrushchev era was ushered in by disturbances in the Gulag which resulted eventually in mass releases and wholesale (though not universal) rehabilitations. The nearest thing to a civil uprising came in the solidly working-class Ukrainian town of Novocherkassk in early June 1962. Local discontent over a wage cut, food supplies and prices turned into a mass strike movement which took over the town. In action reminiscent of the Lenin period, armed security troops had to go in and recapture the occupied civic buildings. Some 24 people died in the fighting and 39 were wounded. A few ringleaders were singled out and executed. Local officials were blamed by the centre for letting the situation get out of hand. Food supplies were brought in to defuse popular discontent. All news of the event was suppressed, surprisingly successfully because the story did not trickle out until some months afterwards and the full story only came out almost thirty years later. While the Novocherkassk incident was an exception, many miniature versions, such as strikes, took place on a wide scale. The full history of them is yet to be written but we have enough examples to make a few tentative generalisations about their significance for our theme. They were more often than not sparked off by flagrant local abuses – outrageous work schedules, diversion or lack of food supplies, harsh work discipline, unpaid wages, withheld bonuses – which provoked spontaneous 'wildcat' responses. Higher officials and often police would descend and the same formula as at Novocherkassk would be applied. A few ringleaders would be harshly punished in order to maintain the repressive 'credibility' of the authorities. Local officials would be sanctioned, even arrested themselves, for incompetence and as a sop to the strikers. Food supplies would be rushed in or wages increased to satisfy immediate demands. The combination was, it seems, highly effective because there were no disturbances which ever threatened the stability of the system. As we have already had occasion to remark, Soviet society as a whole seemed to be firmly under control and there appeared to be no potential force within capable of generating enough energy to cause a shift. Even nationalism, which was to wreak so much havoc just a few years later, showed no sign of stirring on a scale sufficiently large to destabilise the system. It should be firmly noted that there were absolutely no mass national uprisings or disturbances under Khrushchev or Brezhnev.

It seemed, in the words of the famous stage direction from the opera *Khovanshchina* which was frequently referred to at this time, that *narod molchat* – 'the people are silent'. If it were to come at all, change would have to emerge from an unexpected quarter and that is exactly what happened.

The conditions of Khrushchev's instrumentalist 'thaw' and the slothful laxity of the Brezhnev years had allowed the Russian intelligentsia to recreate itself. While much attention has been devoted to the dissident movement, intellectual debate went much further than them and it was their wider audience, including educated ministry and party officials at the highest level, who were, in the end, more effective in implementing change and, consciously or unconsciously, opening the way for the system's collapse. In order to elucidate these areas we need to look not only at the dissident movement but also at officially and semi-officially tolerated critics, at party reformers and at the peculiar ideological twists and turns of the regime itself in the late 1960s and 1970s.

The main features of the dissident movement can be seen in the lives and careers of three of the leading figures, Alexander Solzhenitsyn, Andrei Sakharov and Roy Medvedev. Each became a prominent spokesperson for the main branches of the movement – Slavophile, liberal and socialist respectively.

In the 1960s and early 1970s Solzhenitsyn was undoubtedly the best-known dissident within the Soviet Union and in the wider world. In part, this was because he had been officially published and had gained a worldwide reputation for his story *One Day in the Life of Ivan Denisovich* which propelled him overnight into the role of leading revealer of hidden truths of the Stalin era. Solzhenitsyn's claim to the role did not arise from a literary career or background but from his personal experiences. Born in 1918 he was a product of the Soviet era. His life had been indistinguishable from that of many of his contemporaries – provincial upbringing, unremarkable childhood and youth, a developing sympathy with the goals of socialism, conscription into the Soviet army to fight against the invaders – until he was arrested in 1945 for making derogatory remarks about Stalin in a letter read by the military censorship. He spent the next eight years going through the terrible experiences, including a brush with cancer, recorded in his literary work. *Pace* the postmodernists, Solzhenitsyn's writings, though imagined rather than reproductive of 'reality', were anything but 'fiction'. The road of direct accounts of the camps was closed off by censorship so the novel and short story were the only way to present such experiences to the Soviet public and the world. His aim was to uncover the secret and shame the past and current leadership of the country into corrective and restitutive measures. Indeed, from the formal point of view, Solzhenitsyn's writings were not very distinguished. They had few pretensions to subtlety of plot or stylistic embellishment beyond presenting previously hidden camp jargon as a sub-branch of the Russian language, thereby familiarising the world with expressions such as *zek*, meaning a political prisoner, and *Gulag*, the short name for the camp system. What they did have was a characteristic foreign to much late twentieth-century art and literature, riveting moral authenticity. *First Circle* presented intensely lived debates about the meaning of the Soviet experience conducted by scientific intelligentsia inmates of a special camp (*sharashka*) set up to produce a scrambler phone system for the leadership. One of the highlights was the unforgettable mock show trial of the medieval hero Prince Igor as an agent of the Polovtsian intelligence services. *Cancer Ward* related Solzhenitsyn's experiences of the disease and of his release from the Gulag, also interspersed with brilliantly reproduced debates between different prisoners' views about what they were all enduring. Though pressure was put on the authorities and the most avant-garde Soviet journal *Novyi mir* (*New World*) was ready to publish, neither of Solzhenitsyn's major works appeared in the USSR. In the end, the Brezhnev regime purged the editorial board of *Novyi mir* in 1970.

From the end of the Khrushchev era which had provided Solzhenitsyn's opportunity, nothing of his was published in the Soviet

Union until the time of Gorbachev. In the intervening years his historical mission came to the forefront. He was busy gathering and authenti-
cating the experiences of thousands of camp victims eventually
published in the three volumes of *The Gulag Archipelago*. It was largely
for this work that the authorities sanctioned him through forcible expulsion in 1974. In exile he focused his work on a historical project on the
revolution, *The Red Wheel*. While certain parts of it have been received
with interest, notably his portraits of certain historical figures of the time
including Lenin, the project as a whole has commanded less and less
attention. In part this is because there is little desire for a linked set of
novels *à la* Balzac or Zola and also because the issue has been bedevilled
by Solzhenitsyn's implicit self-image as a new Tolstoy. While he shares
few of Tolstoy's ideas or stylistic genius, he does claim the same moral
stature. As his career developed Solzhenitsyn drifted away from a vague
socialism to become a more and more overt moral preacher drawn
increasingly to the Russian Orthodox religion, though not to the church
leaders whom, true to form, he thoroughly castigated for moral cowardice in bowing to the hurricane of Soviet persecution. There were very
few targets, including friends and crucial helpers in getting him published, whom Solzhenitsyn did not come to castigate. At first, in exile,
he was lionised, especially by the budding new right. His scathing and
morally irrefutable denunciations of the Soviet system past and present
were music to their ears. He was awarded a Nobel prize in 1970. The
love affair between himself and the right began to sour when he turned
his coruscating gaze on America itself and, in the showcase of the
Harvard commencement ceremonies of July 1978, suggested that moral
cowardice was a fast-developing feature of American life.

From that point on, Solzhenitsyn was less and less paraded in public.
His status as favourite dissident of the new right passed to Vladimir
Bukovsky, exiled in exchange for the imprisoned Chilean communist
leader Luis Corvalan in 1976. Bukovsky also produced riveting memoirs
of a Soviet childhood, declining faith in communism and experience of
persecution which, by Bukovsky's time, was more in the form of forced
incarceration in psychiatric hospitals rather than the full-blown camp
system. Unlike Solzhenitsyn, who believed moral force was greater than
material force, Bukovsky could be relied upon to heap praise on every
anti-Soviet initiative of the west, including armed interventions round
the globe aimed at 'containing' communism, the arms race in general
and its last baroque twist, Star Wars, in particular and see no serious
faults in capitalism itself. By the end of the 1970s Solzhenitsyn had

become overtly Slavophile in his outlook. As for its nineteenth-century proponents, Russia, for Solzhenitsyn, was still a beacon for the world calling it to repentance, renunciation of materialism and providing an example of the *reductio ad absurdum* of modernism and modernisation. Industry and western education had ploughed up a morally sound traditional peasant-based Russia. Instead of taking on the ideological burdens of world revolution and construction of socialism, Russia's task, Solzhenitsyn urged, was to turn its back on the outside world and develop the resources, moral and material, on its doorstep, for example in Siberia. Rather oddly, the main feature he criticised in his letter to the Brezhnev leadership of 1974 was its enthralment to ideology. Just cast that off, Solzhenitsyn suggested, and return to the values of orthodoxy and all would be well. Democracy, human rights, material well-being were not of concern to him, or, more exactly, they were very much subsidiary to religious and moral soundness. In many respects, not only in his tall, gaunt, bearded appearance, he was beginning to emulate the prophets as represented in icons. When he eventually returned to Russia he funded his own fifteen-minute nightly television slot in which he harangued his audience. Sadly, in the end, the repetitious and 'outdated' monologues/sermons had most viewers reaching for the channel change button. Despite the collapse of his reputation Solzhenitsyn remains of prime importance. His early works are brilliant portrayals of the times he lived through and the reputation of the Soviet system never recovered from the assault he led on it. True, his positive values of Orthodoxy and moral rectitude have not been implemented, at least to Solzhenitsyn's satisfaction, but it is largely the fate of prophets to cry in the wilderness.

Other dissidents presented a much less heady brew and, particularly in the case of Andrei Sakharov, one which matched much more closely the values of the west, perhaps a reason why, unlike Solzhenitsyn, Sakharov was not forcibly exiled because he would have fitted in better with the flow of western ideas, whereas it was predictable that Solzhenitsyn's nineteenth-century mentality would attract only a limited attention span in the wider world. The ostensible reason for Sakharov's detention within the Soviet Union was that, as a prominent nuclear physicist and key developer of the Soviet hydrogen bomb, he was in possession of state secrets. Indeed, given his formation, Sakharov should have been one of the least likely dissidents. He had no background of persecution by the state before he began to criticise it and had, on the contrary, been one of its golden youths. Born in 1921 into an educated professional intelligentsia family, he was, by 1945, a graduate student at the elite Soviet Academy of Sciences, eventually enjoying all the material advantages, status and protection that the Academy could provide. However, he is the personal encapsulation of Deutscher's telling point. The regime needed to educate and produce figures such as Sakharov, but there was no guarantee that they would not push the limits of the system which had produced them and become critical of the restraints within which the leadership tried to contain society. Sakharov's first, and indeed only, extended manifesto was published in samizdat in 1967. Its title, *Progress, Co-existence and Intellectual Freedom*, betokened something quite different from Solzhenitsyn's mystic moralising. At the core of Sakharov's ideas was the acceptance rather than rejection of core western democratic values. Human rights and legality were vital to Sakharov. He was also imbued with some of the ideas of the time about convergence of capitalist and socialist societies. According to this view the imperatives of modernisation and industrialisation – urbanisation; rising living standards; the need for regulation, for instance, to protect the environment; the increasing size of enterprises; the need for advanced education and many others – would lead to the differences between socialist and capitalist societies diminishing. Capitalism was increasingly adopting control and regulation and moving away from antiquated free-market utopian liberalism, and socialism would have to relax the command economy in favour of greater market influence. The result, in the title of a book by one of the leading proponents of convergence, J. K. Galbraith, would be *The New Industrial State* in which differences between capitalist and socialist ownership of the means of production would be increasingly blurred. While such ideas were blown off course by the bizarre resurgence in the west of eighteenth-century free-market utopianism, itself a reaction to social democracy and the explosion of 1968, they were clearly within the scope of western discourse in a way that Solzhenitsyn's were not.

Sakharov's ideas became a main focus of a form of liberalism which evolved out of a strategy pioneered by another scientist–dissident, the mathematician Alexander Esenin-Volpin. The centrepiece was that the system's own laws should be the basis for pressure. The lawmakers should be held to account and made to uphold their own laws and be shown to have broken them wherever that was the case. Despite initial scepticism the tactic became very widespread and influential. Groups focused on deprivation of rights guaranteed in Soviet law. New repressive techniques devised under Brezhnev, such as avoidance of the legal system in favour of orders confining certain dissidents to psychiatric hospitals, were in part a response to the new tactics and were also open to challenge on the new terms. The struggle was widened to include, for example, attempts to ostracise Soviet psychiatry from the world community though, like many such campaigns, there was a serious division of opinion in the outside world between those who proposed embargoes and those who believed that it was more effective to maintain such contacts as were becoming available. The dilemma was never resolved. However, what is clearer is that the regime was subjected to pressure from this unexpected quarter and it was particularly embarrassing for it to be caught out on grounds of not upholding its own laws. The tactic was so successful that it influenced foreign diplomacy towards the Soviet Union. As part of the Helsinki agreements of 1975, 'basket three' incorporated a decision by all the parties that they would uphold human rights and monitor the situation in each of their countries. The result was the formation of 'Helsinki watch' committees all over the Soviet bloc which claimed legitimacy from the treaty. The Soviet government was even moved, in part as a lumbering attempt to quell the new tactics, to introduce, in 1977, a new constitution deemed less foolproof by the authorities in that it contained a number of catch-22s limiting the exercise of the rights it appeared to promote.

Nonetheless, a clear human rights movement had emerged. It formed important links with religious, national and feminist dissent which all set out to protest being deprived of the rights granted by the UN charters ratified by the Soviet government. A series of *Chronicles of Current Events* was set up, publicising apparent breaches of human rights norms. The main chronicle, published in samizdat and quickly made available abroad, focused on all aspects of human rights violations and highlighted individual cases of persecution. Another chronicle enumerated violation of the rights of Roman Catholics in Lithuania. Many other religious groups were also represented and religious dissent – largely associated with Baptists, Catholics and a few Orthodox – was probably the largest single category of dissent. The majority of those imprisoned for reasons of conscience were of religious inspiration, especially those whose beliefs brought them into direct conflict with the state over issues of medical intervention for children and conscription. Liberal nationalists also appeared who demanded national self-determination and the establishment of democratic norms in their republics. Ukrainian dissenters like Vyacheslav Chornovil, Ivan Dziuba and Valentin Moroz wrote coruscating critiques of the subordination of their republic and, in Moroz's *Report from the Beria Reserve*, one of the most penetrating analyses of Stalinism produced by the movement. As time went on, feminist critics also added their voice to the growing number pointing to violation of basic rights though it remained, in itself, a smaller category of the dissent movement. Most women dissidents associated themselves with the movement in a non-gender-specific way. The particular problems of women – notably the excessive burden of being expected to work and to be the chief maintainers of the household and nurturers of children in the nightmare conditions of Soviet life where shopping alone was almost a full-time activity, let alone washing and food preparation in cramped apartments – were highlighted in many branches of the dissent movement.

The third, socialist, branch of the dissent movement was much smaller in number but was of considerable significance because ideas overlapped into the ruling circles. Its leading figure was Roy Medvedev. He was born in 1925 into a committed Leninist family who named him and his twin brother after the radicals M. N. Roy, a Comintern stalwart from India, and Jean Jaurès, the French socialist leader assassinated on the eve of the First World War. The centrepiece of Medvedev's writing as a dissident was the first independent biography of Stalin and analysis of Stalinism by someone living in the Soviet Union. Where Solzhenitsyn had claimed that all forms of Bolshevism, including Leninism, were flawed theories palmed off on Russia by failed western radicals, Medvedev argued against Stalin and for a renewed Leninism. Where Solzhenitsyn claimed that Stalinism was identical with Leninism and Marxism in general for that matter, Medvedev stressed that Stalin had deviated from Leninism in many respects. He went much further than Khrushchev in promoting this line of argument, exposing issues like the violence associated with collectivisation, the famine of 1932–3, the falsity of the show trials, the disasters of Stalin's 1930s diplomacy, his wartime failures and many other questions which Khrushchev had glossed over. Medvedev looked for a return to socialist democracy based on a democratic and humanist understanding of Marx and the Marxist tradition. Though he had relatively few followers in the Soviet Union, where, for understandable reasons, most critics were impatient with all forms of the 'socialism' that had been thrust down their throats, when the system began to break up under Gorbachev the early steps were taken in the guise of a 'return to Leninist norms'.

This reminds us of an important and often overlooked aspect of dissidence. While heroic figures like those mentioned above put their heads above the parapet and risked prison, psychiatric incarceration and forced exile, there were many others who sympathised with aspects of the movement but were not prepared to overly risk their often privileged position in Soviet life. Far from being full-time dissidents' such people were important officials in major ministries and the party itself. Only since the emergence of Gorbachev have we been able to produce a fuller picture of how, particularly in the lax Brezhnev years, key dissident ideas penetrated deep into the Soviet elite.

In the Brezhnev years the metropolitan elite and many of its counterparts in the republics and Russian provinces were becoming schizophrenic. The way of life to which they aspired was increasingly westernised, the ideas they professed increasingly nationalistic and Slavophile. As we have already mentioned, the Soviet elite did not spend time agonising about how to build socialism, rather it scanned imported shop catalogues and availability lists from special shops to see where its new colour television, hi-fi, video, dishwasher or BMW car was coming from. On a personal note, Soviet friends preceded me in the purchase of all these items. Even at the time of writing, unlike them, I do not have a mobile phone (or a BMW, for that matter). Foreign travel was an opportunity to buy up scarce goods. Even travel within the Soviet Union might feed some of their appetites. It was a common sight to see VIPs returning from Tbilisi in Georgia to Moscow, having numerous cases of wine loaded onto airliners. Country retreats were *à la mode*. The furnishings of such places would often be indistinguishable from their counterparts abroad, apart from the occasional icon, the slightly risqué reproduction (or original for the real McCoy) of an unofficial or marginal artist, a shelf of unread Marxist–Leninist classics and a picture or two of Lenin. In other words, the elite was deeply in thrall to western bourgeois values of consumption and also, although it was much more difficult than in the west, privatisation of personal and family life, that is, cutting it off from wider social values and responsibilities. Not only the regime railed at these developments (even though few of the leaders were themselves free of these characteristics). Solzhenitsyn, too, was scathing. According to him, one reason by which the intelligentsia excused itself from active dissidence was on the grounds that it would jeopardise the well-being of the young. Far from damaging the welfare of children, he urged, what better education could they have than to see their parents take a firm moral stand against evil. Making rude signs at the regime from inside one's pocket, as Solzhenitsyn put it, was not good enough.[1]

One might as well have tried to stop a railway train by exhortation. In its way, the Soviet Union was increasingly focused on consumerism.

While shopping and the acquisition of basic goods was a headache for the majority, and one can understand their obsession with shopping, even when things became easier, the same values – of increasing one's own living standard through accumulation of goods as the first priority in social life – continued to hold. In this sense, the Soviet Union was deeply westernised long before its collapse.

The last great ideological chieftain of the Soviet system was Mikhail Suslov. Born in 1902 and, interestingly, coming from an Old Believer background (that is, from a group which split from mainstream Orthodoxy in the seventeenth century and came to represent a combination of conservative religious belief, a more distant attitude to progress and worldly values, plus a 'protestant' reputation for thrift, sobriety and hard work) he rose to prominence in the late Stalin years. Throughout the Brezhnev years he tried to urge the leadership to hold to a more ideological line, though even he had to become increasingly pragmatic as reality unfolded. The result was that, in the Brezhnev years, ideology became a complex, ambiguous and contradictory area. The large claim, that Marxist ideology was already dead to all intents and purposes, has already been made above. However, it still remained the official shell around all government activities and could, from time to time, be raised up as a ghost to frighten the leaders or, as we shall see, to shame them. However, the prevailing ideology of the Brezhnev period could not be called Marxism. What, then, was it?

Not surprisingly, its chief component was complacency. The Soviet Union, it implied, had not done so badly. It had defied the laws and great powers of capitalism and built a modern society free of the scourges of capitalism – exploitation, unemployment, poverty – in which the rights of citizens were not only granted on paper, but realised in practice by facilitating access of all not only to education and healthcare but to many cheap goods – housing, heating, gas, electricity, public transport, basic food products, tickets for theatre, film and sporting events and access to cultural institutions such as art galleries, museums and historic buildings. In the light of Russia's history these were not inconsiderable achievements. In addition, underdeveloped areas of the Soviet Union had advanced much further than their neighbours, as a glance across the Soviet border into northern Iran, eastern Turkey or Afghanistan would immediately verify. The jump up in living standards there was as obvious as the jump down in comparison with advanced western countries. In other words, although it did not match western living standards (not least, so the semi-official ideology went, because it did not have colonies to exploit – indeed, after the oil price rises of 1973 it even subsidised its eastern European dependencies), it had achieved a basic, modern living standard for all its citizens. Its scientific achievements, symbolised by space travel, rivalled those of the United States. In international affairs, its voice was heard as never before. With the acquisition of 'strategic parity' with the United States it had been confirmed as a world superpower. The main aim of the leadership, so the ideology concluded, was to ensure that these gains were not jeopardised and to increase living standards across the board. The whole thing could be called 'developed socialism' but Marxism no longer had much to do with it.

As with most successful forms of propaganda, the half-truths in the above made it more effective than out-and-out lies. There were, of course, many silences in the official ideology, notably about the costs of Stalin's mistakes. However, the official view was that the past was gone and there was no point raking it up to destabilise the present. Also, if suppression of free speech and of democratic rights was needed, it, too, was a price worth paying. Indeed, there was, given the poorly developed liberal-style political culture in most of the Soviet Union, some support for this proposition. Why waste energy on political argument? The point was for politicians to get together and solve problems. Most westerners who spoke in some depth to ordinary Russians will have encountered such assumptions. Since the fall of communism, as we shall see, they have bedevilled attempts to construct a western-style democracy, and the outside world, especially those pronouncing the 'end of history' and the universality of western models, have been guilty of a degree of cultural imperialism which fails to recognise their existence.

Such were the main propositions of the actual, as opposed to the formal, ideology of the Brezhnev years. Not everyone subscribed to them. The limited toleration of dissidents did not only allow 'progressive' voices to be heard. Extreme right-wing ideas based on traditional Russian sources can also be traced. A nationalism even cruder than that of the authorities was expressed. Contempt for non-Slavic minorities, especially Jews, Germans and the Baltic peoples and foreigners in general, found a number of echoes not only in military and KGB circles but also in the writings of Solzhenitsyn, for whom the revolution was a foreign-led event foisted on the unfortunate Russians by a coalition of Lithuanians, Jews and idolisers of western philosophies. As for its nineteenth-century predecessors, the fount of Russianness was to be found in the church, which itself had a record of anti-Semitism and xenophobia which could still be found within it. While the party leadership certainly did not accept any rehabilitation of the church, it did pull back on the active anti-religious drive of Khrushchev's later years. Churches were not reopened but they did function. Anti-religious pickets were held at Easter, and watch was kept to ensure members of the *nomenklatura* and other important personnel, like schoolteachers, were not attending churches. Even so, relations between church and state were as good as they had ever been in the Soviet period. The church leadership professed loyalty to the Soviet system and became a mouthpiece of the Soviet authorities in international peace campaigns.

In any case, Marxism, although moribund in the leadership, was not entirely dead. As the official, if little regarded, ideology of the state, it was still officially promoted and could produce true believers and, perhaps more important, pretend believers who could use it to criticise the decaying leadership of the country in the late Brezhnev years.

As far as the first category was concerned, it was more likely to be younger people who were starry-eyed about the real building of socialism and criticised their elders for shabby compromises. It was often Young Communist (Komsomol) groups who were most active in picketing churches and spreading anti-religious ideas under the aegis of the propaganda apparatus in, for instance, the Znanie (Knowledge) society for scientific education. However, many of them were doing this to curry favour for their careers, since, as we have already had occasion to remark, it remained necessary to kowtow to the ideology even if it was recognised as a hollow gesture – the result being massive hypocrisy to the point of schizophrenia.

The chances of genuine Marxists emerging was slight. It was my own experience that the Soviet Union was the one country I visited around the world where I hardly ever met a genuine Marxist. A few personal anecdotes might illustrate the peculiarities of the time. I have had no more contact over the Soviet years with officials than I have had to. In March 1983, however, I was approached by one of the country's main propaganda agents, Radio Moscow, and asked if I would allow myself to be interviewed. It appeared politic to agree and I duly did so. When the interviewer arrived he had no idea of a topic. It was I who pointed out, to his surprise, even though it was being widely commemorated officially, that it was the eve of the centenary of Marx's death. Maybe a few questions about the influence of Marx on British historians would be an idea? The interviewer seemed surprised that there was any, but I was able to discuss Hill, Hobsbawm, Thompson and others. How could it be that an important ideological agent such as the Radio Moscow inter-viewer could have so little knowledge of the elements of what he was propagandising? Others of my experiences throw some light. My room-mate during my first prolonged research visit to the Soviet Union in the 1970s was studying to be a teacher of dialectical materialism. His thesis topic was the influence of Hegel in Lenin's *Philosophical Notebooks*. This seemed, at least, to be an intellectually respectable topic and I com-mented that it sounded interesting. My room-mate simply said it was not and never mentioned it again. He, and others in the hostel study-ing with the same goal, confirmed that the teachers of ideology were often the least able, the least motivated and the least respected (intel-lectually) members of the educated classes. The field of *diamat* (dialecti-cal materialism) was seen as a soft option. The regime had allowed the interpretation of its sacred texts to fall into the hands of uninspired careerists.

A final story illustrates to perfection the regime's success in killing off the enthusiasm of its own supporters. In the late 1970s a good friend of mine told me that he had, in his youth, been an idealistic supporter of the building of socialism. However, he eventually came to see that those people spreading the gospel did not themselves believe a word of it. As a result, his own belief in it was undermined. Like many other talented people, he nonetheless remained an active party member, because progress in his career depended on it. Some months after telling the story he came to me with a look of ironic amusement in his eyes. 'Guess what?', he told me. 'My workplace have asked me to lead the ideologi-cal training of staff.' The system had perfectly reproduced the prevail-ing scepticism. My friend had himself become one of those unbelieving teachers who devalued faith in the official state religion. It was not even that his workplace was an insignificant one. He was employed by no less an arm of Soviet propaganda than Tass, the official Soviet news agency, and he even had connections with the Central Committee apparatus.

However, as we have said, the official ideology was a source of politi-cal manipulation for a variety of ends, not least of which was the strug-gle for power. An assault on ideological laxity in favour of a crusade for renewed fervour was a ploy which no one in the party could seriously challenge, even if it was something they did not relish any more than a clergyman could oppose an evangelisation drive. As Brezhnev's health deteriorated, the struggle for his succession brought guarded criticism of his lack of ideological grip. Suslov himself would have been involved had he not preceded Brezhnev into the next world by a few months.

Nonetheless, the successful candidate, Yurii Andropov, wrapped the mantle of ideological rectitude firmly around himself. His reign from November 1982 to February 1984 was too short to bring about any significant changes beyond the fact, whose implications neither he nor anyone else could foresee, that he had one of his protégés, the young provincial party secretary from Stavropol' in south Russia, Mikhail Gorbachev by name, brought into the Politburo. Energy, strength of character and competence appeared to be Gorbachev's chief characteristics. He also had a sense of dissatisfaction at the declining economic performance and falling morale of the country. However, could anyone do anything about it?

10

DISSOLUTION

Speaking at a seminar at the London School of Economics in the early 1970s shortly after his own release from the camps and forced exile, the dissident son of Maxim Litvinov, Stalin's foreign minister, was giving an account of the ideas and tactics of the leading dissidents. Solzhenitsyn wanted to revive the Orthodox Church. Sakharov looked for a renewal of democratic institutions. Medvedev was waiting for the Soviet Dubček. A ripple of gentle amusement passed around the room. The thought that the grim, grey, conservative ranks of the Brezhnev party could spew forth a radical reformer was just too unlikely for those of us present to take seriously. But that is what happened. As we have seen, the system was chronically, but not necessarily terminally, ill. Although the accumulating problems were evident, there was no sign of a political force able to circumvent the powerful institutions and cultures which acted as its life support. Without an individual such as Gorbachev, there was no apparent way the life support might have been turned off.

Some have portrayed Gorbachev as a blundering surgeon who forced his way into the operating theatre and accidentally kicked out the plug of the life support machine, thereby unwittingly killing the patient he wanted to save. Such misinterpretations largely arise through a failure to appreciate the complexity and subtlety Gorbachev required, particularly in the early years, arising from the difficult conjuncture which had brought him to power, and the ambiguity he had to preserve in order to stay there. As we have seen, no Soviet leader since Stalin had absolute power – they had to maintain support at least in the Politburo and Central Committee. Even Stalin felt the need to manipulate institutions to get his way in his last months. Especially as he established himself, a Soviet leader needed a form of consensus. Gorbachev was no exception and he never had the freedom to do as he liked. It is important to remember this at all points in his career. It is also important to understand the ambiguous pressures which had brought him to power in the first place.

Brezhnev's complacency, which had not been overturned by Andropov because of lack of time and which had enjoyed a farcical coda under Chernenko, had been based on appeasing the cadres. The accumulating problems, especially the economic slowdown, had, however, alarmed two major wings of the party leadership, the neo-Stalinists and the reformers, who, otherwise, were far apart and agreed on little else but the need for some kind of remedial action. For the neo-Stalinists, whose leading spokesman was Yegor Ligachev, the solution lay in rejuvenating the existing system by restoring morale, especially among the workers, and reviving the socialist dream with the command economy and productionism as its practical means. Standing up to western cultural imperialism, reasserting Soviet patriotism and leading an assault on vodka culture were key policies to achieve the desired ends. A touch of 'Slavophile' Messianism lingered in the thoughts of the neo-Stalinists. Soviet Russia would once again be a beacon of liberation from exploitation. Reformers, on the other hand, were more 'westernisers'. They had compared the impact of the suppression of initiative and enterprise in the Soviet Union with the buoyant freedom of democratic societies which had become leaders in technological innovation, rising productivity and cultural development of both elite and mass. They even produced more vigorous Marxist debate, for example in the emergence of Eurocommunism, than the Soviet Union itself. Reformers believed that some loosening of central control over politics, culture and the overplanned economy would free up enterprise and create a new positive relationship between leaders and people. They were much impressed by the Prague Spring and had deplored its suppression. Ever since, many of them had nurtured its principles and hopes in their own hearts but had had to negotiate many obstacles in expressing them. They were also encouraged by Eurocommunism which adapted Marxist–Leninist principles to the democratic norms of Western Europe. Indeed, many said it abandoned Leninism through such acts as the French Communist parties' abrupt abandonment of the principle of the 'dictatorship of the proletariat' in 1976 and the Italian Communists' encouragement of a 'historic compromise' with the long-ruling Christian Democrats. The rapprochement was sabotaged by terrorists (apparently of the ultra-left but, according to some, perhaps linked to the CIA-backed ultra-right) who, in 1978, abducted and murdered its chief advocate among Christian Democrats, the former Prime Minister Aldo Moro. His body was symbolically left in the boot of a car in a Rome street halfway between the Christian Democrat and Communist Party headquarters. Although, in the west, this helped turn the rising tide of Eurocommunism and fed into the renewed Cold War and aggressive 'new right' of the 1980s, in the communist world the idea of a 'third way' between Stalinism and unrestrained capitalism continued to evolve. The hope was to combine the gains of the Soviet revolution – notably the economic and social rights of people to secure employment without exploitation plus basic education and healthcare denied to the majority of the world's non-communist population – with democratic political and human rights norms – notably free speech, free elections and the rule of law. Clearly, the recipes of the two groups were very different. The neo-Stalinists were also much more firmly within the political culture of Soviet communism and, some would say, of autocratic and nationalist elements in traditional Russian political culture. Clearly any alliance between them would be tricky and the reformers had very much the weaker hand. If they had any ace at all it was that the neo-Stalinist approach had been tried before, even by the early Brezhnev regime, and had come up short, therefore something more radical must be tried. However, before 1985 the country did not look to have much of a taste for radicalism. In the early, pre-*perestroika* days of Gorbachev's leadership, the neo-Stalinists had the upper hand and it was necessary for the new leader to be especially wary.

A remarkable example of what had brought the two wings together can be found in a film of this period, the documentary directed by Yuri Podnieks entitled *Is it Easy to Be Young?* Throughout the film the camera is addressed by a variety of young people, starting with a punk rocker who trashed a railway carriage after a pop concert and then moving on to an avant-garde artist, a Buddhist postman, an Afghanistan veteran and many others. As if the point was not already being made sufficiently obvious a central moment is made up of a series of talking heads in a main square in Riga, the capital of the Soviet Republic of Latvia where the film was made. In front of an enormous statue in honour of the Latvian Riflemen – noted as early and robust supporters of the Bolshevik revolution in 1917 – teenagers tell the audience that they do not know who the statue is for, what the significance of the Riflemen is and that they are not interested in politics. The implications of the film were clear. It promoted a message on which both reformers and neo-Stalinists could agree. The Brezhnev years had reduced the spiritual and ideological commitment of the population to zero and created a confused and apathetic younger generation, with all that that implied for the future of the Soviet project.

It portrayed ideological cynicism and a multitude of channels through which people were building 'alternative' cultures around which they based their lives, cultures which closely resembled those of their counterparts in the west. Incidentally, the extraordinary variety of microcultures presented also undermined totalitarian views of the system which over-stressed central control which, had it been effective, would have prevented the evolution of such microcultures. While Latvia, as a republic which had only been absorbed into the Soviet Union during the war, was not typical, the message was applicable to much of the Soviet Union.

While reformers and neo-Stalinists could agree on the problem, the solutions were quite different. For the former, radical innovation of an as yet unspecified kind was required. For the latter, a return to the principles of the past, notably of wartime and the pioneering spirit of the First Five-Year Plan, were essential. Neither side was yet strong enough to impose itself on the other, and they had to hang together in order to survive against the conservatives who wanted to preserve the Brezhnevite status quo. It is not surprising that, in the early stages, the reform process was presented in forms which could unite both sides for the time being, in particular a return to Leninism, the resurrection of the principles of 1917 and qualified praise for the Khrushchev period. Ultimately Gorbachev went far beyond such constraints but, as he said to the economic reformer Abel Abanbegyan who questioned (as so many others have done) whether Gorbachev was really committed to radical change since he started out with such limited and traditional-looking policies, 'What else could I do? They had me surrounded.'[1] It is no surprise that, as he built up his own platform, Gorbachev could go no further than ambiguous signs and gestures. Gorbachev's policies had to unfold as he went along for at least two reasons. First, had he unveiled his intentions too soon he would have been dismissed. Second, the task ahead was enormous, unprecedented and extraordinarily difficult. A wisecrack of the time put it thus: 'It's easy to make fish soup out of an aquarium but how does one make an aquarium out of fish soup?' That was the scale of Gorbachev's task. Improvisation was unavoidable. Let us look first at the way the policy of reform developed and then turn to the, ultimately fatal, obstacles it encountered.

The Development of the Reform Process

After lingering at the gates of the next world for some weeks, Konstantin Chernenko finally died on 10 March 1985. His death was announced the following day at 2.00 p.m. after Moscow had been magically and apparently instantly decorated with ceremonial flags and black drapes. However, as acute Soviet observers immediately noted, the television announcer had not been wearing a black tie. In the conditions of the time this was an unmistakable symbol that mourning would not be prolonged. Three hours after the announcement, that is, with unprecedented rapidity, the appointment of Gorbachev to replace him was made public. In a speech, quite uncharacteristic in that it was short, Gorbachev laid down a number of markers, notably the need for democratisation, openness (*glasnost'*), convalescence (*uzdorovlenie*) and socialist legality. While the language was in itself unremarkable the tone was unmistakably different. For the first time in decades the new General Secretary seemed to mean what he said. In another apparently trivial but potent gesture, he attended Chernenko's funeral wearing a grey woollen astrakhan hat, rather than the conventional Russian fur *shapka* worn by all the other leaders on the podium. It was a small gesture but it spoke of individuality, self-confidence and unconventionality.

Gorbachev's first year was one of political consolidation. At the end of it he had a leadership almost free of influential figures of the Brezhnev years. Even those crucial to his appointment, like Gromyko, were dismissed. In Gromyko's case the sinecure of the Soviet presidency was his reward. New appointments were made – Ligachev, Ryzhkov, Yeltsin and others were brought in, often from the provinces, to take up key positions at the centre and maintain the fragile balance of reformers and neo-Stalinists. Persistent questions from western correspondents asking when the reforms would begin were met by a blank wall. Reforms? What reforms?

The tone changed abruptly in late 1986 and early 1987 when it was announced that 'revolutionary changes' were afoot. New words soon entered the world's vocabularies – *perestroika* (restructuring) and *glasnost'* which had, of course, already made its debut – together with Stalinist-sounding terms like *uskorenie* (speeding up). It is very important to grasp what the process meant at this point. First of all, there was no hidden blueprint, nor could there have been one. No one had infallible answers to the Soviet Union's problems. There was a spirit of improvisation and pragmatism. However, certain fateful strategic decisions had already been made. Above all, precedence was being given to political and cultural over economic reforms on the assumption that only a freer and more open society could identify priorities and implement the necessary changes in economic and social life. Behind this was another fateful assumption. The chief enemy of change would be the Brezhnevite bureaucracy which, as we have seen, had done reasonably well in the atmosphere of corruption and hypocrisy. If the bureaucratic machine was the enemy, what force could be exerted on it? Here, the crucial importance of *glasnost'*, socialist legality and democratisation, become clear. Only a concerted campaign by ordinary citizens – who knew intimately what the problems were and who needed the security and confidence of a framework of legality and human rights to allow them to express them – could take the process forward. At one level *perestroika* was saying to the population, 'Here is your chance to reform the system. If you don't take it the reforms will fail.' The passivity, even indifference, of the population to the process was an important cause of ultimate failure. We should note here that this was exactly the opposite strategy from that implemented in China, which also faced the problem of crawling out from under a decaying Stalinism. In China, the bureaucracy was used to implement economic reform while political and human rights reform was stamped out. In July 1989, when Gorbachev was the hero of the Tienanmen demonstrators, his path seemed the more feasible. At the beginning of the twenty-first century, however, the long-continuing success of Chinese economic reform suggests they have the better of it. However, the Soviet Union and China were different entities with different cultures, and democracy was perhaps more deeply rooted in the Soviet Union. In any case, the Chinese leadership still has to face the immense challenge of political reform which could yet bring its economic advances to nought if the country were to enter a period of prolonged political dispute.

The second preliminary point to note, especially from our point of view, is that the old Stalinist shortcomings were the prime targets. In the forefront was the command economy or, in the new phraseology of the time, the administrative command system, that is, the emergence and enforcement of decisions in a completely undemocratic way. Excessive centralisation, unnecessary secretiveness, the suppression of initiative were in the forefront of problems to be dealt with. The process of *perestroika* began with the identification of problems and the promotion of principles on which solutions should be based – democracy, the rule of law, *glasnost'*. It did not have practical measures to hand. The point was to allow them to evolve from greater public discussion and ever-widening popular participation.

A key question from our point of view is: where did our old friend 'productionism' fit into the new developments? This is not easy to answer, especially in the early stages. Many observers who are not very

sympathetic to Gorbachev suggest he was just another promoter of traditional productionism, a reformer who wanted to get the economy
straight in order to continue (or, for those who saw him as a Brezhnev in
a shiny suit, pretend to continue) the process of socialist construction. In
the early days, there was even a new Five-Year Plan (approved in early
1986) and a Khrushchev-style perspective plan to the year 2000. Also,
as has been mentioned, the slogans of a renewed Leninism and a return
to the principles of 1917, notably peace, bread, land and Soviet democracy, became the order of the day. However, not to see the originality in
this would be a mistake. First of all, there were the important tactical
considerations which made a traditional framework and vocabulary necessary for the time being. After all, it was over his agreement to the Five-
Year Plan that Gorbachev had made his remark to Aganbegyan that he
had no choice because he was surrounded. Second, the principles themselves were revolutionary in the existing context. Attempting to restore
Soviet democracy had been at the heart of Roy Medvedev's dissident critique of the Brezhnev years. Land to peasants and factories to workers
had wide-ranging ramifications in the Soviet context, akin to privatisation, in that direct state ownership was being brought into question. Not
to see these differences turns Gorbachev into Ligachev. Ligachev and his
supporters were increasingly aware that Gorbachev was aiming for
something much more than one more Stalinist heave to get the system
going again. In fact, although improved living standards were deemed
an important part of *perestroika*, the broader aim of creating a 'healthy'
and 'normal' society in the Soviet Union – in which citizens would take
greater responsibility for their own lives and 'civil society' would take
over many of the state's functions – was at least equally important to
Gorbachev.

Such were the broad principles of *perestroika*. How were they transferred into everyday political, cultural, social and economic change?

The imaginative breadth and originality of *perestroika* can best be seen
in the spheres of politics, culture and foreign policy. In a major speech
in 1987, on the seventieth anniversary of the October revolution,
Gorbachev declared there would be no blank pages in Soviet history.
True, his own *tour d'horizon* of Soviet history in the speech did little to fill
them in. It was, however, a signal for the biggest outpouring of historical analysis of the system in its history. At first, it was, not surprisingly,
the Stalin period which was the centre of attention. Some observers still
argue that Gorbachev was motivated only by the same instrumentalist
aims as Khrushchev. However, there were none of Khrushchev's

confining conditions. The debate tumbled out into the open and raged, beyond control, in the press, in books, on television, in the very streets. Organisations were set up to commemorate the past and bring together camp survivors. Makeshift memorials were established to remember the victims. One was set up on Lubianka Square facing the KGB headquarters. All previous taboos on the 1930s were quickly broken. Bukharin was not only rehabilitated but appeared, for a short time, to be the patron saint of *perestroika*, which was being presented as a kind of updated NEP. Writings of Trotsky appeared in bookshops by 1988. By 1989 the heritage of Lenin himself was being brought into question. The different camps of interpretation of Gorbachev argue two ways about this. For the sceptics, it was a sign of the process simply running out of control and going beyond the limits set for it by the General Secretary. Others point to promptings from the Kremlin itself encouraging radical reassessment of the role of Lenin.[2] In any case, the holy of holies was being desecrated. The censorship apparatus was virtually abolished in 1988, an unequivocal sign of the leadership's commitment to deep radicalisation. There can be no argument that this was in any sense a neo-Stalinist measure and, as we shall see, the unease of the neo-Stalinist wing of the party was getting more and more obvious.

The years 1988 and 1989 were the high points of *perestroika*. The economy was still functioning. Cooperatives were bringing a new range of goods to city streets. Political organisations of all kinds were set up. Anarchists took over the Moscow square named after their mentor Kropotkin to make speeches denouncing Marxism and to sell their newspapers. Liberals formed a powerful Democratic Union which eventually organised the biggest independent mass demonstrations in the streets and squares of Moscow and Leningrad since the revolution itself. As well as political works, bookstands sold works by formerly banned Soviet authors – Solzhenitsyn and Pasternak being the most symbolic. Foreign writers like Freud were freely available for the first time. Self-help books on everything from herbal medicines to how to build your own dacha became available. Erotic and pornographic books and magazines appeared. An enormous number of independent newspapers were published. It would be no exaggeration to say that, at the time, the Soviet Union had the freest press in the world, since resources to set one up could still be found fairly easily and there were no laws, even of libel, to limit what could be written. Soviet people bought up the papers by the bucketful, often buying several a day to see what was happening. The explosion of sales even affected the rejuvenated official press led by

Pravda, the party newspaper, *Izvestiia*, the central government newspaper and stalwarts such as the Writers' Union and army newspapers, *Literaturnaia gazeta* and *Krasnaia zvezda*. The Communist Youth League paper *Komsomolskaia pravda* was, for a while, considered one of the most avant-garde. The explosion of reading soon led to a shortage of paper – seen by sceptics as a means to limit the outpouring – and it was a scramble to get the limited number of copies of favoured papers as they appeared in kiosks.

Religion, too, was fully rehabilitated. After facing some scepticism on the part of believers, the state Religious Affairs Committee became a partner in the reopening and restoration of churches, mosques and synagogues. For the first time in Soviet history religious texts, sacred works, liturgical books and religious classics became freely available. The Orthodox Church set up a series of kiosks on the streets which also sold religious artefacts. It was a heady moment for everyone.

The main fruit of this period of massive openness was the Congress of People's Deputies elected in March and convened in May 1989. Although sceptics pointed out that it was based only on indirect elections, it was, nonetheless, one of the freest talking shops in the world. It had no real powers, but every shade of Soviet opinion was represented. If Gorbachev had wanted deputies to come together to identify the Soviet Union's problems, he was not disappointed. Every aspect of Soviet life was examined and, for the most part, denounced. In particular, religious, nationalist and ecological themes emerged with full force. The country was riveted to live television broadcasts of its meetings. However, if there had been any hope of it proposing solutions, they were not fulfilled. It tended to be highly negative. Any proposals for steps forward were few and far between by comparison and were, in any case, contradictory. It was easier to describe the fish soup and demand explanations about how it had been produced than it was to reconstitute the aquarium.

The year of 1989 was also the peak of the international dimension of *perestroika*. Even in the ambiguous early days bold international initiatives were announced, eventually labelled 'New Thinking'. These included a moratorium on nuclear testing, a renewed urgency to limit nuclear weapons, and a call for the eventual total abolition of nuclear weapons. The Soviet Union even proposed that all foreign bases of every power should be abolished. In response to Reagan's appeal over Berlin to 'tear down that wall' Gorbachev had announced that nothing was forever. In December 1988, Gorbachev announced at the United

Nations that the Soviet Union would not interfere in the internal affairs of any other state, in effect finally turning the Brezhnev doctrine upside down. Gorbachev's spokesman, Gennadi Gerasimov, added fuel to the flames by glossing the new policy as the Sinatra doctrine – each country would have to do things its way. Sceptics argued that such overtures were just warmed-over Soviet peace rhetoric and were part, as ever, of an ideological campaign to wrong-foot the west at little cost to the Soviet Union. However, 1989 was an *annus mirabilis*. It opened when a promise to withdraw from Afghanistan by February, deemed to be pure window-dressing by the sceptics, happened on schedule. Then the really unthinkable happened. On 3 July 1989 Poland voted in its first non-communist government of the post-war era and the first in the Soviet bloc for four decades. Moscow's reaction? An invitation to the new premier, Mazowiecki, to visit Moscow where he was cordially received and Gorbachev told him that, though it might seem odd to many people, he wished him well in his endeavours. The communist leaders elsewhere in the bloc were scarcely able to believe their eyes. They knew their survival depended ultimately on the knowledge that Moscow would back them by force if necessary. If Moscow was no longer prepared to intervene there was no hope for them. The dramatic events of the autumn saw the peaceful surrender of communist regimes all over the bloc. By and large the greater the influence of Moscow in a particular country, the smoother the transition. In East Germany, where the leaders hated Gorbachev and tried to resist change, events turned on a knife edge, but violence was avoided and, in the most spectacular and symbolic moment, the Berlin wall was, without a murmur from Moscow, torn down. Only in Romania and Yugoslavia, countries long courted by the west and further from Moscow's influence than others, did the confrontations break out into violence, in the latter case with more than a decade of bloody repercussions. While Gorbachev, no more than anyone else, could foresee the full consequences, he never expressed regret about what was happening, nor did he take the slightest step to stop the changes. On the contrary, he argued that those who left it longest would suffer most. Only the international consequences of the reunification of Germany caused serious concern, not the collapse of the communist regime itself. The Kremlin tried to hold out for concessions over German neutrality in return for reunification, but was unprepared to take the serious steps that would have been necessary to stop it, so unification went ahead in the form of the swallowing up of East Germany by West Germany. It was a humiliating moment for Gorbachev but not one of serious consequence. The promised withdrawal of the massive Soviet troop forces in East Germany went ahead on schedule. While the longer-term consequences, in the form of NATO expansion and Russia's role in Europe, have still to be resolved, there can be no doubt that the Yalta agreement was completely dead. No greater break with Stalinist (or Brezhnevite) foreign policy than German reunification could be imagined. The Cold War in Europe was over. In an age of missiles and nuclear rockets rather than tanks, the need for a defensive area and control of land invasion routes was no longer vital. New thinking had certainly come to triumph over old dogmas.

In two years of serious implementation from 1987 to 1989, *perestroika* had destroyed key aspects of the Stalinist system at home and abroad. The planning system was no more. Censorship had been abolished. The secret police were no longer a threat. Major steps had been taken to restore genuine democracy and human rights. A rule of law, to which the authorities were also subject, was being developed. The Soviet bloc was no more. The party still maintained a monopoly of actual power, and the slogans of socialism had not entirely disappeared, but their transformation did not appear to be far off. However, in two more years, the process had collapsed. Gorbachev was out of a job. The Soviet Union itself was no more.

Nemesis

The context in which *perestroika* was introduced could hardly have been worse. The international climate had been poisoned by the second Cold War which had seen successive squabbles over participation in the 1980 Moscow and 1984 Los Angeles Olympic games and had peaked with President Reagan describing the Soviet Union as 'the Evil Empire' and the British Prime Minister Margaret Thatcher comparing Soviet foreign policy to that of Hitler. The shooting down of a Korean airliner that had inexplicably strayed far into Soviet airspace precipitated the worst of this hate campaign even though, as it happens, it was the second time such an incident had happened. In 1978 the Korean Airlines jet was forced down but was able to make a shaky landing at a Soviet military base. The possibility that such tragedies could happen in error was brought home to the United States when it, too, accidentally shot down an Iranian airliner in the Persian Gulf, which may in turn have provoked the bombing of French and American airliners in 1989. Be that as it may, an intense campaign of vilification and doctored tape intercepts was launched by the United States over the Korean jet.

Internally, the sad spectacle of the ailing Brezhnev and the toing and froing of policy in the Andropov and Chernenko periods had led to an exponential growth in cynicism and apathy. The devastating nuclear accident at Chernobyl lowered Soviet credibility abroad even more and, apart from the terrible long-term human cost which has yet to be calculated, it dealt a severe blow to the economy through the cost of containment and the loss of investment and energy capacity. In December 1988, while Gorbachev was at the United Nations in New York, Armenia was struck by a dreadful earthquake which claimed some 25 000 lives and destroyed thousands of buildings. Nothing showed the difficulties of the Soviet Union more clearly than its response to this tragedy. The last comparable predecessor, the Tashkent earthquake of 1966, had seen rapid mobilisation of all-union resources on almost a wartime scale. Construction squads from every republic descended to help the rebuilding. In Armenia, the local government had no resources to match the required tasks and other republics were slow to divert their own, increasingly jealously guarded, assets. It was a reminder that a weakening of central institutions and will was not all beneficial.

Nonetheless, the key difficulties lay elsewhere. The crux of *perestroika* was to release economic energies. But no one knew how. Institutional changes were brought in. In June 1987 a Law on the Enterprise was promulgated, which gave greater freedom to factories to seek out their own resources, pay their employees and dispose of their output, effectively weakening the hold of the central plan which slid quietly out of view. Another law allowed peasants to secede from the collective farm, though the absence of a clear and enforceable law on property rights complicated the issue. Third, a law of May 1988 broke the state monopoly on economic activity by permitting the formation of cooperative enterprises which sprang up quickly, mostly in the form of retail sales kiosks which mushroomed in city streets, and small restaurants which tended to equate more with western norms of quality and service than their traditional Soviet state equivalent.

The next big issue was what to do about ownership of enterprises. While the term 'privatisation' is usually bandied about, many so-called approaches to privatisation would have qualified as socialisation in the capitalist world in that control of institutions was sometimes handed over to employees. Broader strategic plans for extending and speeding up the transformation of state ownership and control into a greater use of market mechanisms abounded. The most loudly touted was the Shatalin 500-day plan for 'shock therapy' which Gorbachev dithered over and eventually implemented in a watered-down version in October 1990. For most Soviet citizens the crucial question was prices. Job security, low personal taxation and state subsidies on key products – bread, meat and many staple foodstuffs plus rents, heating, electricity and public transport – had been essential to their living standards and had been a kind of *quid pro quo* for their economic headaches – scarcities, poor quality, low pay. A transition from a planning and subsidy-based system to an, as yet, unclear set of market relations, offered the unenticing prospect of facing steep price rises as subsidies were withdrawn while the supposed benefits, such as increased production and a better balance between demand and supply, were further down the line. When unemployment and the degradation of public services (transport, medicine, education) also began to feed into the equation, the population as a whole wondered what good would come out of it for them. Although, at the end of 1989, the worst was yet to come, the beginnings of inflation, unemployment and severe economic contraction were already apparent.

One thing is indisputable. The economy had begun to collapse. In the widely used phrase of the time, there was plenty of shock, but no therapy. There were many contributory factors. The enterprise law was unclear and revised several times. The newly formed cooperatives were hated by the ordinary population because they charged substantially higher prices than the state and were seen as a disguised form of price rise. For example, meat would still be sold at the old prices in state shops, but less and less would be available since producers were increasingly free to get better prices from the cooperatives which became well-supplied but charged considerably more. The onus on supplying state shops also fell increasingly on local authorities whose success depended on the resources they could command and their energy in facing up to the task. Ill-run city districts had empty shops while more successful ones had better supplies just around the corner, in some cases.

The law allowing collective farmers to set up independently also failed. Here the explanation points in part to the difficulty of changing cultures. The number of farmers wanting to take the risk of separation was small and they were faced with a mountain of obstacles, not least the reluctance of the collectives to release their land to them. In a curious way, the collectives had become the new communes and as the peasants had forced those who had separated under the Stolypin legislation of 1907–9 back into them as a priority in 1917 and had clung to the communes in the 1920s, so, ironically, the collectives they had fought so hard to stay out of in 1929–30 had become the focus of their still-strong collectivist interest. The survival of the collective, most farmers thought, offered a better chance of survival than its break-up. In any case, the new project may itself have been flawed in that the idea of turning back to individual peasant agriculture at the end of the twentieth century seems anachronistic in the extreme. In the event, the collectives, freed of state direction, muddled on as best they could. Rural areas were hit particularly badly by the collapse of subsidised services (buses, shops, medical facilities) and the large proportion of pensioners saw their small fixed incomes eroded savagely in the face of inflation.

Damaging as the above phenomena were, there was one other area which caused even greater, and even less solvable, problems. The most devastating and uncontrollable force unleashed by *perestroika* was also one of the least expected. It first emerged in the Caucasus in the Armenian enclave of Nagorno-Karabakh, whose status had been laid down in 1923 and which had been quiescent ever since. No one predicted the reemergence of nationality conflict in such a forgotten corner, but memories were long. Fighting broke out in the main town, Stepanakert, in February 1988 over attempts to reunite the enclave with Armenia. Counter-riots broke out in Azerbaidzhan and in the town of Sumgait Azeris massacred Armenians. Demons were emerging. It was the prelude to widespread chaos.

The role of nationalities in the derailing of *perestroika* is as complex as it is important. First of all, as we have already seen, it was not the outburst of nationalism which led to the crisis, but the crisis which led to the outburst of nationalism. In other words, it was a secondary force aroused, from its slumbers by the loosening of the grip of the centre. That said, once aroused, it showed itself to be a still-powerful monster. A full account of the survival, reemergence and impact of nationality issues is beyond our scope but a number of further observations need to be made.

The most obvious fact about nationalities in the Soviet Union – their great number and diversity – is not the most important. Even the authorities had difficulty in saying how many ethnic groups there were, the number fluctuating wildly. In 1929 there were said to be 194; in 1939, 97; in 1959, 126 and in 1979, 92.[3] However, their significance lies elsewhere. Up to now, we have had little cause to mention the variety of nationalities as a significant feature promoting or hampering the development and decline of the Soviet system. From the formation of the

USSR to 1988, nationality issues remained secondary. Horrors were certainly inflicted on them as they were on a variety of class, religious and social groups. Within the barbarous logic of Stalinism, whole ethnic groups were made to pay, by mass deportation, for the supposed potential treachery of some of their members in the Second World War. Chechens, Crimean Tatars and Volga Germans suffered in particular. Monstrous as their treatment was, it was probably of little impact on the wider currents of history. It was also the case that the benefits of the Soviet system could fall more heavily on some minorities. For example, the Central Asian population made more dramatic advances into the Soviet form of modernisation than any other group. Urbanisation, transport infrastructure, level of industrialisation, education, health services and so on were far more developed than across their immediate borders in Iran, Afghanistan and eastern Turkey, though in pre-Soviet times, the standard of living had been very similar across the border.

The main reason for nationality issues remaining secondary was that the vast majority of them were very small in number. The core of the Soviet Union consisted of Russians, Ukrainians and Belarussians who made up 75 per cent of the population and did not feel as ethnically distinct from one another as, say, Armenians and Estonians. Even at the beginning of the twenty-first century, when grouped in separate independent states, the sense of separation between these three core groups remains ambiguous and ill-defined. Only minorities seemed to assert full national independence. The remaining 100 or so nationalities only composed a quarter of the Soviet population and were immensely diverse and lacked any common interest. In fact, the feuds between them have, in almost all cases, proved more damaging than resentment of Russians. Connected with this is the fact that very few ethnic groups enjoyed a clear-cut national territory. Most of them had internal minorities. Many Armenians lived in Azerbaidzhan. Georgia had a Muslim minority in Abkhazia which claimed autonomy. Latvians were almost outnumbered by Russians in their own republic. Eastern Ukraine, including the Crimea which had been symbolically returned to Ukraine by Khrushchev in 1954, was predominantly Russian. Some nationalities were arbitrarily divided by existing boundaries. Ossetians dreamed of uniting the north of their land, which was in Russia, with the south, which was part of Georgia. Russia itself had as many nationalities within its borders as the Soviet Union itself. Tadzhiks, Uzbekhs and Kazakhs were dispersed valley by valley in the southern mountains. Tadzhiks and Kazakhs were also divided by international boundaries with Afghanistan and China respectively. In other words, the Soviet Union was composed of a large number of mini-Soviet Unions, and clean breaks were the exception.

It should also be borne in mind that it was some of the smallest minorities that became the most vociferous. In particular, the Baltic States, which of course had only been part of the Soviet Union since the military campaigns of 1944–5, showed the most hostility to Gorbachev's attempted renewal of the union. Altogether the indigenous Baltic ethnic groups – Estonians, Latvians and Lithuanians – comprised barely 2 per cent of the Soviet population and less than a fraction of 1 per cent of its land area. Equally intractable were the re-emerging problems of the Caucasus divided between four and a half million Armenians, four million Georgians (both of whom were Christian, though of different traditions) and seven million Azeris of Muslim background. In reality, these groups were highly secularised, but deep-rooted feuds had managed to survive across the generations even though, for example, soldiers from all groups had, with no great difficulty, fought side by side in the Soviet army in the Second World War. However, as the Soviet containment system lost its power, a wave of ethnic pressures of murderous intensity began to surface. By encouraging the people to speak up, *perestroika* had opened the way to the expression not only of rational, humane and democratic ideals, but also of primeval feelings that would have been better left unspoken.

Horrendously complicated though they were, nationality issues were not the only serious component of the crisis which was wrapping its tentacles around *perestroika*. Before looking at Gorbachev's attempts to formulate policies to deal with the problems, we need to delineate the other dimension of the crisis, since all aspects interacted with each other and solutions would have to embrace all of them.

A particularly vicious, interactive, self-reinforcing downward spiral existed between nationality issues and economic crisis. As the economy declined, nationalities protested against the centre. As nationalities protested they often withheld or interrupted the circulation of commodities, plunging the economy deeper and deeper into recession and contraction. This fed new resentments and further economic obstacles and so on.

There can be no doubt that the chief precipitant of economic crisis was the reform process itself. Although we can discuss economics under separate categories – inputs, outputs, prices, markets, raw materials, labour and so on – in the real world they are all interrelated to the point of inseparability. One cannot reform an economy the way one might renovate a house by, say, moving out, gutting the interior, replacing the roof, renovating the walls and then reoccupying. An economy is permanently 'occupied' and has to continue to sustain the life and well-being of those who live in it even while it is being renovated. *Perestroika* aimed not only to replace the roof but also to rearrange the foundations with minimum disturbance to the life of the occupants, a tricky task by any standards. In addition, a number of unpredictable but damaging external events made the process more difficult – let us think of them as storms which blew down part of the scaffolding during the renovation of our virtual house. In the forefront here was the decline in world oil prices in the mid-1980s, which deprived the Soviet state of crucial revenue, much of it in hard currency, just when it needed it. In April 1986 one of four nuclear reactors at the Chernobyl power station near Kiev got out of control and set off a fierce fire which released uncalculated amounts of highly toxic nuclear materials into the atmosphere. No one has fully calculated the human cost of this disaster but the immediate economic cost was itself substantial. Immense resources had to be deployed to extinguish the fire and protect the other three reactors. Massive quantities of boron had to be dumped on it. An improvised containment system – a concrete sarcophagus – had to be devised. It had to be built below the stricken reactor as well as above, because the fire was burning a hole into the ground and there was a danger of massive pollution of the water table. An area thirty kilometres in radius had to be abandoned immediately. Workers within the zone could only work for very short periods despite wearing protective clothing. After the completion of the emergency measures, the structure had to be constantly maintained and monitored. Incredibly, such was the demand for power in Ukraine that undamaged reactors at the plant were reopened. The disaster was also damaging because allegations of secrecy and cover-up were made, though these terrible twins are no strangers to the nuclear programmes of many other countries.

Chernobyl was the last disaster to occur under traditional Soviet conditions, that is, under which deployment of resources was made from right across the Union. For example, the heroic firefighters who succeeded in mastering the blaze came from all parts of the country. The next disaster, the Armenian earthquake of 1988, had, as we have seen, the sad privilege of being the first to occur under the new conditions of non-cooperating republics. Armenia was, by and large, left to cope alone with some help from the international community.

The fall in oil prices, nuclear disaster and earthquake were costly and diverted attention from *perestroika* but they were not the main causes of the deepening crisis. The difficulty of reform was the chief problem. It was easy to enumerate the problems – falling productivity, slow techno- logical innovation, falling growth rates, wild fluctuations in agricultural production, demand outstripping supply, arthritic structures for distrib- ution and marketing, a decaying transport infrastructure and many others – but where did one start? Setting enterprises free of central control was a leap into the unknown, dependent upon managers with no expe- rience of such conditions. Raising prices would severely alienate the public whose support for the renewal process was crucial. This opened up a crucial political question. Reform would entail pain in terms of falling living standards and even unemployment, breaches of the Soviet social contract in which economic shortcomings were compensated for by minimum levels of personal and economic security. How far would the population go along with this in the hope of better times emerging as a result? The technical issues were enormous. How and to what degree could market relations be introduced and where did one start? With big industries? With small enterprises? With services? Shouldn't a rule of law be laid down first with a new law of property? Wouldn't even that take years, maybe decades, to establish itself? No one had the answers, or, worse, everyone had different answers. The initial steps of the government were not encouraging in that they were timid and often unsuccessful. The law on the enterprise offered very limited indepen- dence and managers showed that, as predicted, they did not want to be bothered with new responsibilities of dubious provenance and effective- ness. Provisions were made to allow farmers to withdraw from collectives but there were no clear means to enable them to do so in that the oppo- sition of local soviets and the collectives themselves often made the law unrealisable. Under the loosely comparable Stolypin provisions of the post-1905 years, the state put its full weight behind separators from the communes since it was determined, for political reasons, to break them up. No such energy was put behind this, or indeed any, of the specific reform proposals. A law on cooperatives allowed new forms of indepen- dent (that is, non-state) associations to be set up. They mainly evolved in the service sector, setting up retail outlets – often kiosks scattered untidily and with minimal supervision of standards and trading prac- tices – in city centres and residential suburbs. A whole new variety of products quickly emerged, from bananas to Scotch whisky. Cooperative restaurants also mushroomed, sometimes offering speedy and efficient service without the surliness that often characterised state restaurants and canteens. However, such luxuries were only available at a price and did little for low-income groups like pensioners. The cooperatives were, as mentioned above, hated as agents of concealed price rises. Indeed, as dislocation of the traditional economy deepened, inflation began to speed up. The rock-like official stability of the traditional, non-convertible rouble had seen it rise steadily against pound, dollar and Deutsche Mark in the 1970s and early 1980s but in 1988 it began to waver. After 1991, hyperinflation and the daily devaluation of the rouble were ongoing.

By late 1989, *perestroika* had brought about the end of the Cold War, the dissolution of the Soviet bloc in Europe, a conclusion to Soviet intervention in Afghanistan and the first steps towards democracy and the rule of law within the Soviet Union. The dissolution of the Stalinist system had already been accomplished. The command economy and censorship were no more. The party no longer had even a pretence of unanimity, and political differences were out in the open. Productionism was forgotten about. The building of Leninist socialism was marginalised and a broader humanist ideology based, in Gorbachev's words from his first speech as General Secretary, on the principle of 'all in the name of humanity, all for the good of humanity' had replaced class struggle. The removal, in February 1990, of Article 6, the guarantee of the party's leading role in society, was a more dramatic sign of change than the fall of the Berlin Wall. It removed the political bedrock on which the Soviet political edifice had been built. Not only the Stalinist, but also the Leninist, heritage was thereby jettisoned. Remaining stalwarts of the old style were massacred at the polls in March 1990 when it was stipulated that party officials had to win the support of 50 per cent of the electorate (not just the electors) to stay in public and party office. At the same time Gorbachev, having declared the separation of party and public office, opted for the Soviet presidency, a state post from which he hoped to keep *perestroika* together, especially since the party's position in society had been weakened by the repeal of Article 6. However, he did not submit himself to direct election to obtain a mandate, no doubt fearful of the mischief Yeltsin could employ if he did, and contented himself with being elected by the partially reformed Supreme Soviet, promising a full-scale direct presidential election in four years' time. But, counteracting these massive achievements, the country was plunging into an ever-deepening economic crisis and entanglements arising from one of the last remaining vestiges of the Soviet system, the conditions of union itself. The social fabric was tearing. Devaluation of pensions, unemployment, delayed wage payments, rising prices for some – but not all – basic commodities began to reverse the indices of social development. Forgotten diseases began to reappear. Alcoholism rose to new heights. Strikes began to disrupt production even further. Declining regulation and freedom from fear of reprisal led to a rise in accident rates. Environmental considerations were cast aside in a rush to maximise economic growth – no longer in the traditional productionist form of building socialism but to ensure minimal supplies of foodstuffs, raw materials and heating fuel to stave off disaster. By late 1989 and early 1990 these processes had barely begun to make themselves felt but they became the ghostly shadows that dominated the 1990s for the majority of the Soviet population. Astonishing institutional, cultural and international reforms were being contradicted by potential economic disaster. Could *perestroika*, in its Gorbachevian form at least, survive? Could the master improviser work his way out of the crisis?

The Final Collapse

Gorbachev sceptics had been predicting that, in the unlikely event of him actually meaning what he said and really changing the system, he would be faced with a coup led by the usual suspects, the 'hard-liners' or 'conservatives' (that is, the Stalinists in the bizarre vocabulary of official Sovietology), the military and the KGB. By the end of 1989 Gorbachev had proved effective beyond the sceptics' wildest imaginings. Where was the coup?

The defenders of the Stalinist system had begun to grumble more openly about the way things were going in 1988, ironically taking advantage of a policy of *glasnost'* they wished to reverse. The focal point was a letter published on 13 March in a Leningrad newspaper by an obscure party traditionalist named Nina Andreeva who expressed alarm at the erosion of Stalinist values, especially of social discipline, central control and proletarian chauvinism, and called for a more 'balanced' assessment of Stalin. It was widely assumed that she was a stalking horse for Yegor Ligachev and those even more traditionalist than he. The protests remained amazingly muted throughout the 'year of miracles' through a combination of traditional discipline and loyalty to the leader, stunned incomprehension of what was happening and a failure to produce a sustainable alternative. However, Gorbachev had to continue with them in

his camp. A precipitate move from his central balancing act into the
growing reform camp would remove the restraints from the neo-Stalinist
wing of the party which did, indeed, remain strong in the central
bureaucracy, the military leadership and the KGB. Gorbachev could not
yet survive open conflict with them and they doubted whether they
could survive without Gorbachev. He represented a less bad option than
the reformers, grouping increasingly around Boris Yeltsin who, despite
having been flung out of the Politburo for insulting Ligachev in late
1987, was still a member of the Communist Party Central Committee. It
was he who had promoted the abolition of Article 6.

Thus Gorbachev still had to maintain support on both sides. During
1990 this became increasingly difficult in the face of growing claims of
national independence. The Baltic and Caucasus crises ground on. In
January 1990 Soviet troops went into Baku, the capital of Azerbaidzhan,
to overthrew a self-proclaimed popular front and to put an end to horrendous massacres of Armenians, the survivors of which fled the
province – one of the first examples of post-communist 'ethnic cleansing'. In March, the most confrontational of the Baltic States, Lithuania,
under a popular front elected in March led by Vytautas Landsbergis,
declared its independence. This led to a long-drawn-out embargo and
ill-tempered negotiations which damaged all concerned. The March
elections had also brought a new role for Yeltsin as the leading member
of the Russian Supreme Soviet, which elected him Speaker, a position
from which he was determined to make as much trouble as possible for
Gorbachev for whom he seemed to have developed a pathological
hatred. He threw a very large spanner in the works by declaring Russian
'sovereignty' in June 1990. While gratitude is a virtue almost absent
from any politics, it is rather stunning that so many beneficiaries of
Gorbachev's reforms should think mainly of turning them against him.
It has also been held against him that he went about sawing off the
branch on which he sat, by democratising the country before it had been
economically reformed. If economic reforms were to succeed, then the
draconian central powers of the traditional apparatus would, so the
argument goes, have enforced the changes. However, Gorbachev and
his supporters were less sanguine, believing that the traditional apparatus was not a potential mechanism for reform but the chief obstacle to it
which had to be broken up. Once again, the Chinese reform process
provides a directly contrary example.

It has also been suggested that Gorbachev should have faced the
nationality crisis by quickly granting independence to the Baltic and

Caucasus states. On the face of it, there is a great deal to be said for such a policy, but Gorbachev was held back by two considerations. In the first place, it is unclear whether the hard-liners would have worn it. It might have precipitated the much vaunted coup at a time when it still had a chance of success in spring or summer 1990. In truth, the tide was turning so quickly that the chances of stopping it by means of a coup were becoming more Canute-like with every passing month. The Soviet restorationists were missing their moment. Though it is a moot point as to exactly when *perestroika* could be considered irreversible, it was not clear in mid-1990 that it had reached the point of no return, and Gorbachev continued to try to keep the neo-Stalinists on board. Giving away sovereign Soviet territory, a cause dearer to the heart of Brezhnevites than the struggle for socialism, was unlikely to impress them.

Gorbachev's second constraint from accepting independence was a more positive one. He tried to sell the reform process to the dissident states, urging that the Soviet Union from which they wanted to secede was in the process of radical transformation and that it should become a union which the minority nationalities would want to be part of. The logic of the situation was that it would become a kind of Eastern European Union, sharing commitment to democracy, a common currency, a common economic space, shared military and foreign policy and a central judiciary to defend human and constitutional rights. Within this framework the sovereign nations would flourish. However, for many reasons, the small birds were determined to fly. Gorbachev's dream was all very well, but it might not turn out that way. Reactionaries might replace him. Better to flee the cage while the door was open than wait in the hope of better conditions and risk it being slammed shut again.

Ironically, the weaker their chances the more active the reactionaries in the Soviet leadership became. The, from their point of view, horrors of reform and the apathy of the population led them to begin, belatedly, to flex their muscles. They were aided and encouraged enormously by a loss of confidence in Gorbachev by some of his closest supporters. In the forefront was the foreign minister Shevarnadze who, observing the reactionaries' manoeuvre from his privileged position, issued a dramatic warning in December 1990. He portrayed in stark terms his fears of a future coup, berated Gorbachev for his inactivity in the face of it, and resigned his post.

In January 1991 Shevarnadze's prophecies appeared to be coming true. Newly established Internal Ministry troops took an aggressive stance in the Baltic States, to the point of conducting coups in Lithuania and Latvia where communications and television stations were attacked. Massive public demonstrations countered these blundering moves, though some twenty people were killed. One of them was a cameraman working with Yuri Podnieks, the man who made *Is it Easy to Be Young?*, who filmed his own death in the course of making yet another of Podnieks's extraordinary documentaries. The troops were halted, but Gorbachev's position came into question even though he claimed not to have given orders to open fire. Gorbachev sceptics suggest this was a cover. In any case, had they had any political sense, the perpetrators of the Baltic outrages, including Internal Affairs and Security chiefs Bakatin, Yazov, Pugo and Kryuchkov, should have seen that their actions had had precisely the reverse effect to that desired. Rather than intimidate the minnow states into compliance, they had ensured their determination to leave the Union no matter what.

In many respects, Shevarnadze's prophecies had been self-fulfilling. As other reformers like himself left the Gorbachev camp the Soviet president was forced into greater reliance on the enemies of *perestroika* within his government. Ever the master tactician Gorbachev was able to turn this partly to his own advantage in that by keeping them within his government as long as possible they were under partial control. To adapt the colourful expression attributed to Lyndon Johnson with reference to J. Edgar Hoover, better to have them inside the tent pissing out than outside the tent pissing in.

Gorbachev's agenda in early 1991 was exceptionally full. In addition to the multiplying internal crises and the accelerating downward spiral of the economy resulting in longer and longer queues at food shops, he was also trying to implement New Thinking, notably the principle that no state should intervene militarily in the internal affairs of any other, in respect of the crisis following Iraq's invasion of Kuwait in August 1990. Shevarnadze's successor Primakov tried to head off the full application of American military force, but the Soviet Union's status and power had fallen so low and its hopes of American loans was so crucial, that, in the end, it had no independent weight and had to go along with American policy. Nonetheless, the issue was very distracting.

Internally, while little was done on the economic front, Gorbachev put his main effort into untangling the Gordian knot of interrepublican relations since, until an agreement was reached, central authority was increasingly ignored and no progress could be made on other fronts. Increasing tendencies of each republic to limit trade with others deepened the crises. Tractors produced in Belarus remained unusable because Russian suppliers would no longer sell carburettors. Cigarette supplies were reduced because interrepublican trade in filters came to a halt. So it was with many commodities. A new Union treaty was imperative.

Gorbachev and his advisers worked endlessly to try and achieve it. No sooner was a draft apparently agreed than a leading player, usually Yeltsin as President of Russia or Leonid Kravchuk, the President of Ukraine, upped their demands. True to form, Gorbachev tried to circumvent such prevarications of the bureaucracy by mobilising the population, or at least attempting to get a mandate from it. A referendum held in March 1991 produced a massive majority of 76.4 per cent (on an 80 per cent turn-out) in favour of a renewed Union. In April a draft treaty was thrashed out but it was not to be formally implemented until August, a delay which proved fatal.

Throughout Gorbachev's period in office he had presided over a polarising polity. His strength had lain in his position astride the polarisation – each camp, feeling too weak to govern on its own, preferred Gorbachev rather than the other camp. After the publication of the draft Union Treaty, however, the camps split further and further apart. Gorbachev was going to have to jump, but failed to do so in time. At one extreme Yeltsin was touring the republics urging their leaders to take the maximum of power. On the other, anti-*perestroika* forces began to mobilise, led by the intransigents in the government itself including Prime Minister Pavlov and Internal Affairs and Security chiefs Pugo and Kryuchkov. They were able to draw on the Soviet traditions of proletarian chauvinism and Soviet (increasingly a front for Russian) patriotism plus discontent with declining living standards. Worker organisations came onto the streets to protest. In the republics, organisations of Russians, again largely workers, known as Interfronts (Internationalist Fronts), which had first appeared in the Baltic States, grew in strength and were nurtured by the anti-devolutionists. Their leadership represented an alliance of Russian nationalists and backward-looking party apparatchiks.

The continuing withdrawal of radical support for Gorbachev and its reorientation around the unlikely figure of Yeltsin, who was eventually swept to office as first directly elected President of Russia in June 1991, gave the illusion to the anti-Gorbachev forces in the remaining Soviet institutions that their grip on the centre was tightening and, less illusory, that time was running out if they were to preserve it. They mobilised in the Central Committee to attack Gorbachev verbally on 24 April and attempt to reduce his powers but, still able to call their bluff, Gorbachev flaunted his resignation, forcing his opponents to cringingly produce a petition begging him to stay on.

If Gorbachev should have dismissed them at this point then he certainly should have done so shortly after when, on 17 June, Pavlov attempted to get the Supreme Soviet to hand over Gorbachev's presidential powers to himself and the Cabinet of Ministers, in other words to conduct a semi-legal coup. News of the attempt quickly reached Gorbachev who reacted quickly and angrily to get the proposal withdrawn. Incredibly, however, he did not dismiss those who had tried virtually to overthrow him. If anything, this was Gorbachev's fatal mistake. He believed that his two victories had shown they were still under his control and that, in the absence of radical supporters, he had few alternatives. However, his control was less than he thought and the situation led exactly the same group into the tragi-comic adventure which precipitated the final end of the Soviet Union.

Gorbachev left for a much-needed holiday in the Crimea, planning to return for the official signing of the Union Treaty on 21 August (ironically the anniversary of the invasion of Czechoslovakia which had planted the seeds of reform within the Soviet Communist Party). His absence provided his enemies with what they thought was one last chance to save their Soviet Union. In a hopelessly muddled, ill-prepared and half-hearted action on 18 August, Vice-President Yanaev, Prime Minister Pavlov, Interior Minister Pugo and KGB chief Kryuchkov declared Gorbachev released from his functions on grounds of health. Rather like the ill-thought-out Kornilov revolt of 1917 and their own blunderings in the Baltic States earlier in the year, the tragi-comic plotters provoked exactly the opposite of what they desired. The farce collapsed on 21 August. The insane plotters had not only blown apart the remnants of the Union they wanted to preserve, they had also disgraced the name of the party to such an extent that it was outlawed within ten days of the beginning of their mad adventure.

How did this happen? So incompetent were the plotters, they seemed to believe their action would be accepted as a *fait accompli* and took few steps to ensure the support they needed. Instead the coup created immediate division within the Soviet public authorities. A few came out in support. A larger number opposed them. The largest number played a wait-and-see-who's-winning game. Crowds came out onto streets. No one was prepared to open fire. Crack military units disobeyed the coup leaders' orders. Numerous prominent figures gathered at the seat of the Supreme Soviet (loosely the Soviet parliament), the Moscow White

House. After a few careful preliminary phone calls Yeltsin emerged in public and, famously, proclaimed defiance from the top of a tank. In so doing he was able to snatch the initiative from Gorbachev who was being kept incommunicado in the Crimea and even believed his life might be threatened. However, under the pressure of active opposition and massive refusal of support the coup quickly and predictably collapsed – though not before a few foreign governments had appeared almost to welcome it, by quickly accepting if not recognising it. They hoped, perhaps, that it would bring an end to the difficult challenges over principles of international affairs, the issue of foreign military bases and disarmament posed by Gorbachev's New Thinking. The collapse left the plotters cravenly rushing for the airport to head for the Crimea and throw themselves at Gorbachev's feet. A furious Gorbachev at last had them arrested.

When he returned to Moscow, still wearing his holiday clothes and clearly weary from lack of sleep, Gorbachev found himself in the middle of a new situation. At first, it appeared that Yeltsin might be cooperative in that he demanded the immediate implementation of the Union Treaty. However, things changed quickly. Yeltsin was unable to resist the opportunity to humiliate Gorbachev in public ceremonies implementing new policies, notably the banning of the Soviet Communist Party. Gorbachev had tried to resist this. Sceptics have seen it as a sign of his lingering Stalinism, but this overlooks the fact that one of the last things he did before his ill-fated holiday was to get the party at the final Central Committee Plenum on 25 and 26 July to abandon many of its entrenched Marxist–Leninist principles and open itself to a greater compromise with the market. In Gorbachev's words, 'Even those conservatives who longed nostalgically for the old order … realized that … such concepts as the market, civil society, a law-based state, free elections, political pluralism, a multi-party system, human values, integration in the world community and many other ideas of that kind were here to stay.'[4] Some Stalinism! The reformed party was the bedrock on which Gorbachev had planned to bring the Soviet Union to freedom in a more controlled fashion. It was, in any case, the last bulwark of social stability and the last significant all-union institution. To blow it away threatened stability in all respects. Yeltsin, as usual, was blind to such niceties. Bulldoze it out of the way and then see what happens, appeared to be his attitude.

What happened was the plunging of Russia and many of the republics into a chaos from which they have yet to emerge. Seeing the way the wind was blowing, the President of Ukraine, Kravchuk, declared full independence, perhaps mainly to pre-empt Yeltsin from imposing himself on Ukraine. Catastrophic short-termism was the order of the day. Practically all still-functioning institutions – ministries, the security agencies, the military – were subject to a mad scramble of division and grab, led by the increasingly assertive and independent republics. Gorbachev's Soviet Union dissolved under his feet leaving him stranded and entirely without a power base. He attempted to the end to try to restore order to the process, but the final blow was a secret deal by the Russian, Ukrainian and Belarussian presidents to set up a Commonwealth of Independent States, improbably based in Minsk. It was the end. Gorbachev had nowhere else to go. In a dignified speech broadcast on 25 December 1991 Gorbachev resigned. A few days later, at the year's end, the Soviet Union quietly expired. Practically the last Stalinist institution ceased to exist. The Soviet system had reached a definitive end.

11

A NEW TIME OF TROUBLES

In a supreme irony the Soviet system finally ended as it had begun –
through a misconceived, failed coup. In August 1917 General Kornilov
and his supporters, disturbed by the weakness and radicalism of the
Provisional Government, tried to overthrow it. Within two months the
Soviet Government had taken over. In August 1991, Pavlov, Pugo,
Kryuchkov and the other plotters, disturbed by the extent of Gorbachev's
plans to decentralise the Soviet Union, tried to overthrow him. By the
end of the year, the Soviet Union itself was no more. Nowhere could
Marx's aphorism that history repeats itself, the first time as tragedy, the
second time as farce, be more appropriately applied. Except the consequences of the 1991 coup were not a farce for millions whose lives have
been ruined and whose prospects are still ignored by the powerful
within the ex-Soviet Union and the influential without. Since 1991 the
powerful have become rich, the weak increasingly poor, while those in
the middle hover uneasily between the two.

The changes which followed were enormous. A couple of personal
experiences symbolise them. In 1996, I was flying from Birmingham,
England to Moscow via Paris. The passengers, from Paris, were overwhelmingly Russian, many of them clutching large packages with the
best Parisian brand names, especially of haute couture. They badgered
the flight attendants to find room to stow their excess carry-on luggage.
This was an unmistakably New Russian experience. For decades, when
one travelled to the Soviet Union on a western airline it was the exception rather than the rule to meet Russian passengers. At a more mundane but, perhaps, more surprising level, in August 1999, as I was
drafting this book in the small French hamlet of L'Estriverde on the

northern edge of the Loire Valley, I took time off one evening to cycle along the lane to the village of Fontaine Raoul. I was passed by a large truck on its way to the small packing station which was the staple of the local economy. Although the trailer was German I took a closer look at the truck itself. It seemed familiar but unusual. It was Russian. The two drivers had come from Vladikavkaz in south Russia. They had acquired the truck through privatisation of the Sovtransavto fleet and spent months on end in Western Europe hiring themselves out to haul loads around the Continent. They must have been the first Russians to penetrate this tiny corner of France. However, the very next morning, a family on a cycling holiday – two parents and a boy of ten – paused at the crossroads outside the house I was living in to examine the map. After several attempts to find a common language to communicate we stumbled on Russian. They were from St Petersburg and had flown to France, together with their bicycles, and were spending three weeks cycling in northern France. All of these things would have been exceedingly rare, even impossible, in high Soviet times. The best, and some of the worst, aspects of the new Russia are encapsulated in them. It is excellent to find so many Russians abroad but that is not the whole story. Where had the money being spent on Christian Dior clothes come from? How had the drivers actually acquired their truck? Did they have to pay people off for their permits and so on? One family of brave, happy holidaymakers could enjoy France, but how many shared their good fortune?

Within Russia, the ambiguities multiplied. Conspicuous signs of the new wealth in the major metropolitan centres emerged in the form of designer shops, upmarket shopping malls, many large imported cars, numerous nightclubs and casinos. Despite extensive government control of the media, especially broadcasting, a wide range of newspapers and books became available. Foreign films almost wiped out the once thriving domestic film industry. Successful cultural institutions from the Bolshoi Ballet to the Moscow State Circus set up affiliates which spend almost all their time abroad earning hard currency. The Russian Orthodox Church became highly visible in society. Food shops, markets and kiosks were well-stocked but beyond the reach of many. At the same time, law and order broke down. Many public services collapsed. Life expectancy plummeted to make the excess deaths total reach something like that of Stalin's purges. Much of industry collapsed. Agriculture entered a prolonged state of drift. Tax collection was arbitrary. Corruption in government and in law enforcement spread like a cancer. Authority was in dispute at all levels. The crudely conducted war in Chechnya festered on.

Nearly a decade after the collapse, nothing was in prospect to improve the situation. No one appeared to have a strategy for recovery. The election of Vladimir Putin in March 2000 offered little hope. As the creature of the newly rich elite, he was put in place to defend its interests. During the election campaign he refused to outline any policies for dealing with the crisis because, he said, any suggestions would simply be criticised in the press. He was the near-perfect example of a politician elected without revealing any policies. Only a naive and highly manipulated electorate, like that of Russia, could, one hopes, be so easily duped. Within the same time span of its first decade, the Soviet regime had undergone civil war and seen an even deeper collapse than the present one but had also recovered the lost ground and was poised for the Stalin revolution. The first post-Soviet decade saw nothing but decline and drift for Russia. Some of the smaller republics, notably the Baltic States and parts of Central Asia and the Caucasus, showed more resilience and attained modest niches for themselves, even though, in most cases, the achievements fell far short of the expectations of the early days of independence. But overall, the question has to be, what has gone wrong? In answering it, the main focus will be on Russia and on aspects of the post-Soviet situation which throw light on our main theme of the rise and fall of the Soviet system.

New Russia, New Russians

The fundamental feature of the present situation, as Lenin might have put it, is that parts of the old Soviet administrative elite are transforming themselves into a capitalist bourgeoisie. There had been a widespread theory, associated with the Yugoslav dissident communist Milovan Djilas but traceable to Trotsky and even to pre-revolutionary theorists like the Polish radical Jan Wacław Machajski, that the administrative elite of Soviet society was a 'new class' in Djilas's phrase, and, in effect, a ruling class. The limitations of this frequently quoted theory were that there were many restraints on the power and wealth of this elite which were incompatible with it becoming a ruling class in the fullest sense. For instance, property often came with office. A top-quality state dacha, for example, like a company car, would be lost if the job was lost. In any case, such things could not be bought and sold or handed on to children as of right. Ways were often found to hang on to such things, but they were dependent on the goodwill of the authorities.

They were grace-and-favour privileges, not personal possessions. In any case, the levels of privilege were much narrower than those of a normal ruling class. Brezhnev's seven-room apartment in Moscow and his dacha would barely have satisfied a western middle-manager. The luxuries of the system – imported Japanese electronic equipment, German washing machines and fridges and so on – would have been enjoyed by many affluent workers in Western Europe and North America. There were limits on conspicuous consumption and on the way one could spend one's money, for instance on restaurants, nightclubs, casinos and the leisure industry in general which were very underdeveloped in Soviet conditions. Even abroad, discretion was necessary as the surveillance of the KGB and of the host nation might well be operating. In a myriad of ways, while the elites clearly enjoyed a higher standard of living than the masses, they lived relatively modest lives compared to the multi-millionaires and comfortably-off upper-middle classes of the wider world.

Nothing illustrates the shortcomings of the 'new class' theory more than the way in which, since the barriers finally crashed, the elites, not just in Russia but in much of the former Soviet Union and its ex-satellite states, have gone about making up the difference by acquiring the real attributes of a capitalist ruling class. Once Yeltsin fired the starting pistol in 1991, the ambitious and unscrupulous embarked on a vicious scramble to control the assets of the former Soviet state. With ever-decreasing restraint they grabbed whatever could turn a good profit. In the front rank was the vast oil and gas industry with world-leading production worth billions of dollars. For the politically ambitious, television and the media became a target. Airlines, travel agencies, restaurants, leading shops, property, pharmaceuticals were all boom areas. At all levels, down to the lorry drivers mentioned above, the scramble was on to turn state property into profit-making personal property. At the top, private banks were created, which, in the absence of a state bank, even handled government finances. The winners in this race enjoyed massive prizes. Several became US dollar billionaires. Many became millionaires. New services sprang up to cater for the newly rich who were quickly dubbed 'New Russians' in the media. Nightclubs, casinos, prostitution flourished in Moscow as never before. Designer shops proliferated. Estate agents offered dachas around Moscow for millions of dollars which were often paid for in cash rather than through mortgages. One candidate in the 1996 presidential election boasted that he gave his wife US $10 000 pocket money on alternate days of the week. It is hard to see how he expected the impoverished electorate to support him after that.

Of course, not everybody won. Competition was fierce, unrestrained and violent. The new wealth created big-time losers. Wars between bankers cost the lives of several leading figures in the Moscow financial world. Protection rackets proliferated at high and low levels. 'Security' became a major growth industry. At times it was little more than semi-open gang warfare. Corruption spread like wildfire since the stakes were so high. Tax collectors, police, officials at all levels got in on the game. No one seems to have paid their taxes. No one was in a position to control the Gadarene rush.

Unedifying as this spectacle was from any point of view, it was made many times worse in that it occurred against a background of rapidly growing poverty and declining life expectancy for much of the population. Hyperinflation blew away the value of pensions and any modest personal savings people might have had. The collapse of the integrated economy of the USSR and of trade with its former communist partners brought the rapid decline of many major industries, including parts of the defence sector. The result was mass unemployment with no hope of 'restructuring' to create sufficient new jobs to take up the slack. Millions of people continued to work without pay in the hope of preserving their jobs for some moment of recovery in the future. State revenue collapsed. Teachers and academics were not paid for months on end. Printing of money kept the shaky bandwagon rolling at the cost of fuelling inflation even further. Public sector services – education and health – declined. Some went private to make up the shortfall but for rural pensioners not only did their pensions contract but rural shops and bus services disappeared as did travelling medical services. Again, the role of the Soviet state in providing jobs, health, education, housing and a minimum income for all its citizens, including the poorest, was also demonstrated. Crudely speaking, the collapse of the Soviet system was followed by one of the most outrageous and rapid transfers of resources from poor to rich in the history of the modern world. No wonder the impoverished older generation clung nostalgically to the unsavoury new Russian Communist Party to try to turn the clock back. Nothing could show more clearly that the Soviet system had constrained the wealthy and supported the poor. Declining mortality rates are the melancholy symbol of the lot of many in the new conditions. Male life expectancy, driven down by despairing alcoholism and failing medical services, fell from 69 years to 61 years by 1999. Though sources vary and the figures are debatable, in terms of excess deaths (that is, the number of those dying prematurely) the rate is approaching that of Stalin's purges.[1] While one cannot push the comparison too far, since we do not have defined conventions to compare economic mass murder with political mass murder, it is a clear sign of the contemporary disarray.

No serious measures were taken to control the situation, not least because those in government were lining their own pockets without shame. The Prime Minister Chernomyrdin had made a personal fortune from the oil and gas 'privatisation'. The shadowy figure of the billionaire Berezovsky appeared behind the creaking Yeltsin throne and appeared to provide resources for some of its more unpleasant dirty tricks.[2] Yeltsin himself stepped down with a vast, uncalculated, personal and family fortune and the essential accessory of a certificate guaranteeing immunity from prosecution for any wrongdoing in office. In fact, the authority of the state was one of the main victims of the new circumstances. Its collapse opened the road to the ensuing chaos. Lack of ability, and perhaps will, to reconstitute it, has prevented any strategies for improvement on a national scale from taking hold. Given that the state apparatus is highly corrupt, and that law enforcement and the judiciary are subject to bribery and/or official pressure, it is hard to see where a point of application exists for a policy of clean-up. The situation demands answers to the two key questions of nineteenth-century Russia – who is to blame and what is to be done?

Who is to Blame?

Many observers have blamed the remnants of the Soviet system for the current debacle. Indeed, it has a sizeable share of responsibility: low morale, initiative-sapping police surveillance and party control of all areas of life, overcentralisation and bureaucratisation, the slack working and administrative practices of the Brezhnev years, the mighty burden of defence spending, the alienation of much of the population from the state and from political responsibility were undoubtedly very damaging. But at the same time, especially compared to the situation they inherited from tsarism which passed on very similar shortcomings, the system also created certain assets. Part of the legacy of the Soviet system was a well-educated and socially secure population with basic medical provision, extensive industry, a cheap transport network, safe streets, cheap essentials for all such as housing, energy and basic foods. As far as institutions were concerned, the basic state structure itself was not the major problem. The problem was one-party domination of it. On the face of it,

Gorbachev's plan to eliminate the disadvantages and build on the posi-
tives was a defensible one. Gorbachev, whether he realised it or not
when he set out on his epic voyage, had arrived at that most tantalising
of modern mirages; 'the third way', a balance of the advantages of a
democratic market society with the social and economic rights (full
employment, free, universal education to tertiary level, basic housing
and heating for all and so on) which capitalist societies have failed to
deliver. However, it was not to be. Instead, egged on by extensive western support largely denied to Gorbachev, the leading role was taken
over by Yeltsin. Did he have a better strategy?

In truth, it is hard to find any long-term thinking in Yeltsin. He saw
the next barrier and smashed it down apparently without thought for
the consequences. In his early career, as party chief in Sverdlovsk (formerly Ekaterinburg where the tsar and his family had been put to death
in 1918) there had been disquiet that the Ipatiev House, in which the
royal family had died, was a potential site for pilgrimage. Yeltsin was put
in charge of razing it to the ground with bulldozers and a wrecking
crew. This appears to have been his forte. Once he came into central
politics, promoted there by Gorbachev, he used the same bull-at-a-gate
approach. Successive targets were food and transport problems in
Moscow when he was mayor, about which numerous stories circulated;
neo-Stalinist remnants in the Politburo such as Ligachev with whom
Yeltsin prematurely locked horns and nearly wrecked his own career;
Article 6 of the constitution against which he led the charge; Gorbachev
himself whom he clearly had come to detest, a tragic outcome since they
had complemented each other's approach beforehand, Yeltsin as the
icebreaker, Gorbachev as the navigator; the 1991 coup; and, finally, the
Soviet Union itself. By then he had run out of targets.

His record in picking up the pieces has been disastrous.[3] Under his
cunning and conniving eye, the advantages, such as they were, of the
Soviet system were squandered to the great gain, as we have seen, of the
New Russians and at the expense of the poor and the pensioners. Even
the most potent of Soviet institutions, its armed services, declined with
salaries not paid, equipment leaking out onto the world grey market for
arms and tanks, submarines and even nuclear weapons rusting away
without maintenance, a situation highlighted by the tragic loss of the
flag ship submarine *Kursk* in August 2000, and pride eroded by incompetent and dirty campaigns in Chechnya. As we have seen, Yeltsin carefully nurtured the one ex-Soviet institution that could have been most
readily (though not easily) discarded, the KGB, now FSB (Federal

Security Service). Even though its hold internally is nothing like that of its predecessor it has still been a powerful agent of dirty tricks, keeping the superwealthy in power.

Yeltsin, however, was not alone. He increasingly became the creature of his entourage, the front man for the new ruling clique known, absolutely accurately among Russians, as 'the oligarchs', though perhaps 'new plutocrats' would be even better.

Much of the discourse around the Yeltsin years has centred on the word 'transition'. Russia has been said to be in transition, from totalitarianism to democracy and/or from socialism to capitalism (though cynics might point to the incompatibility of the two goals of real democracy and capitalism). Indeed, as we have seen, the whole of Soviet history was itself marked by transition, though in the other direction. While every situation is always in some sort of transition, the term does have specific application not only to Soviet but to post-Soviet times. In both cases, conscious transition policies were being applied. What have they entailed in the Yeltsin years?

The focus of post-Soviet transition has been the economic system, the administrative command system. The first major initiative, the Shatalin 500-day plan, dates back to the late Soviet period and, as we have seen, was only implemented by Gorbachev in watered-down form. We can only speculate on how either of these variants might have worked out in practice because the original remained unadopted and the revised version was caught in the collapse of the Soviet Union. From that moment on, the whole tone of transition changed. The lingering goal of the third way disappeared from view and a headlong rush for an extreme version of free-market capitalism was the battle cry of the new leadership, aided and abetted by western specialists, such as Jeffrey Sachs from Harvard and Richard Layard from the London School of Economics. Many of them had had little or no prior experience of the Soviet economy and, initially at least, had little or no direct knowledge of Russian language, culture and traditions. The governments of Bush (and later Clinton) and Thatcher (later Major) and Helmut Kohl urged maximum 'reform' in the least amount of time. Large international loans and investments, denied to Gorbachev, flooded in. Moscow was rapidly awash with billions of dollars with no institutions of law or economic regulation to control the massive flows of money. The consequences outlined above were almost inevitable. The incentive of superprofits galvanised gangsterism, and the temptations of peculation undermined the successive, western-directed reform programmes of Gaidar and Chubais. The ruthless trampled over the principled, the strong trampled over the weak. The free market had arrived in Moscow.

It was not what Russians had expected. By and large, they were very naive about the outside world, expecting it to be benevolent and to back its rhetoric of support for democratisation and economic transition with concrete assistance. Strangely, even westerners, who might have been expected to know better, shared their optimism. George Soros, for example, bravely admitted that:

> The open societies of the West did not believe in open society as a desirable goal whose pursuit would justify considerable effort. This was my greatest disappointment and misjudgment. I was misled by the rhetoric of the cold war. The West was willing to support the transition with words but not with money, and whatever aid and advice was given was misguided by a market fundamentalist bias. The Soviets and later the Russians were eager for and receptive to outside advice. They realized that their own system was rotten and they tended to idealize the West. They made the same mistake as I did: they thought the West was genuinely concerned.[4]

Tragically, they had picked the wrong advisers, and the transition had happened at a moment when the international conjuncture was still in favour of unrestrained free-marketeers. Russians, like many East Europeans, had naively expected transition to lead towards a comfortable Swedish-style social democracy. Instead, they had been hurled headlong into the Third World, into Brazilianisation, a corrupt, superrich elite presiding over a crudely formed, nouveau riche middle class, and a demoralised and fragmented working class shading into a vast, marginal, impoverished underclass of the cities and the rural areas. It was no coincidence, perhaps, that the western experts, like Sachs and Layard, had made their reputations dealing with the problems of Latin American economies with which, in the beginning, the late and post-Soviet economy had little in common.

What is to be Done?

In August 1998 the gravy train hit the buffers. Massive devaluation wiped out many, but by no means all, paper fortunes. For a while it had a sobering effect. Even the plutocrats realised their linkages to western

capital might have problems. Devaluation stimulated domestic production and put exports out of reach of many. Rising oil prices also
promised some relief to the economy. At last, one hoped, Russians
would begin to take responsibility for their own fate and keep at arm's
length the fashionable nostrums of the west. However, the backlash has
tended to be a narrow nationalist one. Not surprisingly, anti-western
feeling has been growing. Many factors have all added to the sense of
hostility from abroad. In the front rank is the encroaching menace of
NATO, which now embraces several former Soviet bloc nations even to
the point of discussing Estonian membership. The misguided bombing
of Russia's historic ally Serbia (over whose defence Russia had helped
precipitate the First World War) considerably worsened the situation.
One consequence was that, while Russia took a leaf out of NATO tactics
in its 1999 attack on Chechnya, the humanitarian protests of the west
seemed particularly hypocritical from the Russian point of view. After
events in Kosovo, western comparison of Russia's role in Chechnya to that
of Serbia rather than NATO in Yugoslavia, plus and one-sided reporting
of atrocities, were interpreted as consciously hostile acts. The world seemed
to have conveniently forgotten that it was Chechen rebels who, before the
1999 round of fighting began, had deposited the heads of four western
engineers by a roadside and who had murdered many Russian and some
western hostages, leaving aside the murky circumstances of the Moscow
apartment bombings of autumn 1999 which killed hundreds. It was largely
the strength of the backlash which precipitated the near-unknown Putin
into power and raised many questions about the involvement of his supporters in mani-pulating the situation. The internal and external dangers
of a continuation in this vein are obvious, not least the, ironic, strengthening of Russian–Chinese ties which were so weak in the Soviet era.

Roughly speaking, although the alliances between them shift rapidly,
there are three main national political forces in Russia: the ruling 'oligarchs' currently focusing on the newly formed group around Putin and
his supporters; the renovated Communist Party which uneasily com-
bines democratic market principles, Soviet (even Stalinist) nostalgia and
xenophobia; and, third, a weak democratic, anti-plutocratic reformist
bloc currently led by Grigorii Yavlinsky, one of the authors of the
Shatalin Plan, and his Yabloko (Apple) group. However, that is only part
of the story. Much of the task of keeping the social and economic wheels
turning, especially in the absence of strong central government in the
years of Yeltsin's illness and decline, has fallen to strong local figures,
big-city mayors like Luzhkov of Moscow and provincial governors like

Boris Nemtsov of Nizhnii-Novgorod. Can any of them bring fundamental improvements?

Historians cannot look into the future, so perhaps one should suggest
what the current requirements are before assessing whether any group
can deliver them. One fundamental issue remains the implementation of
the rule of law. Russia has never enjoyed this in the full sense. Tsarist and
Soviet law were tainted by arbitrariness even at the best of times and
since 1991 lawlessness has been the order of the day. Nothing would create stability better than the emergence of a genuine rule of law which
applied to government as well as people and which was enforced by an
independent judiciary. The long-term health of Russia starts here.
However, nothing seems less likely in the short to medium term, not least
because, as mentioned above, there is no clear, honest, independent,
trustworthy point of application of such a policy, nor even anything
remotely resembling one. All the potential agencies – central government, police, judiciary – are too deeply entrenched in the current chaos
and corruption to appear capable of rising above it. Certainly, President
Putin has made references to establishing the rule of law and restoring
the authority of the state. Coming from that quarter, however, it would
be foolish to expect a liberal interpretation of the concepts of state
authority and law. Instead, one might have a more dictatorial presidency.
Even that, however, would be difficult. Local oligarchs have entrenched
themselves, and ignoring central decrees has been a national pastime
since the late Gorbachev years. The power needed to enforce such a policy would be incommensurate with its objectives.

One might say that the economic problems of the country should be
high on the agenda. From the point of view of 'national interest', understood as the interest of the largest number of citizens, that would
certainly be the case. However, do those in power care about the wider
interests of the population? If the provinces stay quiet, and the current
exploitative relations they profit from so handsomely are not threatened, they are unlikely to act. If it is necessary to manipulate the electorate through nationalism, as in the Duma elections of December 1999
and the presidential election of March 2000, then that will suffice. Some
economic sops to the masses could back this up. On paper, the opposition, communist and reformist, should be an obstacle to such a policy.
The communists, in particular, have become the voice of the new poor,
especially pensioners, though they have not succeeded in attracting
much support from disillusioned and volatile younger voters who fear a
return to the past. Reformists of all varieties remain too weak nationally

to challenge the oligarchs as, mercifully, does the extreme right associated with the likes of Zhirinovsky, which has been cut off at the knees by Putin who has stolen much of its ethos.

Few of these political groups, the communists being the exception, have much active mass support. There could be no greater contrast between the activity of the masses in 1917 and their relative passivity at the beginning of the twenty-first century. Since the late 1980s, successive waves of ill fortune have swept over them and engulfed many, but there has been no mass resistance. Partly this is because the situation is less desperate today and does not have the menacing background of a catastrophic world war to feed popular fury. But it is also because there is no real leadership or ideology which promises remedies for their plight. Arguably the remnants of the 'third way' offer the best hope, but it is too much associated with yesterday's people (from Gorbachev to the communists) and, in any case, the pressure against it from abroad, and the oligarchs' control of the media, make it difficult for it to succeed. For the moment there is little sign of consistent, self-organised mass activity, as opposed to the occasional powerful spontaneity of major strikes and protests. As in the past, the people are silent but it is a consequence of bewilderment, of confusion over how to deal with the crisis, of shock at what has happened. So far, despite gloomy prognostications, strident nationalism and Fascist-style movements have had no more success than the rest in attracting mass support.

Until broad popular movements do emerge, the oligarchs are likely to continue to have things their own way. Their Achilles heel, however, is each other. Mutual jealousies and internal rivalries have already led to shooting wars between factions. While such dramatic, Chicago-style politics may be less prominent today, the underlying rivalries remain and are a potential source of instability for all. An attempt by any one group or individual to impose is likely to lead to strong resistance from others. An elite divided in this way might be vulnerable. Since the communists represent the largest organised opposition force in the country one has to assume that they would be the most likely beneficiaries of such a split.

Conclusion

In the light of the above, what can we say about the impact of the Soviet system and its legacy? Clearly, the most positive consequence has been the growing application of political and personal rights – freedom of speech, travel, organisation and so on. While these are, as yet, imperfectly enjoyed in Russia they are undoubtedly an improvement on the Soviet years, although some of them, freedom of the press for instance, reached a peak in the Gorbachev period. However, the 1990s also brought into focus other, less recognised, aspects of the Soviet system. Perhaps the most important is that it acted as a kind of vast economic protection system. Now that the ex-Soviet Union is exposed to the full blast of world economic competition, its industrial infrastructure has been devastated. Nostrums about it being a transition from 'inefficient' socialist industry to 'efficient' capitalist production ring increasingly hollow. Instead, it looks more like a classic capitalist attempt to suppress rival production and take over its markets, the fate undergone by India in the mid-nineteenth century. The laws of comparative advantage (producing what is most suited to a particular set of circumstances) and the world division of labour are having their predictable effects. What are Russia's advantages that would attract investment? An educated workforce? A brilliant academic elite? Certainly, but it is easier to attract the best abroad to existing institutions, thereby instituting a damaging brain drain, than to set up new institutions in Russia. What does it have that the world markets want? Oil, gas, gold, diamonds, furs and timber head the list – sufficient to fuel the oligarchs but not to sustain an economy of 150 million people. Its other industries, such as food production, are in a bad way. For potential investors most of Russia is a black hole that would suck resources in without spewing back any profits. Cherry-picking investors might do well but the economy as a whole shows little sign of hope. While Soviet living and production standards were low they were guaranteed to sustain the whole population. For at least a third, and probably more than half of the population, living standards have been in free fall since the late 1980s and there is little or no sign of recovery. Even the present meagre standards often depend on local sleight of hand to keep industries and services running and still-continuing large-scale state subsidies to keep major industries afloat in order to keep the workforce relatively quiet.

The much vaunted 'social and economic rights' achieved by the USSR have been shown to be real. The problem remains, not just for Russia but the world: how does one combine social justice with legal, political and personal rights? Can one set only be bought at the expense of the other? Is the world torn between a consumer-oriented free market and a rigid, planned system? The former delivers for many; but it has to create endless needs and desires rather than satisfaction, otherwise people would stop buying. And it inevitably produces vast inequality – between 'winners' and 'losers', between owners and their associates on one hand, and employees, not to mention the inevitable underclass, on the other. Its incessant drive to produce more and more is increasingly environmentally unsustainable. The planned economy can create an economic safety net but at a relatively low level, and, in the Soviet case, at the cost of repression.

As we have seen in the Soviet case, it was the repression that created the forms of the command economy, not the command economy which created the dictatorship but, nonetheless, when the moment came to reduce the repression, the whole system collapsed. The question of whether they could be better balanced and made complementary to one another, to create free societies with genuine social justice for all, is the great challenge for the beginning of the new millennium. Soviet experience will provide vast material for pondering this question, a vast pool of human experience to be examined and understood. Nonetheless, like any historical event, the Soviet experience is unique and unrepeatable. As we have seen, contingent factors, including the impact of individuals, were influential. Lenin, Stalin or Gorbachev might have taken different decisions which would have had quite different consequences. What would have happened if the August 1991 coup attempt had never taken place? Despite the emergence of virtual history we can never know what might have been, only aspects of what was. Other issues remain to be clarified further. If George Soros could be taken in by Cold War rhetoric, what impact did it have on Soviet historical actors? Can we say for sure that, as we have implied, consumer dissatisfaction was stronger than the desire for human rights?

Many such issues can be clarified further, and only the development of twenty-first-century history will demonstrate the feasibility of combining social justice and freedom more successfully, but it is the firm conclusion of the present study that the structural problems that brought the Soviet system down were there from the beginning. The Soviet experience does not tell us whether or not socialism can be built, but it does tell us it was not built (and probably could never have been built) by a determined minority who, by chance, took control of a vast peasant country. Paradise on earth cannot be based on cruel compulsion of those called upon to construct it.

NOTES

1 BOLSHEVIK DREAMS

1. L. Schapiro, *The Communist Party of the Soviet Union*, 2nd edn (London, 1970), p. 139.
2. Hugh Seton-Watson, *The Russian Empire: 1801–1917* (Oxford, 1967).
3. A. A. Mossolov, *At the Court of the Last Tsar: Being the Memoirs of A. A. Mossolov* (London, 1935), p. 128.
4. See, for instance, the extract from Brezhnev's Party Congress Speech of 1981 (see p. 170).
5. Speech at Second Congress of Soviets, 26 October 1917.
6. This point is well-made in G. Swain, *Russian Social Democracy and the Legal Labour Movement 1906–14* (London, 1983).
7. For a concise account of the significance of these events see Christopher Read, *From Tsar to Soviets: The Russian People and Their Revolution 1917–21* (London, 1996), pp. 53–60.
8. V. I. Lenin, *Farewell Address to the Swiss Workers*, 26 March 1917. (All emphases original unless stated otherwise.)
9. See Read (1996), pp. 164–9.
10. See, for example, the debate around the most recent rebuttal of the accusations: Semion Lyandres, 'The Bolsheviks' "German Gold" Revisited: An Inquiry into the 1917 Accusations', *The Carl Beck Papers in Russian and East European Studies*, No. 1106, (Centre for Russian and East European Studies, Pittsburgh, Penn., 1995).
11. V. I. Lenin, *State and Revolution*, Postscript to the 1st edn.
12. Recent widely differing accounts of the revolution of 1917 include O. Figes, *A People's Tragedy* (London, 1996); R. Pipes, *The Russian Revolution 1899–1919* (London, 1990); Read (1996); and J. White, *The Russian Revolution 1917–21: A Short History* (London, New York, Melbourne, Auckland, 1994).

2 THE SOVIET SYSTEM UNDER LENIN

1. J. Carmichael, *A Short History of the Russian Revolution* (London, 1966), p. 138.
2. See Read (1996), pp. 121–2 and 228–30.
3. E. Heifetz, *The Slaughter of Jews in the Ukraine* (New York, 1921), pp. 175–81, quoted in W. B. Lincoln, *Red Victory* (London, 1991), p. 319.

4. R. Pipes, *The Bolsheviks in Power* (London, 1993), p. 112.
5. See Read (1996), pp. 206–7.
6. T. F. Remington, *Building Socialism in Lenin's Russia: Ideology and Industrial Organization, 1917–21* (Pittsburgh, Penn., 1984), p. 109.
7. See Read (1996), p. 249 for detailed figures.
8. S. Malle, *The Economic Organisation of War Communism, 1918–21* (Cambridge, 1985), pp. 508–11.
9. M. McCauley, *Bread and Justice: State and Society in Petrograd 1917–22* (Oxford, 1991), p. 264.
10. R. Pipes, *Russia under the Bolshevik Regime 1919–1924* (London, 1995), p. 389.
11. Notably by Vladimir Brovkin in *Behind the Front Lines of the Civil War: Political Parties and Social Movements in Russia 1918–22*, (Princeton, NJ, 1994), pp. 298–9.
12. S. Fitzpatrick, 'The Civil War as a Formative Experience', in A. Gleason, P. Kenez and R. Stites (eds), *Bolshevik Culture: Experiment and Order in the Russian Revolution* (Bloomington and Indianapolis, 1985), pp. 57–76.
13. Tim McDaniel, *The Agony of the Russian Idea* (Princeton, NJ, 1996).
14. V. I. Lenin, 'One of the Fundamental Questions of the Revolution', *Between the Two Revolutions: Articles and Speeches of 1917* (Moscow, 1971), p. 379.
15. L. Trotsky, *My Life: An Attempt at an Autobiography* (Harmondsworth, 1975), p. 355.
16. *The Bolsheviks and the October Revolution: Minutes of the Central Committee of the Russian Social-Democratic Labour Party (Bolsheviks) August 1917–February 1918*, trans. A. Bone (London, 1974), pp. 136–40.
17. V. I. Lenin, 'The Immediate Tasks of the Soviet Government', in *Selected Works*, Vol. 2 (Moscow, 1967), p. 645.
18. E. H. Carr and R. W. Davies, *Foundations of a Planned Economy 1926–1929*, Vol. 1 (Harmondsworth, 1974), pp. 380 and 851–2.
19. V. Serge, *Memoirs of a Revolutionary 1901–1941* (London, Oxford, New York, 1963), p. 74.
20. A significant exception is D. Orlovsky, 'State Building in the Civil War Era: The Role of Lower-Middle Strata', in D. Koenker, W. Rosenberg and R. Suny (eds), *Party, State and Society in the Russian Civil War: Explorations in Social History* (Bloomington and Indianapolis, 1989), pp. 180–209.
21. The classic account of this process remains T. H. Rigby, *Lenin's Government: Sovnarkom (1917–1922)* (Cambridge, 1979). The figures for the frequency of meetings can be found on p. 182.
22. Lenin, *Collected Works*, Vol. 44 (Moscow, 1970), p. 445.
23. See E. A. Rees, *State Control in Soviet Russia* (London, 1987).
24. J. Bunyan and H. H. Fisher, *The Bolshevik Revolution 1917–1918: Documents and Materials* (Stanford, Calif., 1934), p. 296.
25. V. I. Lenin, 'The Tasks of the Revolution', in *Between the Two Revolutions: Articles and Speeches of 1917* (Moscow, 1971), p. 388.
26. V. I. Lenin, 'Economics and Politics in the Era of the Dictatorship of the Proletariat', *Pravda*, No. 250, 7 November 1919, reprinted in V. I. Lenin, *Selected Works*, Vol. 2 (Moscow, 1967), pp. 274–82.

3   THE NEP YEARS: ECONOMIC RETREAT, CULTURAL ASSAULT

1. For an excellent detailed account of these processes in an important provincial area see James R. Harris, *The Great Urals: Regionalism and the Evolution of the Soviet System* (Ithaca, NY, 1999). For a compilation of articles pointing to the greater complexities of Stalin-period politics and society see S. Fitzpatrick (ed.), *Stalinism: New Directions* (London, 2000).
2. A. Nove, *An Economic History of the USSR*, 2nd edn (Harmondsworth, 1989), p. 84.
3. See Christopher Read, *Culture and Power in Revolutionary Russia: The Intelligentsia and the Transition From Tsarism to Communism* (London, 1990), pp. 51–93.
4. K. Marx, 'A Contribution to the Critique of Hegel's Philosophy of Right: Introduction', in K. Marx and F. Engels, *Collected Works* (London, 1975), p. 174.

4   TOWARDS THE STALIN SYSTEM: THE 'GREAT TURN', 1928–32

1. For a classical view see J. P. Sontag, 'The Soviet War Scare of 1926–27', *Russian Review*, Vol. 34 (1975). For a more recent view based on archival revelations see N. S. Simonov, 'The "war scare" of 1927 and the Birth of the Defence–Industry Complex', in M. Harrison and J. Barber (eds), *The Soviet Defence–Industry Complex from Stalin to Khrushchev* (London, 2000), pp. 33–46.
2. However, a British diplomatic observer of the time described the scare as 'a genuine not a constructed fear'. Quoted in Lennart Samuelson, *Plans for Stalin's War Machine: Tukhachevsky and Military Economic Planning (1925–1941)* (London, 2000), p. 35.
3. Harrison and Barber (2000), p. 35.
4. Schapiro (1970), pp. 313 and 318.
5. R. W. Davies, *The Socialist Offensive: The Collectivisation of Russian Agriculture 1929–1930* (London, 1980), p. 258; M. Fainsod, *Smolensk under Soviet Rule* (London, 1958).
6. It is this hierarchical interrelatedness of the whole society which has raised the debate about 'totalitarianism' and made such an unsatisfactory word difficult to replace. While the concept leaves a lot to be desired it is the best we so far have to point to the peculiarities of the system at this time. We will return to it later.
7. S. Fitzpatrick, 'Cultural Revolution as Class War', in S. Fitzpatrick (ed.), *Cultural Revolution in Russia, 1928–1931* (Bloomington, Ind. and London, 1978), p. 37.
8. The issue is dealt with more fully in the next section.
9. Fitzroy Maclean, *Eastern Approaches* (London, 1964), pp. 36–7.

5   STALINISM TRIUMPHANT

1. M. Lewin, *Lenin's Last Struggle* (New York, 1968).
2. R. Tucker, *Stalin as Revolutionary 1879–1929* (London, 1974), p. 135.
3. R. H. McNeal (ed.), *Resolutions and Decisions of the Communist Party of the Soviet Union*, Vol. 2 (Toronto, Buffalo, 1974), pp. 115 and 118.
4. J. Stalin, 'The Tasks of Business Executives (Speech Delivered at the First All-Union Conference of Managers of Socialist Industry, 4 February 1931)', in *Problems of Leninism* (Moscow, 1945), p. 356.
5. The classic formulation of the question was by Alec Nove, 'Was Stalin Really Necessary?', in *Encounter*, April 1962.
6. Most notably in M. Djilas, *Conversations with Stalin* (London, 1962).
7. D. Volkogonov, *Stalin: Triumph and Tragedy* (London, 1991), p. 103.
8. J. Stalin, 'Dizzy with Success (Problems of the Collective-Farm Movement)', in *Problems of Leninism* (Moscow, 1945), p. 327.
9. See, in particular, J. Barber, *Soviet Historians in Crisis 1928–32* (London, 1981).
10. E. Ammende, *Human Life in Russia* (London, 1936). Ammende first alerted the outside world in a letter published in an Austrian newspaper on 26 June 1933: ibid., p. 19.
11. R. Conquest, *Harvest of Sorrow: Collectivisation and the Terror–Famine*, (London, 1986).
12. See the exchange in *Soviet Studies* between S. Rosefielde (in vol. 33, no. 1 (January 1981), pp. 51–87) and Stephen Wheatcroft (in vol. 33, no. 2 (April 1981) and vol. 35, no. 2 (April 1983)). More recently Wheatcroft has revised his estimate of famine victims upwards, having the good grace to accept that his earlier calculations were no longer sustainable – something none of the other interpreters has, up to the present, been prepared to do. See S. Wheatcroft, 'More Light on the Scale of Repression and Excess Mortality in the Soviet Union in the 1930s', in J. Arch Getty and Roberta T. Manning (eds), *Stalinist Terror: New Perspectives* (Cambridge, 1993), pp. 275–90.
13. S. Wheatcroft, M. Tauge and R. W. Davies, 'Stalin, Grainstocks and the Famine of 1932–1933', *Slavic Review*, vol. 54, no. 3 (1995), pp. 642–57.
14. See note 12 for references.
15. A. Nove, 'Victims of Stalinism: How Many?', in Getty and Manning, (1993), p. 271.
16. See E. Bacon, *The Gulag at War* (London, 1994); S. G. Wheatcroft, 'Victims of Stalinism and the Secret Police: The Comparability and Reliability of the Archival Data – Not the Last Word', *Europe–Asia Studies*, vol. 51, no. 2 (1999), pp. 315–45; and R. Conquest, 'Comment on Wheatcroft', *Europe–Asia Studies*, vol. 51, no. 8 (1999), pp. 1479–83.
17. This was the point of view of Isaac Deutscher, expressed in a number of his works including *Stalin: A Political Biography* (Oxford, 1967).
18. E. Ginzburg, *Into the Whirlwind* (London, 1967); Lev Kopelev, *The Education of a True Believer* (New York, 1980); Joseph Berger, *Shipwreck of a Generation* (London, 1967); Karlo Stajner, *Seven Thousand Days in Siberia* (Edinburgh, 1988). I am grateful to Roger Chetwynd for drawing my attention to the last reference.

19. L. Trotsky, *The Revolution Betrayed: What is the Soviet Union and Where is it Going?* (London, 1967), pp. 283–5.
20. S. Fitzpatrick, *Everyday Stalinism* (Oxford, 1999), p. 85.
21. If true this would not be the only example of Stalin borrowing from the arch-enemy. Hitler's 'night of the long knives' preceded the Soviet blood purge and increasing militarisation of Soviet parades followed the Nazi practice mythologised in the films of Leni Riefenstahl.
22. O. Khlevnyukh, 'Reasons for the Great Terror: The External Political Aspect', unpublished paper presented to the Economic and Social History Seminar (SIPS), Centre for Russian and East European Studies, University of Birmingham, 28 January 1998.
23. This is confirmed by documents published in J. Arch Getty and Oleg V. Naumov, *The Road to Terror: Stalin and the Self-Destruction of the Bolsheviks, 1932–1939* (Annals of Communism) (New Haven, Conn. and London, 1999).
24. F. Chuev, *Sto sorok besed s Molotovym: Iz Dnevnika F.Chueva* (Moscow, 1991).
25. R. Tucker, *Stalin in Power: The Revolution from Above 1928–41* (New York and London, 1990), pp. 377–8.
26. E. A. Rees (ed.), *Decision-Making in the Stalinist Command Economy, 1932–37* (London and New York, 1997).
27. I. Deutscher, *Stalin: a Political Biography* (Oxford, 1961), p. 569. It was written in 1948–9.
28. For an account that emphasises the normality of life in the 1930s see R. W. Thurston, *Life and Terror in Stalin's Russia 1934–41* (New Haven, Conn. and London, 1996). For one which stresses extraordinary abnormality see Fitzpatrick (1999). The truth probably lies somewhere in between.
29. Notably Hiroaki Kuromiya, *Stalin's Industrial Revolution: Politics and Workers 1928–1932* (New York, 1988) and C. Ward, *Russia's Cotton Workers and the New Economic Policy: Shop-floor Culture and State Policy 1921–1929* (Cambridge, 1990).
30. D. Filtzer, *Soviet Workers and Stalinist Industrialisation: The Formation of Modern Soviet Production Relations, 1928–1941* (London, 1986).
31. See Lewis Siegelbaum, *Stakhanovism and the Politics of Productivity in the USSR, 1935–41* (New York, 1988).
32. S. Kotkin, *Magnetic Mountain: Stalinism as Civilization* (Berkeley, Calif., 1995), p. 104.
33. Kotkin (1995), pp. 125–7.
34. Vera Dunham, *In Stalin's Time. Middleclass Values in Soviet Fiction* (Cambridge, 1976).
35. S. Fitzpatrick, *Stalin's Peasants: Resistance and Survival in the Russian Village After Collectivization* (New York and Oxford, 1994) and Lynne Viola, *Peasant Rebels under Stalin: Collectivization and the Culture of Peasant Resistance* (New York and Oxford, 1996).

6   FROM WORLD WAR TO COLD WAR

1. G. Roberts, *The Soviet Union and the Origins of the Second World War: Russo-German Relations and the Road to War, 1933–41* (London, 1995);

C. Kennedy-Pipe, *Russia and the World 1917–1991* (London, 1998), ch. 2, pp. 36–56; J. Haslam, *The Soviet Union and the Struggle for Collective Security in Europe 1933–39* (London, 1984); G. Gorodetsky (ed.), *Soviet Foreign Policy 1917–91: A Retrospective* (London, 1994).

2. See, for example, the account of Karlo Stajner (1988), p. 101.
3. S. Wheatcroft and R. W. Davies, 'Population', in R. W. Davies, M. Harrison and S. Wheatcroft (eds), *The Economic Transformation of the Soviet Union 1913–1945* (Cambridge, 1994).
4. German eyewitness at Prokhorovka on 12 July, quoted in R. Cross, *Citadel: The Battle of Kursk* (London, 1993), p. 215.
5. M. Djilas, *Conversations with Stalin* (London, 1962), p. 133.
6. For a moving account of this moment see Primo Levi, *The Truce* (London, 1987).
7. Alec Nove in C. Read, *Stalin: Terror and Transformation*, Warwick History Video, University of Warwick, Coventry, 1992.
8. D. Holloway, *Stalin and the Bomb: The Soviet Union and Atomic Energy 1939–1956* (New Haven, Conn. and London, 1994), pp. 144–7.
9. The most extraordinary example was the deportation of whole ethnic groups. Robert Conquest gives a grand total of 1.65 m deportees from Chechen, Ingush, Karachai, Balkar, Kalmyk, Volga German and Crimean Tatar peoples. An area of 62 000 square miles was vacated: R. Conquest, *The Nation Killers* (London, 1972), pp. 65–6.
10. Figures from T. H. Rigby, *Communist Party Membership in the USSR 1917–1967* (Princeton, NJ, 1968), pp. 52–3.
11. M. Gorbachev, *Memoirs* (London, New York, Toronto, Sydney, Auckland, 1997), pp. 40–2.
12. D. Yergin, *Shattered Peace: The Origins of the Cold War and the National Security State* (Cambridge, Mass., 1977).
13. D. Volkogonov, *Stalin: Triumph and Tragedy* (London, 1991), pp. 525–8.
14. A. Nove, *An Economic History of the USSR* (London, 1969) and R. Suny, *The Soviet Experiment: Russia, the USSR and the Successor States* (Oxford, 1998), p. 333.
15. The account of Stalin's last days is based on that given in Volkogonov (1991), pp. 571–3 except that this source gives the time of death as 9.50 a.m.

7 SUCCEEDING STALIN

1. Isaac Deutscher, *Russia after Stalin* (London, 1969), p. 73.
2. Ronald Kowalski and Dilwyn Porter, 'Political Football: Moscow Dynamo in Britain, 1945', *The International Journal of the History of Sport*, vol. 14, no.2, (August 1997), pp. 27–45.
3. Walter Ciszek SJ, *With God in Russia* (New York, 1966), pp. 221–41 gives an eyewitness account of events in Norilsk.
4. See, for example, Bernard Guetta, ' Et l'URSS entra en agonie: La Prague Connection', *Le Nouvel Obzervateur*, no, 1763, 20 August 1993, pp. 32–9.

8   DE-STALINISATION HALTED

1. Central Soviet Archive of the Ministry of Defence f. 32. op. 11 302. D. 62, l. 546, quoted in Volkogonov (1991), pp. 473–4.
2. J. Keep, *Last of the Empires: A History of the Soviet Union from 1945–1991* (Oxford, 1996), p. 204; and G. Hosking, *A History of the Soviet Union 1917–1991. Final Edition* (London, 1992), p. 377.
3. R. Service, *A History of Twentieth-Century Russia* (London, 1998), p. 410.
4. Z. Mlynar, *Night Frost in Prague: The End of Humane Socialism* (London, 1980), pp. 240–1.
5. R. Suny, *The Soviet Experiment: Russia, the USSR and the Successor States* (New York and Oxford, 1998), p. 423.
6. Notably Alexandre Bennigsen and Chantal Lemercier-Quelquejay, *Le soufi et le commissaire: Les confrères musulmanes en URSS* (Paris, 1986).
7. Hélène Carrère d'Encausse, *L'empire éclaté: La révolte des nations en URSS* (Paris, 1978).

9   SOVIET SOCIETY SINCE THE LATE 1950s

1. A. Solzhenitsyn, 'The Smatterers', in A. Solzhenitsyn *et al.* (eds), *From under the Rubble* (London, 1976), pp. 255 and 277–8.

10   DISSOLUTION

1. A. Brown, *The Gorbachev Factor* (Oxford, 1996), p. 148.
2. V. Shlapentokh, *Soviet Intellectuals and Political Power: The Post-Stalin Era* (Princeton, NJ, 1990), p. 239.
3. B. Kerblay, *Modern Soviet Society* (London, 1983), p. 39.
4. Gorbachev (1997), p. 782.

11   A NEW TIME OF TROUBLES

1. G. Palast, 'Failures of the 20th century: see under IMF', *The Observer*, 8 October 2000, Business supplement p. 7 suggests that 1.4 million a year has been added to the Russian death rate.
2. George Soros, 'Who Lost Russia?', *New York Review of Books*, vol. XLVII, no. 6 (11 April 2000), p. 16 [pp. 10–16].
3. There are numerous accounts but see, in particular, Tatyana Tolstaya, 'The Way They Live Now', *New York Review of Books* (24 April 1997); David Remnick, *Resurrection: The Struggle for a New Russia* (New York, 1997) and Service (1998), pp. 509–43.
4. Soros (2000), p. 10.

SELECT BIBLIOGRAPHY

The literature on the Soviet Union is enormous. To make it more manageable the following bibliography is tilted towards recent and relatively broad-ranging works in English which pick up themes central to the present volume. Many of them contain more specialised bibliographies.

1 General Works

Acton, E., *Russia: The Tsarist and Soviet Legacy*, 2nd edn (London, 1995).
Andrlè, V., *A Social History of Twentieth-Century Russia* (London, 1994).
Daniels, R. V., *The End of the Communist Revolution* (London, 1993).
Hosking, G., *A History of the Soviet Union: 1917–1991 Final Edition* (London, 1992).
Hosking, G. and R. Service (eds), *Reinterpreting Russia* (London, 1999).
Kenez, P., *A History of the Soviet Union From the Beginning to the End* (Cambridge, 1999).
Malia, M., *The Soviet Tragedy: A History of Socialism in Russia 1917–1991* (New York, 1994).
Nove, A., *An Economic History of the USSR*, 3rd edn (London, 1992).
Sandle, M., *A Short History of Soviet Socialism* (London, 1999).
Service, R., *A History of Twentieth-Century Russia* (London, 1997).
Suny, R., *The Soviet Experiment: Russia, the USSR and the Successor States* (Oxford, 1998).

2 Lenin, the Revolution and the 1920s

Acton, E., *Rethinking the Russian Revolution* (London and New York, 1990).
Berdyaev, N., *The Origins of Russian Communism* (Ann Arbor, Mich., 1966).
Brovkin, V., *Behind the Front Lines of the Civil War: Political Parties and Social Movements in Russia 1918–1922* (Princeton, NJ, 1994).
Brovkin, V. (ed.), *The Bolsheviks in Russian Society: The Revolution and the Civil Wars* (New Haven, Conn. and London, 1997).
Carr, E. H., *The Interregnum* (London, 1954).
Carr, E. H., *Socialism in One Country 1924–6*, 2 vols (London, 1958–9).
Carr, E. H., *The Bolshevik Revolution*, 3 vols (Harmondsworth, 1968).

Carr, E. H. and R. W. Davies, *Foundations of a Planned Economy 1926–1929* (London, 1969).

Carrère d'Encausse, H., *Lenin: Revolution and Power* (London, 1982).

Chamberlin, W. H., *The Russian Revolution*, 2 vols (New York, 1965).

Chase, W., *Workers, Society and the Soviet State: Labour and Life in Moscow, 1918–1929* (Urbana, Ill., 1987).

Cohen, S., *Bukharin and the Bolshevik Revolution: A Political Biography (1888–1938)* (New York, 1973).

Danilov, V. P., *Rural Russia under the Old Regime* (London, 1988).

Erlich, A., *The Soviet Industrialization Debate* (Cambridge, Mass., 1960).

Figes, O., *A People's Tragedy: A History of the Russian Revolution* (London, 1996).

Fitzpatrick, S., *The Russian Revolution* (Oxford, 1982).

Fitzpatrick, S., A. Rabinowitch and R. Suny (eds), *Russia in the Era of NEP* (Bloomington, Ind., 1991).

Goldman, W., *Women, the State and Revolution: Soviet Family Policy and Social Life 1917–1936* (Cambridge, 1993).

Keep, J., *The Russian Revolution: A Study in Mass Mobilization* (London, 1976).

Kenez, P., *The Birth of the Propaganda State: Soviet Methods of Mass Mobilization* (Cambridge, 1985).

Koenker, D. *et al.* (eds), *Party, State and Society in the Russian Civil War* (Bloomington, Ind., 1989).

Lenin, V. I., *Selected Works*, 3 vols (Moscow, 1967).

Lewin, M., *Lenin's Last Struggle* (London, 1969).

Lewin, M., *Political Undercurrents in Soviet Economic Debates* (Oxford, 1971).

Lewin, M., *The Making of the Soviet System* (London, 1985).

Lincoln, W. B., *Red Victory: A History of the Russian Civil War* (London, 1991).

Lukkanen, A., *The Party of Unbelief: The Religious Policy of the Bolshevik Party 1917–1929* (Helsinki, 1994).

Luxemburg, R., *The Russian Revolution and Leninism or Marxism* (Ann Arbor, Mich., 1961).

McCauley, M., *Bread and Justice: State and Society in Petrograd 1917–22* (Oxford, 1991).

McKean, R., *St. Petersburg Between the Revolutions* (New Haven, Conn., 1990).

Malle, S., *The Economic Organization of War Communism (1918–21)* (Cambridge, 1985).

Mawdsley, E., *The Russian Civil War* (London, 1987).

Narkiewicz, O., *The Making of the Soviet State Apparatus* (Manchester, 1970).

Pethybridge, R., *The Social Prelude to Stalinism* (London, 1974).

Pethybridge, R., *One Step Backwards, Two Steps Forward* (Oxford, 1990).

Pipes, R., *The Formation of the Soviet Union: Communism and Nationalism 1917–1923* (Cambridge, 1964).

Pipes, R. (ed.), *Revolutionary Russia: A Symposium* (Cambridge, Mass., 1968).

Pipes, R., *The Russian Revolution 1899–1919* (London, 1990).

Pipes, R., *The Bolsheviks in Power* (London, 1993).

Rabinowitch, A., *The Bolsheviks Come to Power* (London, 1979).

Radkey, O., *The Unknown Civil War in Soviet Russia: A Study of the Green Movement in the Tambov Region 1920–21* (Stanford, Calif., 1976).

Read, C., *From Tsar to Soviets: The Russian People and Their Revolution* (London and New York, 1996).

Remington T. F., *Building Socialism in Lenin's Russia: Ideology and Industrial Organization 1917–21* (Pittsburgh, Penn., 1984).

Rigby, T. H., *Communist Party Membership in the USSR 1917–1967* (Princeton, NJ, 1968).

Russell, Bertrand, *The Theory and Practice of Bolshevism* (London, 1920).

Schapiro, L., *The Origins of the Communist Autocracy: Political Opposition in the Soviet State: First Phase, 1917–22* (London, 1955).

Schapiro, L., *The Communist Party of the Soviet Union* (London, 1963).

Schapiro, L., *1917: The Russian Revolutions and the Birth of Present-Day Communism* (London, 1984).

Serge, V., *Memoirs of a Revolutionary*, trans. and abridged by P. Sedgwick (Oxford, 1963).

Service, R., *The Bolshevik Party in Revolution 1917–1923* (London, 1979).

Service, R., *Lenin: A Political Life*, 3 vols (London, 1985, 1991, 1994).

Service, R. (ed.), *Society and Politics in the Russian Revolution* (London, 1992).

Service, R., *Lenin: A Biography* (London, 2000).

Service, R., *The Russian Revolution 1900–1927*, 3rd edn (London, 2000).

Siegelbaum, L., *Soviet State and Society Between Revolutions, 1918–1929* (Cambridge, 1992).

Smith, S. A., *Red Petrograd: Revolution in the Factories 1917–18* (Cambridge, 1983).

Stone, N., *The Eastern Front 1914–17* (London, 1975).

Sukhanov, N. N., *The Russian Revolution: An Eyewitness Account*, 2 vols, trans. and edited by J. Carmichael (New York, 1962).

Swain, G., *The Origins of the Russian Civil War* (London, New York, 1996).

Trotsky, L., *History of the Russian Revolution*, 3 vols (New York, 1932).

Trotsky, L., *Terrorism and Communism* (London, 1975).

Tumarkin, N., *Lenin Lives! The Lenin Cult in Soviet Russia* (Cambridge, Mass., 1983).

Voline, *The Unknown Revolution 1917–21* (Detroit and Chicago, n.d.).

Volkogonov, D., *Lenin: A New Biography* (New York, 1994).

White, J., *The Russian Revolution: A Short History* (London, 1994).

Williams, B., *The Russian Revolution (1917–1921)* (Oxford, 1987).

Williams, B., *Lenin* (London, 2000).

Yaney, G., *The Urge to Mobilize: Agrarian Reform in Russia 1861–1930* (Chicago and Urbana, Ill., 1982).

3   The Stalin Years

Andrle, V., *Workers in Stalin's Russia: Industrialization and Social Change in a Planned Economy* (Brighton, 1988).

Bacon, E., *The Gulag at War* (London, 1994).

Barber, J. and M. Harrison, *The Soviet Home Front, 1941–45* (London, 1991).

Bialer, S. (ed.), *Stalin and His Generals* (New York, 1969).

Carrère d'Encausse, H., *Stalin: Order Through Terror* (London, 1982).

Cohen, S., *Rethinking the Soviet Experience: Politics and History Since 1917* (New York, 1985).

Conquest, R., *The Nation Killers* (London, 1970).

Conquest, R., *The Great Terror: A Reassessment* (Oxford, 1990).
Cooper, J., M. Perrie and E. A. Rees (eds), S*oviet History 1917–53: Essays in Honour of R.W. Davies* (London, 1995).
Davies, R. W., *The Industrialization of Soviet Russia*, 2 vols (London, 1980).
Davies, R. W., *The Soviet Economy in Turmoil: 1929–30* (London, 1988).
Davies R. W., M. Harrison and S. Wheatcroft (eds), *The Economic Transformation of the Soviet Union 1913–1945* (Cambridge, 1994).
Davies, S., *Popular Opinion in Stalin's Russia: Terror, Propaganda and Dissent, 1934–39* (Cambridge,1997).
Deutscher, I., *Trotsky: The Prophet Armed 1879–1921* (Oxford, 1959).
Deutscher, I., *Trotsky: The Prophet Unarmed* (Oxford, 1959).
Djilas, M., *Conversations With Stalin* (London, 1962).
Dunham, V., *In Stalin's Time: Middleclass Values in Soviet Fiction* (Cambridge, 1976).
Dunmore, T., *The Stalinist Command Economy: The Soviet State Apparatus and Economic Policy 1945–53* (London, 1980).
Erickson, J., *The Road to Stalingrad* (London, 1975).
Erickson, J., *The Road to Berlin* (London, 1983).
Fainsod, M., *Smolensk Under Soviet Rule* (London, 1958).
Filtzer, D., *Soviet Workers and Stalinist Industrialisation* (London, 1986).
Fitzpatrick, S. (ed.), *Cultural Revolution in Russia 1928–1931* (Bloomington, Ind., 1978).
Fitzpatrick, S., *Education and Social Mobility in the Soviet Union 1921–1934* (Cambridge, 1979).
Fitzpatrick, S., *Stalin's Peasants: Resistance and Survival in the Russian Village After Collectivisation* (Oxford, 1994).
Fitzpatrick, S., *Everyday Stalinism* (Oxford, 1999).
Fitzpatrick, S. (ed.), *Stalinism: New Directions* (London, 2000).
Franklin, B. (ed.), *The Essential Stalin: Major Theoretical Writings 1905–52* (London, 1975).
Getty, J. A., *The Origins of the Great Purges. The Soviet Communist Party Reconsidered, 1933–1938* (Cambridge, 1986).
Getty, J. A. and Roberta T. Manning, *Stalinist Terror: New Perspectives* (Cambridge, 1993).
Getty, J. A. and Oleg Naumov (eds), *The Road to Terror: Stalin and the Self-Destruction of the Bolsheviks 1932–1939* (New Haven, Conn., 1999).
Gill, G., *The Origins of the Stalinist Political System* (Cambridge, 1990).
Gleason, A., *Totalitarianism: The Hidden History of the Cold War* (New York, 1995).
Hahn, W., *Postwar Soviet Politics: The Fall of Zhdanov and the Defeat of Moderation* (Ithaca, NY, 1982).
Harrison, M., *Soviet Planning in Peace and War* (Cambridge, 1985).
Harrison, M., *Accounting for War: Soviet Production, Employment, and the Defence Burden* (Cambridge, 1996).
Harrison, M. (ed.), *The Economics of World War Two: Six Great Powers in International Comparison* (Cambridge, 2000).
Harrison, M. and J. Barber (ed.), *The Soviet Defence–Industry Complex from Stalin to Khrushchev* (London, 2000).
Hoffman, D., *Peasant Metropolis: Social Identities in Moscow 1929–41* (Ithaca, NY and London, 1994).

Holloway, D., *Stalin and the Bomb: The Soviet Union and Atomic Energy, 1939–1956* (New Haven, Conn., 1994).

Khlevniuk, O., *In Stalin's Shadow: The Career of Sergo Ordzhonikidze* (Armonk, NY, 1995).

Khrushchev, N., *Khrushchev Remembers*, 2 vols (London, 1977).

Knight, A., *Beria: Stalin's First Lieutenant* (Princeton, NJ, 1993).

Kotkin, S., *Magnetic Mountain: Stalinism as a Civilization* (Berkeley, Calif. and Los Angeles, 1995).

Kuromiya, H., *Stalin's Industrial Revolution: Politics and Workers, 1928–32* (Cambridge, 1988).

Lampert, N. and Gabor Rittersporn (eds), *Stalinism – Its Nature and Aftermath: Essays in Honour of Moshe Lewin* (Armonk, NY, 1992).

Levi, P., *The Truce* (London, 1987).

Linz, S. (ed.), *The Impact of World War II on the Soviet Union* (London, 1985).

Lukkanen, A., *The Religious Policy of the Stalinist State: A Case Study: The Central Standing Commission on Religious Questions, 1929–1938* (Helsinki, 1994).

Mandelstam, N., *Hope Against Hope* (London, 1970).

Mandelstam, N., *Hope Abandoned* (London, 1974).

Medvedev, R., *Let History Judge: The Origins and Consequences of Stalinism* (London, 1971).

Molotov, V., *Molotov Remembers: Inside Kremlin Politics, Conversations with Felix Chuev* (Chicago, Ill., 1993).

Overy, R., *Russia's War* (London, 1998).

Rees, E. A., *State Control in Soviet Russia* (London, 1987).

Rees, E. A. (ed.), *Decision-Making in the Stalinist Command Economy, 1932–37* (London, 1997).

Rigby, T. H. and P. Reddaway (eds), *Authority, Power, and Policy in the USSR: Essays Dedicated to Leonard Schapiro* (New York and London, 1980).

Rosenberg, W. and L. Siegelbaum (eds), *Social Dimensions of Soviet Industrialization* (Bloomington, Ind., 1993).

Samuelson, L., *Planning for Stalin's War Machine: Tukhachevskii and Military–Economic Planning 1925–41* (London, 2000).

Siegelbaum, L., *Stakhanovism and the Politics of Productivity in the USSR 1935–1941* (Cambridge, 1988).

Siegelbaum, L. and R. Suny, *Making Workers Soviet: Power, Class and Identity* (Ithaca, NY and London, 1994).

Solzhenitsyn, A., *The Gulag Archipelago*, 3 vols (London, 1974–7).

Stajner, K., *Seven Thousand Days in Siberia* (Edinburgh, 1988).

Stalin, J., *Problems of Leninism* (Moscow, 1945).

Thurston, R., *Life and Terror in Stalin's Russia, 1934–1941* (New Haven, Conn., 1996).

Trotsky, L., *The Revolution Betrayed* (London, 1937).

Tucker, R. C., *Stalin as Revolutionary 1879–1929* (London, 1974).

Tucker, R. C. (ed.), *Stalinism: Essays in Historical Interpretation* (New York, 1977).

Tucker, R. C. *Stalin in Power: The Revolution from Above 1928–41* (New York, 1990).

Viola, L., *Best Sons of the Fatherland: Workers in the Vanguard of Soviet Collectivization* (Oxford, 1987).

Viola, L., *Peasant Rebels Under Stalin: Collectivization and the Culture of Peasant Resistance* (Oxford, 1996).

Volkogonov, D., *Stalin: Triumph and Tragedy* (New York, 1988).
Ward, C., *The Stalin Dictatorship* (London, 1998).
Ward, C., *Stalin's Russia*, 2nd edn (London, 1999).
Zaleski, E., *Planning for Economic Growth in the Soviet Union, 1918–1932* (London, 1980).
Zaleski, E., *Stalinist Planning for Economic Growth, 1933–1952* (London, 1980).
Zubok, V. and C. V. Pleshakov, *Inside the Kremlin's Cold War* (Cambridge, Mass., 1995).

4 From Stalin to the Present

Aganbegyan, A., *The Challenge: The Economics of Perestroika* (London, 1988).
Alexeyeva, L., *Soviet Dissent: Contemporary Movements for National, Religious and Human Rights* (Middletown, Conn., 1985).
Alexeyeva, L., *The Thaw Generation* (London, 1986).
Beschloss, M. and S. Talbott, *At The Highest Levels: The Inside Story of the End of the Cold War* (London, 1993).
Bialer, S. (ed.), *Inside Gorbachev's Russia: Politics, Society and Nationality* (Boulder, Colo, 1989).
Boldin, V., *Ten Years That Shook The World: The Gorbachev Era as Witnessed by His Chief of Staff* (New York, 1994).
Breslauer, G., *Khrushchev and Brezhnev as Leaders: Building Authority in Soviet Politics* (London, 1982).
Brown, A., *The Gorbachev Factor* (Oxford, 1996).
Brown, A. and M. Kaser, *Soviet Policy for the 1980s* (London, 1982).
Brumberg, A. (ed.), *In Quest of Justice: Protest and Dissent in the Soviet Union Today* (New York, 1962).
Burlatsky, F., *Khrushchev and the First Russian Spring: The Era of Khrushchev Through the Eyes of His Advisor* (New York, 1988).
Cohen, S. (ed.), *An End to Silence: Uncensored Opposition in the Soviet Union: From Roy Medvedev's Underground Magazine 'Political Diary'* (New York, 1982).
Cohen, S., R. Charlet and A. Rabinowitch (eds), *The Soviet Union Since Stalin* (Bloomington, Ind., 1980).
Cook, L., *The Soviet Social Contract and Why it Failed* (Cambridge, Mass., 1993).
Crankshaw, E., *Khrushchev: A Career* (London, 1966).
Dallin, A. and Lapidus, G. (eds), *The Soviet System in Crisis* (Boulder, Colo, 1991).
Davies, R. W. (ed.), *Soviet History in the Gorbachev Revolution* (London, 1989).
Davies, R. W. (ed.), *Soviet History in the Yeltsin Era* (London, 1997).
Djilas, M., *The New Class: An Analysis of the Communist System* (New York, 1957).
Dunlop, J., *Faces of Contemporary Russian Nationalism* (Princeton, NJ, 1983).
Ellis, J., *The Russian Orthodox Church: A Contemporary History* (London, 1986).
Feshbach, M., *The Soviet Union: Population Trends and Dilemmas* (Washington, DC, 1982).
Goldman, M., *The USSR in Crisis: The Failure of an Economic System* (New York, 1983).
Gorbachev, M., *Memoirs* (London, 1996).
Grachev, A., *Final Days: The Inside Story of The Collapse of the Soviet Union* (Boulder, Colo, 1993).

Gromyko, A., *Memoirs* (New York, 1990).

Gunther, J., *Inside Russia Today* (New York, 1958).

Hopkins, M., *Russia's Underground Press: The Chronicle of Current Events* (New York, 1983).

Hosking, G., *The Awakening of the Soviet Union* (London, 1990).

Kaiser, R., *Russia: Hopes and Fears* (London, 1975).

Kaiser, R., *Why Gorbachev Happened: His Triumphs and His Failures* (New York, 1991).

Keep, J., *The Last of the Empires: A History of the Soviet Union, 1945–1991* (Oxford, 1995).

Kerblay, B., *Modern Soviet Society* (London, 1983).

Kerblay, B., *Gorbachev's Russia* (New York, 1989).

Lane, C., *Christian Religion in the Soviet Union: A Sociological Study* (London, 1978).

Leonhard, W., *The Kremlin Since Stalin* (London 1968).

Lewin, M., *Political Undercurrents in Soviet Economic Debates* (Princeton, NJ, 1973).

Lewin, M., *The Gorbachev Phenomenon* (London, 1988).

Ligachev, Y., *Inside Gorbachev's Kremlin* (New York, 1993).

McCauley, M. (ed.), *The Soviet Union After Brezhnev* (London, 1983).

McCauley, M. (ed.), *Khrushchev and Khrushchevism* (London, 1987).

McCauley, M. (ed.), *The Soviet Union Under Gorbachev* (London, 1987).

Matlock, J., *Autopsy on an Empire* (New York, 1993).

Matthews, M., *Privilege in the Soviet Union* (London, 1978).

Matthews, M., *Class and Society in Soviet Russia* (London, 1982).

Matthews, M., *Education in the Soviet Union: Policies and Institutions Since Stalin* (London, 1982).

Medvedev, R. and Zh., *Khrushchev: The Years in Power* (Oxford, 1977).

Micunovic, V., *Moscow Diary* (London, 1980).

Morrison, J., *Boris Yeltsin: From Bolshevik to Democrat* (New York, 1991).

Nove, A., *Stalinism and After* (London, 1975).

Nove, A., *Glasnost in Action* (London, 1989).

Post, L. van der, *Journey into Russia* (London, 1964).

Reddaway, P., *Uncensored Russia* (London, 1972).

Rigby, T. H., *The Changing Soviet System* (London, 1990).

Roxburgh, A. (ed.), *The Second Russian Revolution* (London, 1991).

Sakharov, A., *Memoirs* (London, 1990).

Sakwa, R., *Gorbachev and His Reforms 1985–1990* (London, 1990).

Smith, H., *The Russians* (New York, 1976).

Smith, H., *The New Russians* (New York, 1990).

Suny, R., *Revenge of the Past* (Cambridge, 1993).

Tatu, M., *Power in the Kremlin From Khrushchev to Kosygin* (London, 1969).

Voslensky, M., *Nomenklatura: Anatomy of the Soviet Ruling Class* (London, 1984).

Walker, M., *The Waking Giant: The Soviet Union Under Gorbachev* (London, 1986).

White, S., *Gorbachev and After* (Cambridge, 1991).

Yeltsin, B., *The Struggle for Russia* (New York, 1994).

INDEX